Christian Schmaltz

A Quantitative Liquidity Model for Banks

GABLER RESEARCH

Christian Schmaltz

A Quantitative Liquidity Model for Banks

With a foreword by Prof. Dr. Thomas Heidorn

GABLER

RESEARCH

Bibliographic information published by the Deutsche Nationalbibliothek
The Deutsche Nationalbibliothek lists this publication in the Deutsche Nationalbibliografie; detailed bibliographic data are available in the Internet at http://dnb.d-nb.de.

Dissertation Frankfurt School of Finance and Management, 2009

1st Edition 2009

Editorial Office: Claudia Jeske | Anita Wilke

Gabler is part of the specialist publishing group Springer Science+Business Media.
www.gabler.de

Umschlaggestaltung: KünkelLopka Medienentwicklung, Heidelberg
Printed on acid-free paper
Printed in Germany

ISBN 978-3-8349-1822-2

Para mi princesa

Foreword

Liquidity is a core resource and its management is a core activity of banks. Nevertheless, liquidity management has not received much attention during the last decades, as liquidity has not been perceived as scarce. This perception has clearly changed during the financial crisis 2007/2009. Facing dried interbank markets, many banks were desperately looking for liquidity. Despite its crucial role, the modeling techniques for bank liquidity are so far rather simple, which sharply contrasts the sophisticated techniques used for other risks as credit or market. Furthermore, German regulators now allow banks to use internal liquidity models for regulatory reporting. This leads to the need to develop a liquidity model for banks that uses advanced stochastic techniques, incorporates all liquidity key variables, discusses internal liquidity allocation and optimization. The work of Christian Schmaltz closes this gap in the literature.

There are three major contributions:

1. Key liquidity variables are derived.
2. An innovative way to internally allocate liquidity is developed.
3. Transfer prices of liquidity are calculated.

The key variables are derived from the liquidity condition of banks and the channels to generate additional cash flows. Customer deposits and credit, funding spread and funding capacity, haircuts and short term interest rates are identified as key liquidity variables. Liquidity risk is the consequence of the non-deterministic nature of these variables, which may take large adverse values (liquidity crisis). Having identified the key variables, a liquidity model is set up by assuming a particular stochastic process for each variable. The focus lies on the customer cash flows which are modeled by a jump-diffusion process. With this general type of process it is possible to describe stochastic objects that have an expected component and two unexpected components. One unexpected component accounts for small and the second for sudden large deviations. Customer cash flows can be modeled this way. The expected component can be interpreted as contractual or expected cash flows, the small deviations come from the liquidity option banks provide for their customers and the large deviations are confidence-driven (individual or systematic liquidity crisis). In contrast to previous authors, Christian Schmaltz models cash flows on the product level instead of using an aggregate. This allows him to discuss the interdependence between products and to analytically describe the aggregation and disaggregation of liquidity risk.

The model is applied to internal liquidity allocation and optimization. The thesis proposes to separate the cash flow components and to allocate them to different departments. In particular, the expected cash flow is allocated to the asset liability management, the unexpected component to the money market and the confidence-driven part to the risk controlling department. The asset liability management manages long-term cash flows facing funding spread uncertainty. The money market department manages the short-term unexpected component using money market loans and deposits. This department has to maintain a (central) reserve. The risk controlling department pools the confidence-driven component. It balances the risk with a decentral reserve. The departments are connected by a new liquidity transfer price system that reflects the cost of a passive strategy. This system ensures that the liquidity allocation is adequately accounted for in the profit and loss calculations. Transfer prices are of practical importance as they are an integral component of recent regulatory initiatives in liquidity management.

The addressees of this work are numerous: the model could inspire liquidity managers and controllers in banks for their own internal models. Furthermore, it might serve regulators for their assessment of these models. Finally, it invites researchers to generalize many assumptions that have been made during the development of this particular approach.

Being convinced of the promising solutions and their practical relevance, I hope that Christian Schmaltz' approach to liquidity risk will find a wide acceptance in the industry and research community.

Prof. Dr. Thomas Heidorn

Acknowledgements

This thesis is a joint effort of my brain and fingers, but it benefited from many other people intellectually, financially, and personally.

Intellectually, I am very grateful to my supervisor Prof. Dr. Thomas Heidorn for having given me the opportunity and freedom to focus on the exciting subject of liquidity management for the past three years. When we seemed to hit a wall, we brainstormed and found a way out. I thank Prof. Dr. Ursula Walther for interesting insights into the behavioural aspects of liquidity and her acceptance of my co-supervision. Furthermore, I am also grateful to Prof. Stephan Dieckmann who accepted the external supervision despite his recent move to a new town and university. My special thanks go to Prof. Dr. Wolfgang Schmidt for his altruistic help and impulses with respect to stochastic optimization.

Furthermore, I want to express my gratitude to HSH Nordbank AG for raising a topic of practical relevance, providing a network of liquidity practitioners, and for sponsoring this thesis. It is true that while contracts are made between institutions, contacts are made between people – therefore, my thanks to HSH are equally shared between Dr. Carl Heinz Daube, Prof. Dr. Dr. Marcus Porembski, Armin Schneider, and Dirk Schröter. Furthermore, I thank TriSolutions' Dr. Peter Bartetzky, Dr. Holger Thomae, and Dr. Tobias Ihde for their suggestions and valuable comments during my first liquidity project.

Not only am I grateful to my office, but to the colleagues in its vicinity. I highly appreciate the inspiring conversations about filtrations, processes and beyond with colleagues and my friends Christoph Becker, Natalie Packham, and Carlos Veiga.

I am further indebted to Mildred Fehlberg and my friend Stefan Hirth for proof-reading and questioning all the points that seem to be self-explanatory while they are not.

Personally, I am grateful to my friend and training partner Dierk Dennig for setting the pace in both marathons and research. Furthermore, I thank Matthias Hilgert for nice runs, nice conversations, and nice venues.

I thank my parents for teaching me that life is a pool of options rather than of obligations. I chose the option to pursue a PhD in full consciousness of the fact that any other option would have found their full support as well. Finally, I am grateful to my future wife Maria, for her sunshine on rainy days – but this is beyond words anyway.

Christian Schmaltz

Contents

List of Figures

List of Tables

Symbols

Notation	Description
$1-\alpha$	Origination, Fraction of Roll-Over Volume
$B_{t_{k+1}}$	Money Market, Cumulated Cash Flow Balance
β	Origination, Long-term Funding Capacity
$C(.)$	Jump Transfer Price, Required Collateral
CF_t^+	Incoming Cash Flow at t
CF_t^-	Outgoing Cash Flow at t
$c^R()$	Brownian Transfer Price, Cost Function
$c(t_1,t_2)$	Credit Spread for period $[t_1,t_2]$
$d_t^{+/-}$	Money Market, Interbank Loan (-)/ Deposit (+)
$\delta(t_1,t_2)$	Market Illiquidity Premium for period $[t_1,t_2]$
η	Liquidation Model, Market Resiliency
$FC(.)$	Brownian Transfer Price, Required Funding Capacity
FC_t	Available Funding Capacity at t
γ	Brownian Transfer Price, Diversification Systematic/ Non-Systematic
γ^p	Brownian Transfer Prices, Diversification Product i/ Product j
$H(i)$	Liquidation Model, Characteristics of Asset i
HC	Haircut
HC^{ON}	Liquidation Model, Market Depth
$J_{t_k}^i$	Product Cash Flow, Compound Poisson Process
l	Brownian Transfer Price, Secured Fraction
λ^i	Product Cash Flow, Jump Intensity

Notation	Description
LC_t	Liquidation Capacity at t
L_t^a	Liquidation Value of Asset a at t
MMD	Money Market Department
$\mu_{t_k}^A$	Aggregated Cash Flow, Drift
$\mu_{t_k}^i$	Product Cash Flow, Drift
$N(t_k)$	Counting Model for Compound Poisson Process.
n_1	Transfer Prices, Time Without Exercises
n_2	Transfer Prices, Number of Exercises
OD	Origination Department
p	Brownian Transfer Price, Confidence Level
p^c	Money Market, Probability of Distressed Funding
p^{CF}	Money Market, Probability of Inflowing Cash Flow
$\Phi()$	Standard Normal Distribution
PV_t	Present Value at t
P&L	Profit & Loss
q_k	Time Index for Quarterly Variables
$r(t_1,t_2)$	Gross Funding Rate for $[t_1,t_2]$
$r_f(t_1,t_2)$	Risk-free interest rate for $[t_1,t_2]$
RC	Risk Controlling
s	Origination, Penalty Spread
s^A	Aggregated Cash Flow, Jump Component
s^{bas}	Bid-ask spread
s^i	Product Cash Flow, Jump Scaling Factor
σ^A	Aggregated Cash Flow, Brownian Component
σ^i	Product Cash Flow, Brownian Volatility
σ^M	Systematic Brownian Risk across all Products
σ^P	Unsystematic Brownian Risk across all Products
T	Transfer Prices, Product Maturity
t_k	Time Index for Daily Variables
ϑ_1^i	Confidence Model, Expected Jump Size
ϑ_2^i	Confidence Model, Jump Size Variance
$TP^B()$	Brownian Transfer Price
$TP^D()$	Drift Transfer Price
$TP^J()$	Jump Transfer Price

Notation	**Description**
V	Liquidation Model, Transaction Volume
v_{t_k}	Liquidation Model, Volume liquidated at t_k
W_{t_k}	Wiener Process
$\Delta W_{t_k}^{i,p}$	Product Cash Flow, Product-specific Liquidity Shock
$\Delta W_{t_k}^{m}$	Product Cash Flow, Systematic Liquidity Shock
$X_{t_k}^{i}$	Inventory of product i at t_k
Y_j	Jump Size Model for Compound Poisson Process

Chapter 1
Introduction

1.1 Motivation

Banks are intermediaries between liquidity supplying depositors and liquidity demanding borrowers.[1] Furthermore, they provide contingent liquidity in the form of loan commitments and liquidity backup lines. Importantly, liquidity is a core resource for banks that needs to be actively managed. For that purpose, we will develop a quantitative model of bank liquidity. Consequently, our model must be stochastic, complete, and will incorporate bank particularities. Here, completeness refers to the fact that the model encompasses product and aggregate as well as short and long-term liquidity. Significantly, an important particularity of banks' business that our model addresses is confidence. Incidentally, liquidity modelling is only the starting point for liquidity management, and we therefore discuss modelling, managing and optimizing liquidity.

Liquidity does not matter in perfect capital markets[2]: symmetric information ensures that agents have a perfect knowledge of banks' asset quality and asset value. The ability to raise external funds is only limited by the true asset value and not by the value that agents estimate. Moreover, assets are perfectly liquid and can always be sold at their true value. As a consequence, banks are not needed in perfect capital markets.

By contrast, the true asset value of banks is unknown to investors in real markets. These investors have to replace the true value with an estimate that could be heavily biased by rumours. Thus, any bank could face funding problems if the bank is exposed to adverse rumours.[3] Furthermore, other banks could hoard their liquidity as they face funding difficulties themselves. Additionally, liquidity is important for banks since they are the exclusive liquidity channel for central banks. The channel must function effectively to ensure that economy works smoothly. Besides, banks have mutually high liquidity exposures. The failure of one bank can easily encroach on other banks. Finally, liquidity is for banks what commodities are for corporations: an input factor for their (loan) production function. Hence, liquidity is important for banks in general.

---

[1] Chapter 2 provides a thorough definition of liquidity.

[2] For a definition of Perfect Capital Markets, see [Hartmann-Wendels et al., 2007, p.19].

[3] A recent example is that of the Bank of East Asia. Rumours of the imminent bankruptcy circulated via text messaging. As a result, customers stormed the bank to withdraw their savings and the bank had to credibly communicate its financial robustness, as the rumour was without any base. See [FTD, 2008c]. [BCBS, 2008, p.6] stressing that even banks that look solvent might face liquidity problems.

Institutional changes during the last decade require a readjustment of banks' liquidity management. Important changes are:[4]

- Disintermediation
  On the liability side, the traditional funding by retail deposits is shrinking and successively replaced by wholesale funds.[5] The implications are threefold: firstly, wholesale funding is more expensive than retail funding, reducing a bank's earnings. Secondly, wholesale investors are more price and rating sensitive, implying a higher funding risk.[6] Thirdly, banks use more Money Market instruments, thereby increasing bank interdependencies for short-term funds.
  On the asset side, large corporations substitute their bank loans with capital market debts. Among these debts, a very popular instrument for the short-end of the market are Commercial Papers (CP).[7] However, CP-issuers buy backup lines from banks in case their CPs are not prolongated (rolled over). Replacing loans by credit lines is a shift from unconditional to conditional liquidity, which increases liquidity risk. Figure 1.1 tracks the growth of the credit line exposure of US-banks. A similar trend (growth of 20% in 1995-2000) has been reported for major UK banks.[8]
- Securitization
  Prior to securitization, banks held loans until maturity. Generally, loans tie resources in the form of liquidity and capital. Securitization provides the opportunity to sell loan portfolios prior to maturity. As a consequence, capital and liquidity are only temporarily tied. As soon as loans are sold, new loans can be originated, re-using the same liquidity and capital as for the first loans.[9] This strategy was very popular among banks as figure 1.2 suggests. However, this strategy relies on the smooth functioning of securitization markets. If planned securitizations cannot be sold, banks are left with more credit risk and higher funding volumes than expected. If funding has been locked in as short-term, banks face an additional roll-over risk. As a result, securitization increases asset liquidity but also the liquidity risk. Banks that outsourced their securitization activities to special purpose vehicles kept the liquidity risk by liquidity backup facilities (see previous point).
- Complex Financial Securities
  Financial engineers developed instruments with complex risk and cash flow structures. Collateralized Debt Obligations (CDO), CDO squared, CPDO (Constant Proportion Debt Obligations) and other leverage products are examples of these.[10] These instruments constitute a new source of liquidity risk because their valuation is based on non-public information and requires sophisticated models. Furthermore, data about their

[4] See [IIF, 2007, p.14ff.], [BCBS, 2008, p.2ff] or [CEBS, 2008, p.16ff.].

[5] See [European Central Bank, 2002, p.6]. An empirical study for British banks was performed by [Wetmore, 2004] while [Weber and Norden, 2006] studied the funding schemes of German Banks.

[6] As ratings become more important for funding, banks are keen to obtain a high rating. Particularly the short-term rating incorporates an assessment of bank liquidity management, which provides an additional incentive to review liquidity management. See [Bank for International Settlement, 2006, p.118].

[7] See [Brealey and Myers, 2000, p.923] for details on Commercial Papers.

[8] See [European Central Bank, 2002, p.11].

[9] The business model is referred to as 'Originate and Distribute'.

[10] The growth of CDS squared in 2004 was estimated at 400% (see [RISK, 2005]). See [British Bankers' Association, 2006] for a discussion and growth statistics of credit risk innovations.

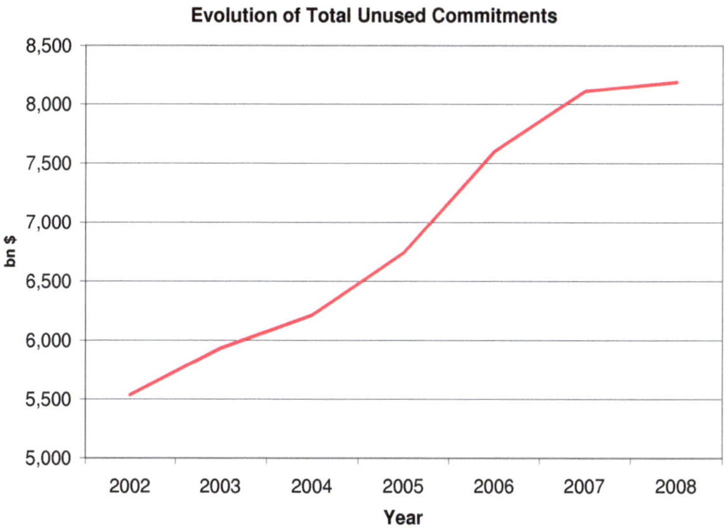

Fig. 1.1 Evolution of Total Unused Commitments of US-FDIC-insured Banks, Reporting Dates: 30.6., Source: Federal Deposit Insurance Corporation (FDIC)

behavior in stressed markets is unavailable. Complex securities have the highest valuation uncertainty and are likely to experience the most violent price shifts in stressed markets.[11] These securities might be difficult to sell in stressed markets because investors wait till valuation uncertainty is reduced. This then implies a liquidity risk for banks that want to sell them (see previous point), but it also implies a risk for banks that want to hold them and value them mark-to-market: valuation uncertainty directly translates into doubts about banks' solvency that might trigger funding problems.

- Collateralization
  To reduce counterparty risk liquidity management increasingly depends on high-quality collateral: central bank funding and a substantial fraction of wholesale funds are only available on a secured basis.[12] Figure 1.3 compares the average daily turnover of secured and unsecured Money Market transactions across time. It suggests that secured transactions are more important in both absolute and incremental terms. Collateral establishes a link between asset quality and funding capacity.
- Internal Liquidity Models
  Since January 1, 2007, German regulators have accepted internal liquidity models for liquidity risk reporting, which provides an incentive to develop an internal liquidity model that can replace the regulatory model.[13]

[11] [Financial Stability Directorate, 2008] discusses the uncertainty-valuation-liquidity relation.

[12] Furthermore, banking activities such as derivative transactions and payment services require collateral.

[13] See [Bundesanstalt für Finanzdienstleistungsaufsicht, 2006b, Paragraph 10].

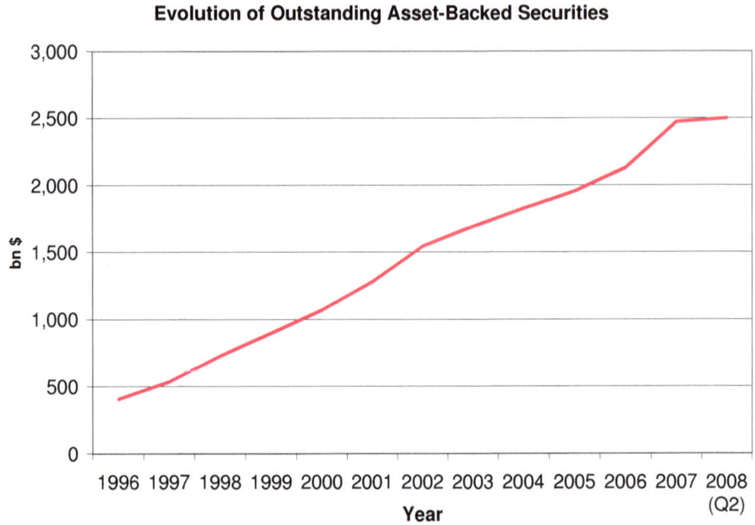

Fig. 1.2 Evolution of Outstanding Asset-Backed Securities (ABS), Source: Securities Industry and Financial Markets Association (SIFMA), Reporting Dates: 31.12.(2008: 30.6.)

Liquidity is even more important today because liquidity risk materialized during the subprime crisis. At the beginning of 2008, liquidity risk was perceived to be the most severe risk.[14] By comparison, it was not even mentioned in the same survey of 2007. In the following, we shortly describe causes, triggers and liquidity impact of the subprime crisis up to September 2008.[15]

The subprime crisis has been caused by US-banks' excessive lending to subprime borrowers.[16] Historically, the proportion of subprime borrowers among new residential mortgages was 8%. In 2006 it went up to 20%. The reasons for an excessive supply of subprime credit risk are threefold: firstly, low interest rates and interest rate teasers made loans affordable to subprime borrowers; secondly, house prices increased considerably in the last decade. Anticipating future price growths, banks did not require initial funds and financed up to 100% of the house price. Thirdly, banks originated loans under the assumption that they would not hold them till maturity, but would sell them shortly after origination. Given that short investment horizon, they lowered their standards for credit risk assessment. The excessive supply met an excessive demand for subprime credit risk. The excessive demand had its origin in two factors: firstly, investors searched yield pickups, as risk-free

[14] This is the result of a survey conducted by the Centre for Financial Innovation with 376 responses (59% bankers, 35% observers and 6% regulators) in February and March 2008. See [Centre for the Study of Financial Innovation, 2008] for details.

[15] We summarize the arguments raised by [Crouhy et al., 2008].

[16] The term 'subprime' refers to borrowers with low credit quality, who are borrowers with a low credit scoring, little credit history and/or with other types of credit impairment. See [Doms et al., 2007, p.1].

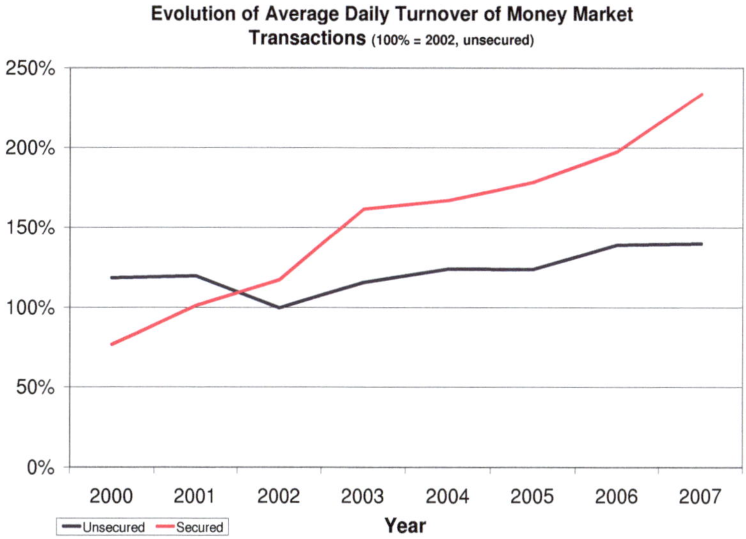

Fig. 1.3 Evolution of Secured and Unsecured Money Market Transactions, Source: Euro Money Market Survey 2007

interest rates were low; secondly, structured subprime securities provided an attractive rating/yield-ratio. High ratings have been favored by securitisation. Securitisation allows to create highly rated tranches out of low credit quality underlying mortgages.

The subprime crisis was triggered by increasing deliquency rates among subprime borrowers. Deliquency rates rose for three reasons: firstly, interest rates went up and increased the mortgage payments of those with variable rates. Secondly, interest rate teasers matured and switched to risk-adjusted rates. Thirdly, house prices started to stabilize or even to decrease. As a result, this made refinancing more expensive or even impossible.

Without securitization, it is likely that the US-made crisis would have remained a US-crisis and that it would not have had a global impact. However, securitization allocated credit risks of subprime borrowers at institutions that do not have direct access to subprime borrowers. As securitized assets have highly complex structures and no valuation has ever been done in stressed economic circumstances, valuation uncertainty among investors rose, leading to substantially reduced security values and market liquidity. Uncertainty did not differentiate between security types. Rating agencies that have been considered to be experts in assessing credit risk increased valuation uncertainty, as they were forced to reassess their methodologies as well.[17] Hence, the attractive rating/yield-ratio turned out to be too optimistic ex-post.

[17] Fitch recorded 128 downgrades (Q1, 2007) and 3683 downgrades (Q1, 2008) for subprime ABS. Moody's downgraded 2988 (Q1, 2008) versus 99 (Q1, 2007). S&P downgraded 5444 (Q1, 2008) versus 115 (Q1, 2007) (see [SIFMA, 2008, p.10]). See [Committee on the Global Financial System, 2008] for a discussion of rating transitions.

The liquidity impact of the subprime crisis was threefold: firstly, investors stopped buying securitized assets, leading to higher funding requirements for banks that planned with their securitization. Secondly, investors were reluctant to lend against these securities as collateral. This implied higher liquidity requirements of special purpose vehicles (SPV) that relied on secured rolling-funding. Via backup liquidity facilities or reputational concerns, the liquidity risk of their SPVs returned to banks. Thirdly, mark-to-market losses led to substantial write-offs and cast doubts on the solvency of banks, deteriorating their funding situation.[18] The main channel for short-term liquidity management, the interbank market, almost evaporated.[19] This is due to two reasons: firstly, banks preferred to hoard liquidity as they did not trust other banks and, secondly, they were uncertain about their own liquidity needs for the near future.[20] One positive aspect of the subprime crisis is that it is a severe stress test for liquidity managers. The crisis renewed the awareness for the oldest bank risk. Furthermore, it made the new sources and propagation channels of liquidity risk transparent. The crisis revealed bank-specific and systematic deficiencies of liquidity management.[21]

1.2 Problem Description

1.2.1 Bank Liquidity Models

A recent development in risk management is the approval of internal models for regulatory reporting. Regulators assume that internal models reflect bank-specific exposures better than a 'one fits all' regulatory model. Internal models have first been approved for credit and operational risk.[22] Nowadays, national supervisors encourage the development of internal models for liquidity risk.[23] German supervisors are the first ones to accept internal liquidity models.[24] Hence, there is an evident need for the development of such models.

[18] A prominent example of those mechanisms is the German bank IKB and its special purpose vehicle 'Rhinland Funding'. The business model was planned as follows: 'Rhinland Funding' buys (illiquid) ABS with high ratings (70% AA or above, only 10% below investment grade) and funds them via short-term asset-backed commercial paper (ABCP). This business model implicitly assumes that the short-term positions can always be rolled over. Because subprime ABS have been downgraded and considerably revalued, Rhineland Funding was unable to roll over the CPs. However, for that scenario, 'Rhineland' has been endowed with a backup credit line by IKB. IKB, however, was unable to raise sufficient funds to cover the credit line drawing, because major lenders cancelled their credit lines (see [Economist, 2007]). [Brunnermeier, 2008] provides a description of the vicious liquidity spirals that underlie the evaporation of funding.

[19] See [FTD, 2008b].

[20] See [FTD, 2008a].

[21] Regulators identified weak points (see [Basel Committee on Banking Supervision, 2008, p.11ff.]) and already responded by publishing new 'Principles for Sound Liquidity Risk Management and Supervision' (see [BCBS, 2008]).

[22] The tendency for internal models has been pioneered by Basel II. See [Basel Committee on Banking Supervision, 2006, p.52] for internal rating models for credit risk. Also see [Basel Committee on Banking Supervision, 2006, p.144] for internal models for operational risk.

[23] See [CEBS, 2007, No. 35] for a survey on liquidity regulation.

[24] See section 1.1.

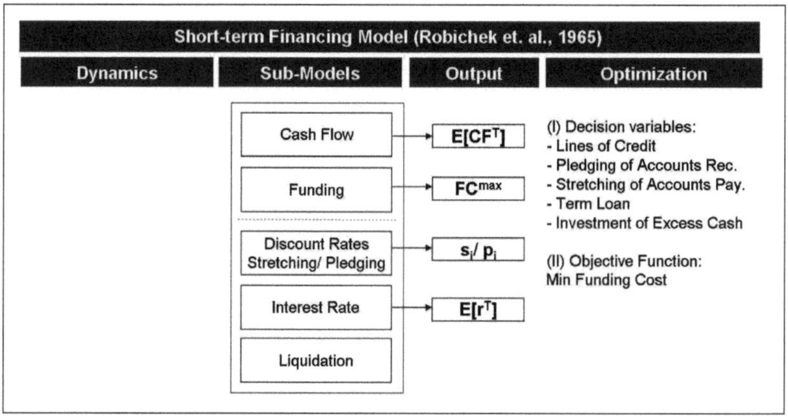

Fig. 1.4 Short-Term Financing Model by Robichek et al. (1965)

1.2.2 Quantitative Liquidity Models

The majority of publications about bank liquidity management is qualitative. In fact, regulators and industry sources postulate qualitative requirements on liquidity models, but do not specify any model.[25] This sharply contrasts with the current modelling stage of other risk types: interest rate, equity and credit risk use sophisticated quantitative techniques. The modelling of bank liquidity has not adopted these techniques yet. As a result, there is a need for the development of quantitative liquidity models.

Quantitative liquidity models exist for corporations. The management of short-term liquidity is described by cash management models.[26] The management of long-term liquidity (funding), on the other hand, is described by debt management models. In the following, we review the literature for both model families and motivate the adjustments that are needed to incorporate bank particularities.

1.2.2.1 Cash Management Models

Deterministic Models

The first generation of cash management models were deterministic, which reduced stochastic variables to their expected values. Figure 1.4 summarizes the short-term fi-

[25] Recent important publications about bank liquidity management are: (1) Supervisors: 'Principles for Sound Liquidity Risk Management and Supervision' ([BCBS, 2008]), CEBSs technical advice to the European Commission on Liquidity Risk Management ([CEBS, 2007], [CEBS, 2008]), (2) German Law Maker: Minimum Requirements for Risk Management, BTR 3 ([Bundesanstalt für Finanzdienstleistungsaufsicht, 2005]), German Liquidity Directive [Bundesanstalt für Finanzdienstleistungsaufsicht, 2006b] (3) Industry Sources: Framework for liquidity risk management ([IIF, 2007]). Textbooks are sometimes more quantitative with respect to selected topics ([Bartetzky et al., 2008], [Matz and Neu, 2007]).

[26] See [Krumnow et al., 2002, p.273].

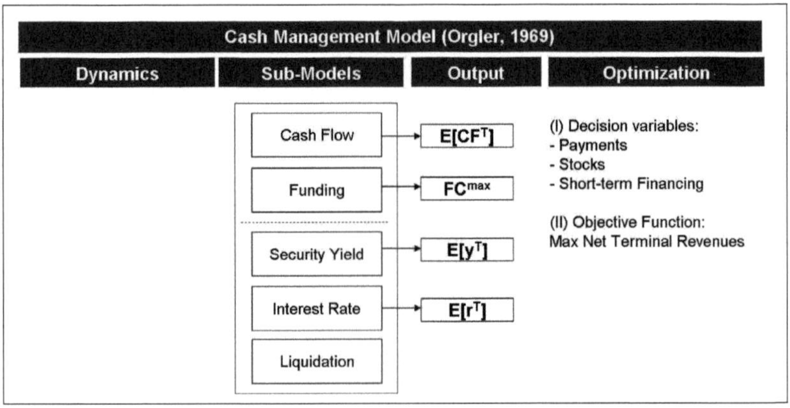

Fig. 1.5 Cash Management Model by Orgler (1969)

nancing model proposed by Robichek et al. (1965).[27] The figure consists of four sections: 'Dynamics', 'Sub-Models', 'Output' and 'Optimization'. Sub-Models contain the key variables that are modelled. Dynamics describes how stochastic key variables are modelled. Key variables that are deterministic do not have a dynamic. The column 'Output' lists the model output and the column 'Optimization' gives a short description of the optimization programme, containing decision variables and objective function. We use this structure for the description of all subsequent liquidity models. This facilitates the comparison of models.

The model describes a corporate treasurer that determines the optimal financing policy for a given cash flow forecast. The treasurer can choose from lines of credit, reporting payables, anticipating receivables, term loans and investment of excess cash. The benefits of reporting payables and anticipating receivables are controlled by the discounts s_i and p_i.

Orgler (1969) extends the investment spectrum by stocks.[28] Figure 1.5 summarizes the model. As the model is deterministic, stock returns are modelled by their expectations. The objective function maximizes net terminal revenues. Robichek et al. (1965) place the focus on the funding side ('Financing Model'). In Orgler's model, funding and investment are both equally important.

Deterministic models are used to optimize liquidity for the 'business as usual' scenario. They do not, however, incorporate stress scenarios and therefore cannot model liquidity risk.

[27] See [Robichek et al., 1965].

[28] See [E.Orgler, 1969].

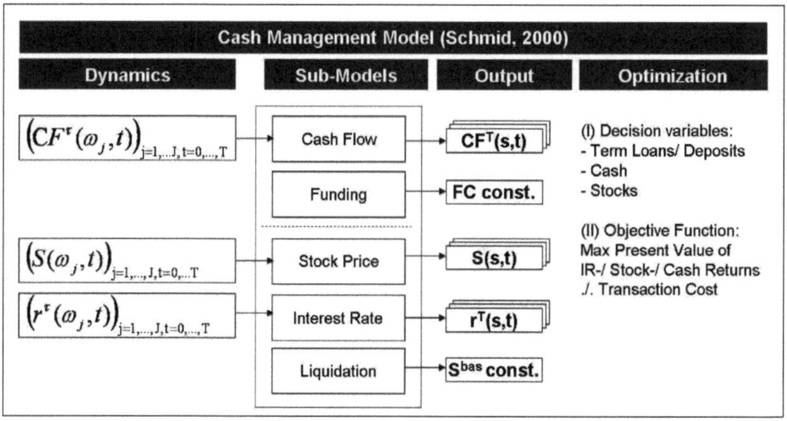

Fig. 1.6 Cash Management Model by Schmid (2000)

Stochastic Models

Deterministic cash management models are extended by replacing expectations with random variables. A recent stochastic cash management model has been presented by Schmid (2000) as summarized by figure 1.6.[29] The model assists treasurers in determining the optimal investment/funding mix given a particular cash flow dynamic. The available instruments (= decision variables) are term loans/term deposits, stocks and cash reserve. The treasurer maximizes the expected present value of future returns after transaction cost. The model contains three stochastic drivers: cash flows, stock prices and interest rates. Less modelling attention is placed on funding capacity (FC) and transaction cost (bid-ask spread s^{bas}), as both are deterministic.

A similar model has been developed by Ferstl and Weissensteiner (2008), summarized in figure 1.7.[30] As in Schmid's model, interest rates and stock prices are stochastic. Ferstl and Weissensteiner minimize Conditional Value at Risk (CVaR), which is the weighted sum of Value at Risk and Expected Shortfall. However, the model operates on expected cash flows. Furthermore, funding is not restricted; Thus, they cannot model liquidity risk. By focussing on the investment aspect of cash management, they are missing important elements for liquidity management. As banks are firms as well, one might infer that (corporate) cash management models are adequate for managing bank liquidity. However, this is not the case. They are of limited use for banks for the following reasons:

1. Product cash flows are not modelled
   Liquidity is managed on the aggregate level. Therefore, cash management models use the aggregate cash flow. However, the modelling of bank liquidity has to start at the product level. In contrast to corporates, liquidity is an input factor in banks' production function. Banks 'produce' loans and deposits using liquidity. The prices of products

[29] See [Schmid, 2000].

[30] See [Ferstl and Weissensteiner, 2008].

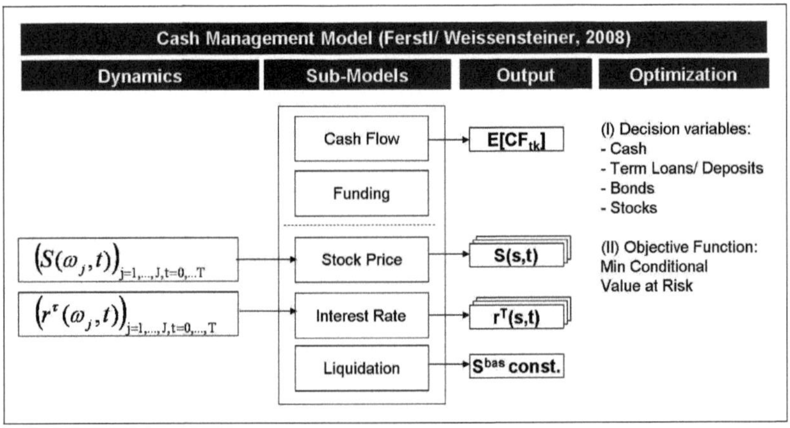

Fig. 1.7 Cash Management Model by Ferstl/ Weissensteiner (2008)

must incorporate the prices of input factors. Hence, banks must determine the price of liquidity and allocate it to products. The allocation depends on the cash flow characteristics of the product. Thus, the starting point of a bank liquidity model must be the product cash flow. Furthermore, the model has to detail how product cash flows are aggregated to the bank cash flow.

2. No confidence-component
   Many banks use deposits for funding. Deposits are liquidity options, as customers can withdraw funds whenever they wish to do so. Customers cannot only withdraw when they need funds, but also when they lose confidence in a bank's ability to repay deposits.[31] Hence, deposit cash flows contain a confidence component that corporate funding lacks. Cash management models do not account for that confidence component. The confidence component can cause stress scenarios that are unlikely for corporations.
3. Stock investments and interest rate management
   In corporations, treasurers have a monopoly on financial transactions. However, banks have specialized departments for different kinds of transactions: proprietory equity trading for stock investments; the swap book for interest rate management; a liquidity book for liquidity management. The liquidity manager of a bank is unlikely to invest in stocks or to manage the interest rate exposure. Banks separate these activities in specialized departments. A bank liquidity model neither has to model stock prices nor long-term interest rates. In that sense, it is a particular case of a cash management model. The internal specialization of a bank requires several departments to be involved in liquidity management. In that case, the model has to specify tasks and benchmarks of the involved departments and describe how liquidity is internally transferred between departments.

[31] A loss of confidence can exacerbate the situation and lead to a bank run, as recently seen at Northern Rock. See [Northern Rock plc, 2007, p.25].

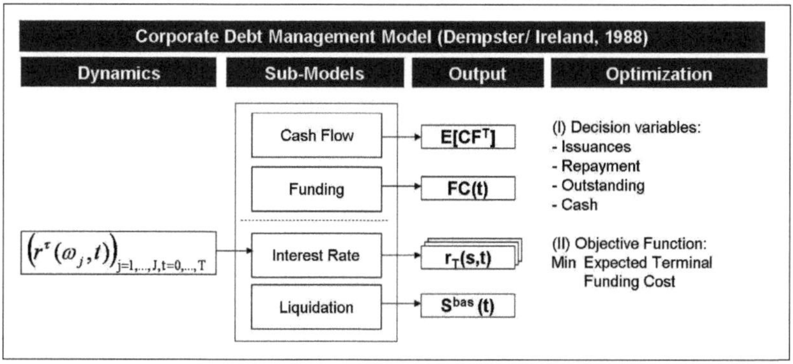

Fig. 1.8 Corporate Debt Management Model by Dempster/ Ireland (1988)

4. Asset liquidation and funding capacity
   As corporations do not provide liquidity options, they are not exposed to the risk of violent cash outflows. Certainly, banks are exposed to them. As a reaction, banks can liquidate assets or raise external funds. However, both measures might be correlated to the cash flow evolution and induce elevated cost. Usually, corporations hold little quantities of liquid assets. Furthermore, their funding capacity is rather stable. As a result, cash management models do not incorporate stochastic funding capacity or stochastic asset liquidation. Admittedly, a bank liquidity model has to account for this.

The arguments suggest that corporate cash management models cannot be used straight away for bank liquidity management. Cash management models have to be adjusted to account for bank particularities.

1.2.2.2 Debt Management Models

The management of the funding profile is described by corporate debt management models. Corporate debt management models assist treasurers in determining the optimal funding mix with respect to type, maturity, terms and timing of debts given a particular interest rate dynamic. Figure 6.8 summarizes an exemplary debt management model presented by Dempster and Ireland (1988).[32] The corporate debt manager decides the volume of issuances, repayments (call options), outstanding and cash. The debt manager minimizes expected terminal funding cost. Interest rates are the stochastic sources of the model; cash flows, funding capacity and liquidation costs are deterministic. We argue that corporate debt models must be adjusted to manage bank debt for the following reasons:

1. Funding profile and interest rates can be managed independently
   Interest rate and debt maturity coincide for fixed-rate issuances. Floating rate instruments decouple interest rate and debt maturity. Thus, the decision concerning interest rate maturity and debt maturity can be taken independently. The variable that is linked

[32] See [Dempster and Ireland, 1988]. For a shorter version, see also [Cornuejols and Tütüncü, 2007, p.282ff.].

to debt maturity is the funding spread. Therefore, the debt management model should use the funding spread as driving variable instead of interest rates.

2. Roll-over risk
   As for cash management models, the funding capacity should be stochastic in debt models. It might be possible that issuances cannot be rolled over.[33] This is an important risk that the debt model should take into account.

Like cash management models, corporate debt models need to be adjusted before using them for banks.

1.2.3 Complete Liquidity Models

In contrast to the literature, we develop a complete liquidity model. Completeness refers to several dimensions:

1. Model covers both short and long-term liquidity
   If the cash and debt management models of the previous section are adjusted for bank particularities, they remain partial models. However, they have a common point: cash flows. Cash management models manage short-term, debt management models long-term cash flows. An integrated model to describe short and long-term cash flows is desirable. Our model accounts for this point.
2. Model describes product and aggregate liquidity
   Liquidity is **managed** on the aggregate level (Liquidity Management). However, liquidity is **priced** on the product level (Liquidity Controlling). In fact, the liquidity cost and benefits of products have to be incorporated in product pricing. In contrast to the literature that starts on the aggregate level, we base our modelling on the product level and subsequently aggregate to reach the management level. The aggregation requires additional assumptions concerning the dependence structures of products and the consideration of potential diversification effects.
3. Model encompasses expected and stress scenarios
   Currently, banks have one model for expected cash flows (planning model) and one model for stress testing. However, it is more desirable to have one stochastic model that is able to describe multiple scenarios. Accordingly, our model is stochastic and covers such a variety of scenarios.

Apart from these completeness criteria, our analysis is unique with respect to another aspect: it describes Liquidity Modelling, Controlling and Management (Optimization). As we cannot build on existing bank liquidity models, we have to describe all steps of liquidity management. We begin with the liquidity model, discuss liquidity controlling and conclude with liquidity optimization. Thus, we discuss neither liquidity controlling nor liquidity management as the literature usually does. Instead, we address both fields.

Our approach closes the gap in complete quantitative liquidity models for banks. It provides a sound analytical basis for liquidity management in banks that had been missing so far. We believe that a first approach has to be complete in order to give other researchers

[33] The roll-over risk materialized during the subprime crisis.

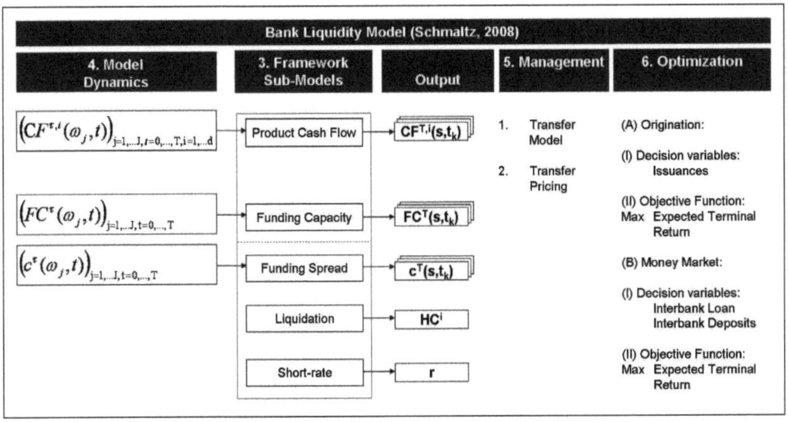

Fig. 1.9 Our Bank Liquidity Model

an understanding of the whole process. Once the process is understood, basic concepts can be replaced by more sophisticated approaches. Thus, we rank completeness above sophistication.

In contrast to other risk classes, liquidity management is based on inhouse variables. Thus, implementation issues vary between banks. Consequently, our analysis does not address implementation issues.

1.3 Objective and Proceeding

The previous section argued that there is a need for complete, quantitative, internal bank liquidity models. We develop a model that satisfies all these criteria. Subsequently, we describe the steps taken to derive such a model.

Chapter 2 studies the different concepts of liquidity. It provides an overview of what is understood by liquidity in the literature. Therefore, we discuss definitions, properties and particularities of each concept. Finally, we analyze interdependencies between them.

After the definitional chapter we elaborate the bank liquidity model. Its structure is given in figure 1.9. The numbered columns correspond to the chapters.

Chapter 3 derives the minimum set of variables that a bank liquidity model should account for. We refer to these variables as key liquidity variables. They represent the sub-models that are needed to describe bank liquidity. A preparatory step introduces fundamental terms and tools of liquidity management that we use in subsequent sections. The key variables are derived from the liquidity strategies that banks run. We formulate them as stochastic processes, and together they form the liquidity framework.

Chapter 4 derives a particular liquidity model by specifying the stochastic process for each key variable. The specification takes three steps for each variable: firstly, we study requirements that the literature postulates for the modelling. Apart from external requirements, we also incorporate our requirements to ensure that the model is complete and that it accounts for bank particularities. Secondly, we discuss advantages and disadvantages of potential modelling approaches. Thirdly, we choose an approach. Each specified process can be considered a sub-model. The complete set of sub-models constitutes our bank liquidity model.

Chapter 5 discusses liquidity management. This is an additional column compared to the models in the literature that assume that liquidity is managed in one department. We analyze whether the one-department structure is suitable for banks. If multiple departments are involved we have to detail how (transfer model) and at which prices (transfer pricing) liquidity is transferred between departments. Furthermore, we describe department objectives and instruments. Our management approach should naturally fit into the banks' organizational setup. In order to allow for local (department-internal) optimization, we have to minimize inter-department dependencies.

Chapter 6 describes the local optimization within departments. In a first step we determine why global optimization can be split up into department-wise optimization. Subsequently, we set up the local optimization programmes and solve them.

Chapter 7 concludes and offers an outlook for further research.

Chapter 2
Liquidity Concepts

Liquidity is a term with distinct but related meanings depending on the context. Traders, treasurers and central bankers use the term 'liquidity', but mean different things.[1] Because of this, it is necessary to de- and refine what we understand by liquidity. The literature distinguishes three liquidity concepts:[2]

1. Asset Liquidity
2. Institutional Liquidity
3. National Liquidity

These concepts are discussed in subsequent sections. For each concept, we provide a definition, components, value range and risk dimension.

2.1 Asset Liquidity

Asset Liquidity is defined as the ease to liquidate an asset quickly with minimal liquidation losses.[3] Therefore, the dimensions of Asset Liquidity are 'time' and 'liquidation value'. An asset can be liquidated by two mechanisms:[4]

1. Self-liquidation
   A maturing asset automatically reconverts to cash at maturity.[5] Self-liquidation does not involve cost.
2. Shiftability
   Prior to maturity, an asset can be liquidated by sale or pledging. Shiftability usually involves liquidation cost.

---

[1] See [Persaud, 2003, p. 86] and [Issing, 2001, p. 169].

[2] See [Reimund, 2003, p. 5ff.],[Körnert, 1998, p. 66], [Issing, 2001, p. 169ff.] and [Krumnow et al., 2002, p. 880]. The latter lists 'International liquidity' as a separate liquidity category.

[3] See inter alia [Brunner, 1996, p. 3f.], [Krumnow et al., 2002, p. 880], [Mankiw, 2001, p. 647], [Saunders and Hugh, 2001, p. 127] and [Timothy W. Koch, 2000, p. 125].

[4] See [Krumnow et al., 2002, p. 880] and [Reimund, 2003, p.7 ff.].

[5] 'Self-Liquidation' is a particular case of 'Shiftability' where the liquidation value is prohibitively small and time to liquidation is maturity.

In self-liquidation, only short-term securities are liquid. Eternal securities (e.g. shares) are illiquid. In self-liquidation, the maturity is known, the payment contractually fixed and (usually) unconditional.[6]

Shiftability decouples maturity and asset liquidity because assets can be liquidated before maturity. However, shiftability involves liquidation cost that occurs as the long-term fundamental value (present value) cannot be realized due to market frictions.[7] In the following, we use 'liquidation' for shiftability, as 'liquidation' is commonly used for selling/pledging assets. If we mean self-liquidation, we explicitly use the term 'self-liquidation'.

In pricing models, market illiquidity is measured by an illiquidity premium. In liquidity management, it is measured by haircuts.[8] We discuss both methods to outline the differences.

Asset Liquidity in Pricing Models

Pricing models introduce an additional parameter for market illiquidity.[9] It can be interpreted as a premium that investors require to be compensated for transaction cost or valuation uncertainty. The present value equation extended for market illiquidity is defined by (2.1):

$$L_t^a = \sum_{j=t+1}^{T} \frac{CF_s^a}{(1+r_f(t,j)+c^a(t,j)+\delta^a(t,j))^s} \tag{2.1}$$

$$\begin{aligned} &\text{being}: \\ CF_s^a &: \text{Future Cash Flows, asset a} \\ L_t^a &: \text{Liquidation Value, asset a} \\ r_f(t,j) &: \text{Risk-free interest rate} \\ c^a(t,j) &: \text{Credit Risk Premium, asset a} \\ \delta^a(t,j) &: \text{Illiquidity Premium, asset a,} \\ &\delta^a(t,j) \geq 0 \end{aligned}$$

The liquidation value (or market price) of asset a at time t is denoted L_t^a. It is the sum of all future cash flows discounted at the risk-free rate $r_f(t_1,t_2)$ plus the premium for credit risk inherent in asset a $c^a(t_1,t_2)$ and a premium for a's potential future illiquidity $\delta^a(t_1,t_2)$. Market illiquidity is measured by delta. Delta is an illiquidity premium, as it takes positive values for less liquid assets and zero for liquid assets.

The present value PV_t^a can be interpreted as the market value for perfectly liquid assets:

$$PV_t^a = L_t^a(\delta^a = 0) \tag{2.2}$$

---

6 If we abstain from credit risk.

7 See [Biais et al., 2005].

8 Haircuts are subsequently explained. Regulators use haircuts to measure asset liquidity. See [IIF, 2007, p.31] and [BCBS, 2008, p.22].

9 For a continuous version for defaultable corporate bonds, see [Longstaff et al., 2005].

Asset Liquidity in Liquidity Management

In liquidity management, asset liquidity is measured by haircuts HC. Note the following relation:

$$PV_t = \underbrace{HC \cdot PV_t}_{\text{Not recovered}} + \underbrace{(1-HC) \cdot PV_t}_{\text{Recovered}} \tag{2.3}$$

PV : Present Value

HC : Haircut

The present value can be decomposed into a fraction that can and a fraction that cannot be recovered in liquidation.[10] Haircuts can take any values between 0 and 1. Similar to delta haircuts are illiquidity measures as they take large values for less liquid and zero for perfectly liquid assets.

Haircuts measure illiquidity in currency units, delta measures illiquidity as discount premium. Both measures are positive. Delta is not limited, whereas haircuts are limited at 1.

Haircuts can be reconciled with bid-ask spreads that are often used as empirical proxies to measure market liquidity in a trading context. The bid-ask spread s^{bas} is the difference between bid- and ask-quotes:

$$\begin{aligned} s^{bas} &:= (P_t^{Bid} - PV_t) + (PV_t - L_t) \\ &= (P_t^{Bid} - PV_t) + HC^{Ask} \\ &= HC^{Bid} + HC^{Ask} \end{aligned}$$

Being:

P_t^{Bid} :Purchase Value, Bid-Quote

L_t :Liquidation Value, Ask-Quote

PV_t :(Fundamental) Present Value

The haircut as defined by (2.3) constitutes one part of the bid-ask spread, namely the difference between present and liquidation value (ask quote). Put into the bid-ask context, it is the ask-haircut. The second bid-ask component is the difference between purchase value (bid quote) and present value. We denoted this difference HC^{Bid}. Thus, the bid-ask spread is the sum of the haircut that the selling and the buying side have to bear. If not stated differently, haircut always means HC^{ask}.

Asset liquidity depends on the institutional setup: marketable assets have a higher liquidity than non-marketable assets. Financial assets are marketable if they are produced on a primary market[11] and not by an intermediary. Theory suggests that intermediaries can produce financial assets at lower cost if primary markets are not perfect. These im-

[10] The fraction that is recovered in liquidation is sometimes denoted 'Moneyness' k (k = (1-HC)). See [Wagner, 2007], [Büttler, 1999].

[11] [Krumnow et al., 2002, p.1048].

perfections include transaction cost, information asymmetries and non-transferable capabilities.[12]

However, the existence of a market is a necessary, but not a sufficient condition for high asset liquidity.

Research has revealed that the following factors reduce asset liquidity:[13]

- Exogenuous transaction cost
  These costs include brokerage fees, taxes or order-processing cost.
- Demand pressure
  Demand pressure occurs when potential buyers are not available in the market. Meanwhile, positions have to be taken by market makers on their inventory. To compensate the inventory price risk, market makers require a price discount.
- Private Information
  If the seller is assumed to have private information, the buyer anticipates that the seller knows that the asset price will deteriorate. The buyer already anticipates this by requiring a price discount.
- Search frictions
  The price discounts consist of search costs to find a counterparty and of bilateral negotiation costs.
- Strategic Behavior of Market Makers[14]
  Market makers should provide market liquidity. However, in certain market circumstances it is preferable for them to absorb liquidity.

In real markets, one or more factors might be present, substantially reducing market liquidity.

The risk side of Asset Liquidity is the risk that asset liquidity suddenly deteriorates or even vanishes. This implies that the liquidation discount increases substantially.

[12] The transaction cost-argument is based on the assumption that an intermediary benefits from economies of scale in transaction costs. Popular (model) transaction costs are search costs and the administration of financial assets. The information asymmetry argument is based on the assumption that an intermediary can realize economies of scale by monitoring borrowers. They have to be monitored because they know the success/failure of their projects whereas the lender does not (Information asymmetry). In an opportunistic way, the borrower could draw his own advantage from the information gap (moral hazard). Monitoring reduces the cost implied by moral hazard. The non-transferability argument is based on the assumption that borrowers have a specific capability/ideas to use the financed asset. They could use this unique capability to blackmail the lender. An intermediary who successively learns the capability reduces the moral hazard cost. For further details, see [Hartmann-Wendels et al., 2007, p.110ff.].

[13] For a literature survey of market liquidity, please refer to [Biais et al., 2005] and [Amihud et al., 2005]. The first survey studies the impact of the institutional setup on market liquidity. The second survey papers deal with the impact of market liquidity on asset prices.

[14] [Amihud et al., 2005], [Biais et al., 2005].

2.2 Institutional Liquidity

'Institutional Liquidity' describes the capacity of an institution to meet its payment obligations when they are due.[15] It is formalized by inequality (2.4):

$$CF_t^+ + FC_t + LC_t \geq CF_t^- \tag{2.4}$$

Payment obligations CF_t^- constitute the right hand side of (2.4). The left hand side contains the sources to cover them. Payment obligations are covered in a natural way by (1) incoming cash flows CF_t^+. If incoming cash flows are not sufficient, additional liquidity actions have to be taken. These actions are (2) asset liquidation LC_t and (3) unsecured external funding FC_t. LC_t stands for liquidation capacity. It is the sum of the liquidation values[16] of assets that have not been taken into account by CF_t^+. Assets can be liquidated by either repo or sale.[17] FC_t stands for funding capacity. The sum of liquidation and funding capacity is termed Counterbalancing Capacity. Note that institutional liquidity is defined on the institutional level. Therefore, all variables in (2.4) are aggregate quantities.

At its origin, institutional liquidity is a binary concept: if (2.4) holds, the entity is liquid, otherwise it is illiquid. A binary statement is unable to support management decisions. Therefore, practitioners use liquidity measures with continuous scales in form of ratios.[18]

The risk dimension of institutional liquidity is that the bank becomes illiquid, i.e. that it cannot meet its payment obligations. Together with insolvency, illiquidity is the second default reason according to the German Bankruptcy Code. As the code distinguishes two reasons, there have to be situations in which an institution is illiquid but not insolvent, or insolvent but not illiquid.

Illiquidity and insolvency are distinct, but closely related. As we focus on liquidity, we briefly delimit both terms. We base our arguments on the German Bankruptcy Code.

The code defines illiquidity as the situation in which an institution is unable to fulfil payment obligations when they are due.[19] An institution is insolvent if its asset value falls below the liability value whereas both positions are valued from a going concern perspective.[20]

The definitions have two implications: firstly, illiquidity is conditional on an (observable) payment event. As a result, it is easy to detect for outsiders. Secondly, insolvency is hard to detect for outsiders as it is based on non-observable quantities. Therefore, the law extends the insolvency definition by forcing board members (insiders) to publicly declare insolvency as soon as they are aware of it.[21]

Clearly, if assets are worth less than liabilities, the institution is insolvent. If there is a payment obligation and assets are liquid, the payment obligation can be honoured; hence, the institution is not illiquid. If assets value more than liabilities on a going-concern per-

[15] s. [Saunders and Hugh, 2001, p. 113], [Reimund, 2003, p. 5ff.], [Krumnow et al., 2002, p. 880f.], [Körnert, 1998, p. 66]. For a legal definition, see [German Bankruptcy Code, 1995, Paragraph 17].

[16] See definition (2.1).

[17] Section 3.1.5 describes and compares repo and sale.

[18] See [Baetge et al., 2004, p.262ff.] and [Küting and Weber, 2001, p.122ff.].

[19] See [German Bankruptcy Code, 1995, Paragraph 17].

[20] See [German Bankruptcy Code, 1995, Paragraph 19].

[21] See [PLC, 2007, Paragraph 401,Sect.1,No 1].

spective (i.e. on a middle to long-term perspective) the institution is solvent. However, if there is a payment obligation and assets are illiquid[22], the institution is illiquid.[23] Obviously, the two valuation methods for assets ('Going Concern' Value/'Liquidation' Value) lead to the distinction between insolvency and illiquidity. The 'Going Concern' value refers to the present value or fundamental value. As defined in section 2.1, assets are liquid if their 'Going Concern' value equals its liquidation value. Assets are illiquid if both values substantially differ. Hence, illiquid assets are at the origin of institutional illiquidity and therefore at the distinction between insolvency and illiquidity. An institution that only holds liquid assets can never be illiquid. However, it can be solvent or insolvent, depending on the asset value.

Institutions with a high proportion of illiquid assets and many (stochastic) payment obligations are exposed to illiquidity. As banks have exactly such an asset/liability profile, they are particularly exposed to illiquidity risk.[24]

In order to avoid liquidation cost, lawmakers do not require self-liquidation of illiquid but solvent institutions. They require a going concern under a liquidator. However, an illiquid, but solvent institution is bankrupt and has to bear bankruptcy costs just like an insolvent institution. Bankruptcy costs can be grouped in direct and indirect costs.[25] Direct bankruptcy costs cover legal, administrative and reorganization cost while indirect bankruptcy costs result from shrunk business and loss of staff top performers. Supposing that illiquidity results from a temporary problem (of a payment obligation of one day), the costs of shrunk business are rather long-term (crisis hysteresis), as lost confidence is difficult to regain. As a bank's deposit business is based on confidence, the indirect bankruptcy cost of shrunk future business makes illiquidity particularly expensive for banks.

2.3 National Liquidity

National liquidity is defined as the sum of central bank money (money basis) plus the liquidity created by commercial banks (book money).[26]

Money basis and book money are best explained by the money supply process.[27] Figure 2.1 describes the two steps of the process: the upper part explains the initial injection of the money basis from the central bank to a commercial bank.[28] The lower part explains the creation of book money as interaction between commercial bank and non-banks.

Our explanation begins with the first step in which the central bank decides on the money basis (central bank money). It can be provided in form of banknotes or deposits (at

[22] The going concern-value is much higher than the liquidation value.

[23] If the law recognized illiquidity as a separate bankruptcy reason, the institution would be forced to self-liquidate till it honours the payment obligation or till it is insolvent (liquidation losses exceed equity). However, the law does not require self-liquidation in case of illiquidity, but encourages for going-concern with a liquidator.

[24] Banks usually hold iilliquid loans and are exposed to stochastic payment obligations from deposits.

[25] See [Brealey and Myers, 2000, p.510ff.].

[26] See [Krumnow et al., 2002, p. 880] and [Körnert, 1998, p. 66].

[27] See [Issing, 2001, p. 56ff.].

[28] We simplify the process by summarizing the whole banking industry as a single commercial bank.

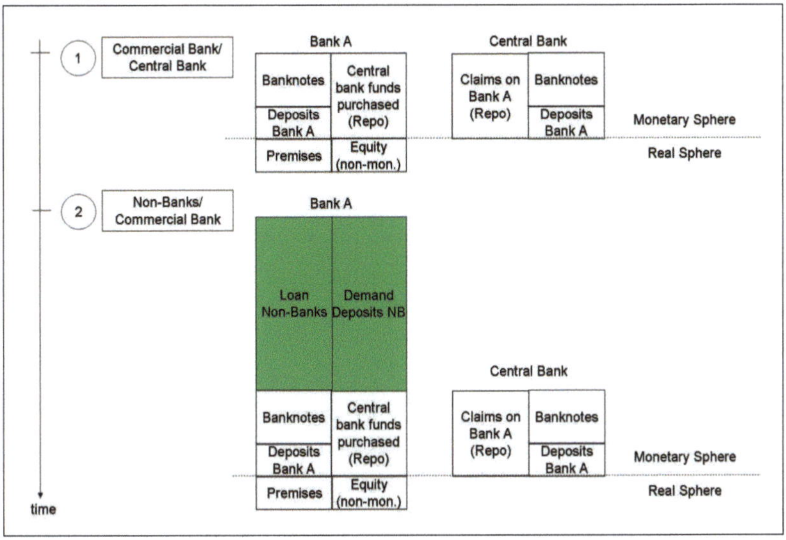

Fig. 2.1 Money Supply Process (Based on [Issing, 2001, p.55ff.])

the central bank).[29] We assume that our central bank only uses banknotes. Furthermore, we abstract from claims/liabilities to foreign countries and transactions with the state. Banknotes are owned by the central bank. They are injected into the economy via secured lending (repo).[30] We assume that bank A is endowed with non-monetary premises and that the central bank accepts them as collateral.[31] The maturity of the repo determines the date by which the banknotes have to be returned to the central bank or the repo has to be rolled over. The repo establishes a claim of the central bank against bank A. Bank A begins with a balance sheet that consists of banknotes that are funded with a repo liability.

Once, the commercial bank is endowed with the money basis, it can grant loans to non-banks. This is the second step of the money supply process (lower part of figure 2.1). We assume that loans are illiquid, i.e. cannot be sold (converted into banknotes). In a cash economy in which non-banks do not hold accounts and all payments are made in cash, the commercial bank can only grant loans up to the amount of banknotes received. In an account economy in which non-banks do hold accounts with bank A, bank A can grant more loans than it received banknotes. The loans are funded by demand deposits. The more account-based the economy, the higher the amount the bank can grant non-cash. The liquidity created by banks is in form of book money.

---

[29] An abstract central bank balance sheet is given in [Issing, 2001, p.56]. The balance sheet of the Bundesbank can be found in the Annual Report (see [Deutsche Bundesbank, 2007, p. 125ff.]).

[30] The ECB's main refinancing operation is a weekly repo (tender). See [European Central Bank, 2006, p. 8]. For a description of repo, see section 3.1.5.

[31] We introduce a real sphere endowment to separate the real and monetary sphere, and to keep the monetary sphere as simple as possible. Any monetary endowment (e.g. securities) would introduce an additonal degree of complexity without gaining any additional insight.

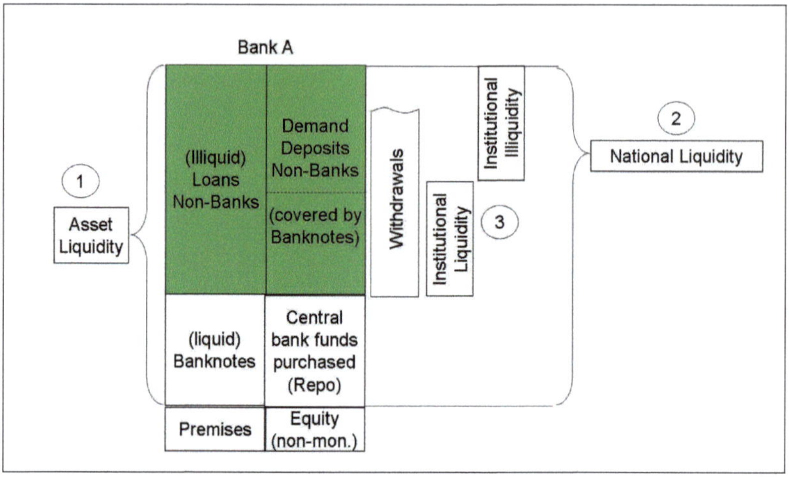

Fig. 2.2 Bank Balance Sheet and Liquidity Concepts

National liquidity comprises the asset side of bank A: the sum of banknotes (central bank money) and (illiquid) loans (book money).

National liquidity is measured in monetary units on a continuous scale.

The national liquidity has a risk potential on both sides: too much money supply creates an inflation risk, insufficient supply slows down economic activity.[32]

2.4 Interdependencies between Liquidity Concepts

At the beginning of this chapter, we stated that liquidity is a term with distinct, but related meanings. After having focused on the differences between liquidity concepts, we now want to emphasize the link between them.

Banks are the natural choice in order to show the interdependencies, as they deal with all three concepts. Our following explanations are based on figure 2.2. Figure 2.2 displays bank A from the previous section. Every liquidity concept is assigned a number to easily locate it within the figure. Asset liquidity (1) refers to the liquifiability of the positions of the asset side. The assets of bank A cover the whole spectrum of asset liquidities from liquid banknotes to illiquid loans. Banknotes are liquid, as they are the official means of payment. Loans are illiquid because there is no market to sell them prior to maturity.

National liquidity (2) comprises banknotes and (liquid) deposits created by banks. Deposits are liquid as they constitute a claim to convert them into banknotes whenever customers feel like it.

[32] See [Holtemöller, 2008, p.287ff.].

Institutional liquidity (3) was defined as the capacity of an institution to meet its payment obligations. The payment obligations of bank A could result from deposit withdrawals and repo repayment. The repo maturity is known. By contrast, deposit withdrawals are unknown. If customers withdraw deposits, they obtain banknotes. However, only a fraction of deposits is backed with banknotes. If withdrawals are lower than the stock of banknotes, the bank is liquid. Otherwise, it is illiquid.

Hence, liquidity concepts are distinct, but related. In a bank, all three concepts come together.

2.5 Summary

Liquidity is a term that subsumes several concepts. The literature distinguishes asset, institutional and national liquidity.

Asset liquidity refers to the cost to liquidate assets. In pricing models, the costs are modelled by discount markups. In liquidity managment, they are modelled by haircuts. Marketable assets are more liquid than non-marketable assets; nevertheless, markets are not a guarantee for perfect liquidity. In fact, liquidity varies across instruments and markets. Market liquidity is difficult to measure as it contains several dimensions. Asset liquidity risk refers to the unexpected evaporation of markets.

Institutional liquidity refers to the ability of institutions to honour payment obligations that are satisfied in a natural way by incoming cash flows. Additionally, the institution can generate liquidity by funding or by asset liquidation. The sum of both is termed Counterbalancing Capacity. Illiquidity is a default reason. The law distinguishes default by illiquidity and insolvency. Illiquidity is defined by payments, insolvency upon going-concern values. Without the attribute 'going-concern', illiquidity would not exist as autonomous default reason, but would always lead to insolvency.

National liquidity refers to the means of payments available in an economy. The initial money endowment of the central bank (money basis) is extended by loan grantings of private banks. The higher the percentage of book-money in the economy, the more national liquidity can be generated by banks.

Asset, institutional and national liquidity are linked. Banks have to deal with every liquidity concept: they hold assets, must stay liquid and operate as intermediary and multiplier of central bank liquidity. Therefore, liquidity management is particularly complex for banks.

Chapter 3
Liquidity Framework

This chapter derives variables that have to be considered by a bank liquidity model. In a preparatory step, we introduce fundamental concepts and tools that are used in subsequent sections. Variables are derived from liquidity strategies run by banks. The variables are stochastic processes. Together, they form the liquidity framework. The framework is not a liquidity model but rather describes a family of models. A model is obtained by specifying the process dynamics. The framework serves as input for the next chapter where our liquidity model is presented.

3.1 Modelling Fundamentals

3.1.1 Stock versus Flow Perspective

Cash flows play a central role in subsequent sections. As the name suggests, cash flows have a flow perspective, which is why we briefly describe the link between balance sheet and cash flows using a simple bank balance sheet.

Figure 3.1a displays a bank that funded its loan business (assets) with equity and deposits (liabilities). The current stock of loans is L_t, the one of deposits D_t. E_t is the current stock of equity. Cash flows are the stock deltas as displayed in figure 3.1b.

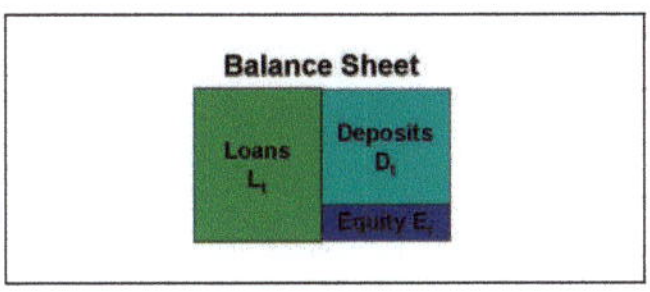

Fig. 3.1a Balance Sheet

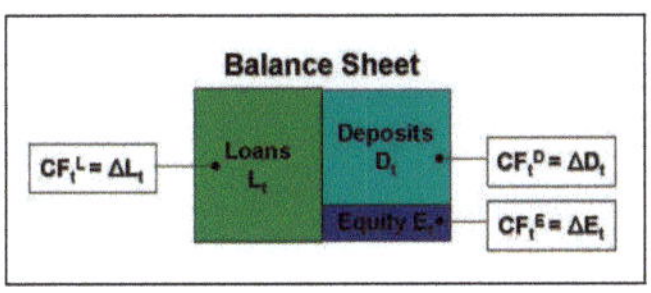

Fig. 3.1b Cash Flow as Stock Delta

Assets generate incoming, liabilities generate outgoing cash flows.

The aggregate cash flow of a bank is the netted delta of positions. It is positive (incoming cash flow) if the balance increases and negative (outgoing cash flow) if it decreases. Furthermore, the aggregate cash flow is zero if the balance amount does not change.

Just as cash flows can be derived from positions, positions can be derived from cash flows: the current positions are the sum of all future cash flows. Hence:

$$\begin{aligned} X_t &= \sum_{t=1}^{\infty} \Delta X_t \\ &= \sum_{t=1}^{\infty} CF_t^X \\ X &\in \{L, D, E\} \end{aligned}$$

Note that X_t is not the sum of discounted values. It is the sum of future (notional) cash flows.

3.1.2 Cash Flow Maturity Ladder

The cash flow maturity ladder is an instrument that is intensively used in liquidity management to visualize cash flows. It plots cash flows across time. Banks construct cash flow maturity ladders, but usually do not disclose them.[1] Cash flow maturity ladders are constructed for several scenarios of which the most common ladder is the one for expected cash flows, which represent the 'business-as-usual' scenario.

Our explanations are based on figure 3.2. It displays (a) the balance sheet, (b) the maturity structure of the balance sheet and (c) the cash flow maturity ladder. The departure point is the balance sheet from the previous section. Knowing the maturity structure, the positions can be split up according to their maturity (see (b)). Plotting the maturity structure across time leads to the cash flow maturity ladder (c).[2] The maturity structure (b) already reveals maturity and volume mismatches between loans and deposits. Even more visible are the mismatches in the maturity cash flow ladder (c): outgoing and incoming cash flows never match.

---

[1] Some banks disclose the maturity of their liabilities, but not the maturity of their assets. For example, Deutsche Bank presents a maturity profile of all liabilities in [ON,3M,12M,5Y,$> 5Y$]-Buckets in the Notes of their Financial Report (see [Deutsche Bank Group, 2007, p.225]). However, they do not disclose the maturity structure of their assets. Note, that the Consolidated Statement of Cash Flows (e.g. for Deutsche Bank, [Deutsche Bank Group, 2007, p.105]) that is an integral component of the Annual Financial Report is not a cash flow maturity ladder. It shows the structure of cash and cash equivalents and their changes during the reporting period, and indicates the free cash available for investments or shareholders. As Commerzbank states:

> As far as banks are concerned, the cash flow statement can be considered not very informative. For us, the cash flow statement does not replaces liquidity planning or financial planning, and we do not look upon it as a management tool.

(See [Commerzbank AG, 2008, p.143ff.]).

[2] For didactic reasons, we assigned 10Y to equity although its maturity is not limited.

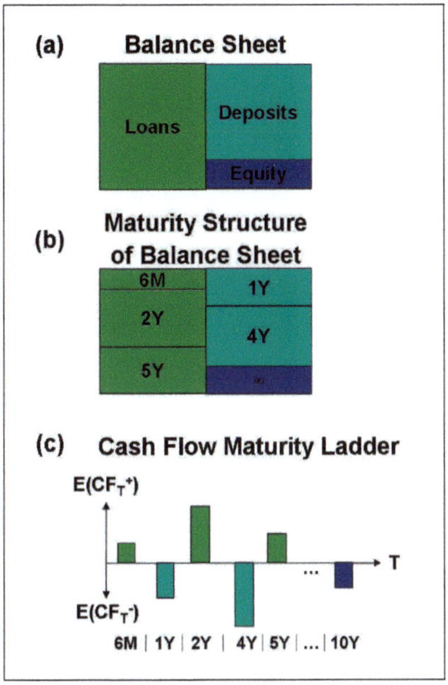

Fig. 3.2 From Balance Sheet to Cash Flow Maturity Ladder

3.1.3 Interest Rates and Liquidity Management

For liquidity management, the liquidity maturity is relevant. The liquidity maturity is the date on which the instrument matures. This contrasts with the interest rate maturity, which is the date on which the interest rate is reset. A 5 year-3M-floating loan has a liquidity maturity of 5 years and an interest maturity of 3 months.

Figure 3.3 displays all possible constellations of liquidity and interest rate (mis)matches. In Bank A, interest and liquidity maturity of assets and liabilities match. Hence, interest rate and liquidity positions are closed. Bank D funds 10Y fixed-rate loans by 5Y-fixed rate bonds. For this reason, interest and liquidity position are open.

The development of interest rate floaters have decoupled interest and liquidity maturity.[3] In Bank C, the liquidity position is closed (10Y) whereas the interest rate position (6M,10Y) is not. Bank C runs an interest rate, but not a liquidity risk.

Bank B runs a liquidity risk (10Y against 5Y), but closed its interest rate position by choosing the same floating rates.

In contrast to floating interest rates, floating spreads do not exist. They would be credit spreads that are reset before liquidity maturity. If floating spread instruments existed, the spread maturity could be managed independently on the actual liquidity maturity.

[3] The interest rate maturity is either less than the liquidity maturity or equal.

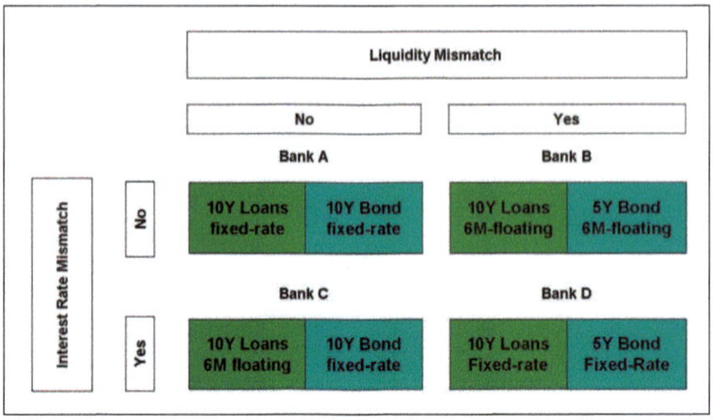

Fig. 3.3 Possible Interest Rate and Liquidity Configurations

With the evolution of interest rate swaps, the interest rate position can be changed without changing the underlying funded position. As standardized credit spread swaps do not exist (floating spread against fixed-rate spread), the spread position cannot be changed without changing the underlying liquidity position.[4] Obviously, interest rate swaps allow the separation of interest rate and liquidity management. In fact, the interest rate position of a bank can be replicated by a swap portfolio without investing any funds.[5] Thus, interest rate and liquidity strategy can be managed in separate books.[6] For that purpose, fixed interest rate cash flows are swapped to the swap book, leaving the cash flow portfolio with floating rates. Hence, if not stated otherwise, our liquidity portfolios bear floating rates. Their value is interest rate-neutral. Thus, liquidity departments operate on a portfolio of floaters. A direct consequence is that long-term interest rates do not have to be modelled for liquidity management.

Concerning the term 'maturity', we use the following convention: maturity always refers to the liquidity maturity if not stated differently. Furthermore, we will use the idea of separating long-term interest rates from liquidity management in future chapters.

3.1.4 Liquidity Options

Bank products vary in the flexibility that they provide to customers. On the one hand, there are products that fix amounts and dates of payments – amortizing loans are an example. There is no flexibility left for the customer. On the other hand, there are products where

[4] A spread swap could be replicated by setting up a CDS-portfolio of long and short-CDS. As CDS are fixed-rate instruments, the floating-leg has to be duplicated by a rolling-CDS strategy.

[5] Swaps do not require an initial investment at origination. We abstract from real world margin requirements as our model is situated in a default free world.

[6] Even if derivatives allow the separation of interest rate and liquidity, interest-rate driven liquidity risk and liquidity driven interest rate-risk are inseparable from derivatives. Interest-rate driven liquidity risk exists if the liquidity maturity is interest-rate dependent. As an example, one might think of depositors that decide upon their withdrawals depending on the interest rate evolution. Liquidity-driven interest rate risk occurs if the bank hedges their interest rate exposure in deposits based on expected cash flows. If depositors withdraw their funds because of unexpected liquidity needs, the realized cash flow profile substantially differs from the expected one. This implies that the interest rate position is not closed. In a first step, we abstract from these spillovers and assume that swaps can perfectly disentangle interest rate and liquidity strategies.

Characteristics	Liquidity Options (e.g. Demand Deposits)	P&L-Options (e.g. American Call Stock Option)
Liquidity Impact	P&L (Option Value) << Liquidity Impact	P&L (Option Value) = Liquidity Impact
Underlying	Liquidity	(Traded) Financial Instrument
Driving Factors	unknown	known
Hedging*	Approximately (Market incompleteness assumpt.: no committed interbank CL) Only an issue in presence of funding constraints (=> funding model)	Ok (Complete Market)
Exercise	1. (usually) exercised 2. Possible irrational exercise (depending on option holder segment) 3. Systematic or unsystematic	1. (usually) unwinded, but not exercised 2. Rational exercise 3. Only systematic

* only Ly Perspective

Fig. 3.4 Comparison of Liquidity and P&L-Options

customers can repay or withdraw whenever they feel like it. Here, loan commitments or deposits are examples. These products provide a maximum of flexibility. The higher the customer flexibility, the more uncertain the product cash flow. The main part of banks' cash flow uncertainty results from these products. We denote these products as Liquidity Options.[7] We denote call and put options on financial assets as 'P&L'-options. Although 'liquidity option' suggests a similarity to P&L-options, both option classes differ in important characteristics. We are not aware of any systematic classification of liquidity options in the literature. As we need a clear understanding of liquidity options in subsequent sections, we provide such a classification.

We define liquidity options as products where the option holder has the right to unexpectedly repay or withdraw funds. Examples are saving deposits or loan commitments.

In a first step, we compare liquidity options to P&L-options. In a second step, we discuss driving factors of liquidity options.

Liquidity Options versus P&L-Options

Figure 3.4 compares liquidity and P&L-options. Subsequently, we step through the characteristics (first column). We illustrate them by product examples. We choose saving deposits as our example for liquidity options. As P&L-options, we use an American call option on a stock. The liquidity impact of an option is the payoff. The P&L-impact of an

[7] The literature does not provide a common term for these products. Deposits are sometimes referred to as non-maturing assets.

option is its price. Prior to maturity, payoff and price differ. For P&L-options, it holds:

$$\begin{aligned} \text{Price} &= \text{Payoff} + \text{Time Value} \\ &\geq \text{Payoff} \end{aligned}$$

As the time value is positive, the option price is greater or equal to the payoff. Hence, the P&L-impact is also larger or equal to the payoff. The payoff of liquidity options is the notional. However, the option price is much lower. If saving deposits are withdrawn, the whole amount is liquidity relevant, but only the interest rate paid on the drawn amount is P&L-relevant.

Liquidity and P&L-options differ in their underlyings. Liquidity options are the right on drawing/repaying liquidity. P&L-options are the right on buying/selling a (traded) financial asset at a fixed price.

Liquidity and P&L-options also differ with respect to the factors that trigger the exercise: the factors that trigger liquidity options are unobservable. We will discuss potential factors more thoroughly in the next section. By contrast, the driving factor of P&L-options is the price of the underlying. The price is observable. For the American call it is the price of the stock.

As financial contracts can only be written on observable factors, no contracts can be written on the driving factors of liquidity options. Thus, they cannot be hedged.[8] If it is possible to identify observable proxies for the factors, approximate hedges can be set up. P&L-options can be hedged due to their observable and traded factors. The call option can be dynamically hedged with a portfolio of stocks and risk-free bonds.

As liquidity options cannot be hedged, they are usually exercised. By contrast, P&L-options are usually closed out (opposite deal). P&L-options are only systematically exercised: either nobody exercises or everybody does. This is a direct consequence from the systematic underlying. Liquidity options know unsystematic (idiosyncratic) and systematic exercises. Unsystematic reasons might be individual liquidity needs, whereas systematic reasons might result from a loss of confidence.

We compared liquidity options and P&L-options. We shortly want to situate callable bonds and target redemption notes in our classification.[9]

The holder of the call option of callable bonds can decide to repay the notional prior to maturity. This satisfies our definition of liquidity options. Usually, the option is exercised depending on the bond value.[10] However, it could be exercised because the option holder needs liquidity, no matter the bond value. This stresses that a callable bond can be exercised for two reasons: value (driving factor: interest rates) or liquidity (driving factor: liquidity needs). The callable bond is a liquidity option with two triggers: liquidity and market factors.

A target redemption note is not an option because nobody holds a right: neither the issuing bank nor the investor. The maturity is 'decided' by the market.

---

[8] The option could be sold to other parties. But this is not what we understand by hedging.

[9] A target redemption note is a structured product that matures as soon as the cumulated sum of coupons exceeds a boundary or at maturity.

[10] If the borrower holds the call option, he calls if the bond value is above par. If the investor holds the call option, he calls if it is below par.

Trigger	Credit Lines	Demand Deposits	Saving Deposits
Liquidity Need (Payment, Surprises, Opportunities)	X	X	X
Bank Inconfidence (in Bank A, in Banking Industry)		X	X
Excess/ Deficit yield to investment alternatives			X

Fig. 3.5 Driving Factors of Bank's Most Popular Liquidity Options

Liquidity options generate the main part of cash flow uncertainty, as their liquidity impact is higher than their P&L-impact. In contrast to P&L-options, their driving factors are unobservable. For the modelling of liquidity options, we have to make assumptions about their driving factors. Due to this, we discuss potential factors in the next section.

Driving Factors of Liquidity Options

We consider the main liquidity options of a bank: credit lines, demand deposits and saving deposits.[11] We assume that holders of liquidity options consider the factors given in figure 3.5. Agents demand liquidity (hold liquidity options) for payment obligations, to be protected against liquidity shocks and to benefit from investment opportunities.[12] The three sources might lead to an unpredictable liquidity need. In that case, depositors exercise their option and withdraw the liquidity. We assume that the need for liquidity is the only reason that triggers the exercise of credit lines.

In contrast to credit lines, depositors are creditors to the bank. Thus, they might also exercise their option due to a credit/confidence trigger even if they do not need the liquidity.

For saving deposits a third factor is likely to have an impact: the relative yield compared to alternative investments. We assume that clients consider demand deposits primarily as liquidity resource.[13] In contrast, saving deposits are hold for a savings objective. However,

[11] The ECB-statistics of Monetary Financial Institutions can serve as data base to analyse whether deposits constitute the main part of banks funding. The ECB-statistics is a monthly aggregate of the balance sheet positions of all banks of the reporting countries. As of August 2008, the representative European bank is funded at 50% with deposits. Deposits from other banks account for 20.5% of total liabilities, from governments for 0.4% and from 'Others' 29.9%. Deposits from banks are not split up into demand, term and saving deposits. Deposits from others are split up into demand deposits (9.8% of total liabilities), term deposits (13.74%) and saving deposits (5.2%). Hence, demand and saving deposits are an important balance sheet position. Unfortunately, the statistic does not contain any off-balance sheet positions. Therefore, we cannot provide figures for credit lines. The statistics can be accessed via the website of the German Bundesbank.

[12] See [Keynes, 1936, p.144ff.].

[13] Holders of credit lines may also changes banks because of the conditions. However, we assume that they do not decide their drawing/repayment because of credit line conditions.

the rate can be set by the bank (pricing option). We assume the deposits rate to be constant. We, therefore, restrict our analysis to the first two factors, namely liquidity needs and bank confidence.

3.1.5 Repo

Repo stands for 'Sale and Repurchase' agreement.[14] In a repo-deal, one counterparty temporarily sells securities on a spot basis to another counterparty and repurchases them on a forward basis. All rates and terms are known at origination. The securities are effectively sold, i.e. the legal ownership is transferred to the buyer. The particularity is that the economic ownership of securities is not transferred: the seller retains the economic benefits and the market risk although he is not the legal owner anymore. As a repo combines two deals, it can either be interpreted as security spot selling and forward repurchase (emphasizing the security aspect) or as secured funding (emphasizing the funding aspect). Both aspects are inseparable, as the security sale is the drawing of the loan and the security repurchase is the repayment of the loan.

In order to analyze liquidity and P&L-implications of a repo, we compare repo to asset sale and unsecured funding. Figure 3.6 uses a bank with a funding gap as starting point (left side). The funding gap can be closed by 'Asset Sale' (1), 'Repoing'(2) or 'Unsecured funding' (3). For each alternative, we discuss liquidity and P&L-impact.

Asset Sale

Assets are sold at their liquidation value.[15] The liquidation value measures the amount of inflowing liquidity. The liquidity is used to cover the funding gap. The balance has shortened, i.e. from a P&L-perspective, the bank loses both security and funding. Hence, it renounces on the security benefits and saves funding costs.

Unsecured Funding

For unsecured funding, the liquidity impact is the notional amount of the funding gap. From a P&L-perspective, unsecured funding requires a higher credit spread than secured funding (repo), as the unsecured lender bears the default risk of the bank and not that of collateral. As the bank keeps its securities, it continues to enjoy the benefits (and risk) of them.

Repo

A repo consists of spot sale and forward repurchase of securities. In contrast to asset sale, the spot sale is not executed at the transaction value, but on the transaction value

[14] A good introduction to repo and repo-markets is [Choudhry, 2007, p.493ff.].

[15] Equation (2.1) on page 16 defines the liquidation value.

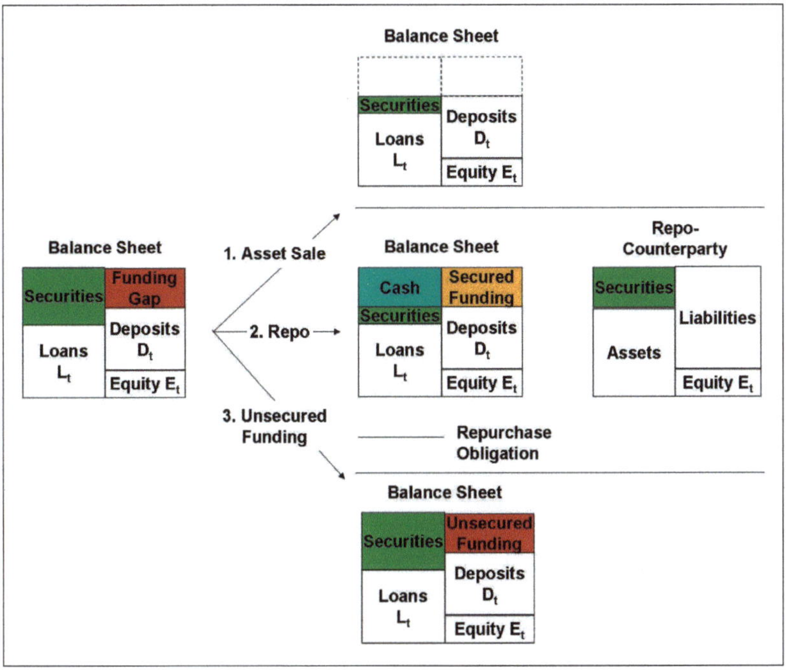

Fig. 3.6 Comparison Repo to Asset Sale and Unsecured Funding

minus a haircut. The haircut depends on the credit quality of the collateral and protects the lender against the collateral's price risk. Table 3.1 gives haircut indications:[16] The

Table 3.1 Rating-Sensitive Haircuts

Rating Range	Haircut [%]
AAA to AA	3.5%
A	5%
BBB	7%
Sub-investment grade	10%

collateral value can deteriorate. A possible scenario is the downgrade of the collateral. The haircut seeks to protect the lender against such value deterioration. For collaterals without haircuts, the liquidity impact of asset sale and repo are identical. For high quality collateral, haircuts are low, implying that the liquidity impact of repoing and asset sale is almost the same. From a P&L-perspective, repoing implies lower funding spreads than

[16] Source: [Choudhry, 2007, p.510]

unsecured funding because the credit risk is lower.[17] The bank keeps the economic ownership. Therefore, it still enjoys the security benefits as any other security holder. Repo can add substantial value if non-marketable assets are eligible as collateral. An example is the recent extension of the collateral definition of the European Central Bank (ECB).[18] Nowadays the ECB accepts certain non-tradable assets as collateral.

Repo is particularly useful in times of distressed financial markets when market values are temporarily under pressure. Under such circumstances, asset sale realizes a loss. A repo retains the chance to increase prices.

To sum up, the liquidity impact of repoing and asset sale are similar for high quality collateral. Repoing has a slight disadvantage in the form of haircut. The P&L-advantage of repoing is twofold: firstly, the funding spread is lower than for unsecured funding. Secondly, repoing avoids liquidation losses in times of market turmoils.

In our setup, we subsume repoing under asset liquidation. We do so as the distinction of repoing and asset sale would make the analysis more complex without providing much insight. This is valid for moderate haircuts and low short-term spreads.

3.2 Liquidity Strategies of Banks

The literature intensively discusses the risk, but merely the return aspect of liquidity.[19] To study optimal liquidity management, we consider it more appropriate to describe the liquidity strategies that banks run and to identify risk **and** return of each strategy. This approach directly leads to the key liquidity variables that form our liquidity framework.

Banks run two liquidity strategies:

1. Maturity Mismatch Strategy
   A bank runs an intended maturity mismatch by granting illiquid, long-term loans out of short-term funding. 'Short-term' and 'long-term' refer to the liquidity maturity, not to the interest rate maturity.[20] This strategy is not an exclusive bank strategy. Corporates and banks' Special Purpose Vehicles run this strategy as well. By choosing short-term funding, they save on funding costs, given an upward-sloping funding spread term structure.[21]

[17] The credit risk in a repo is the credit risk of the collateral. The credit risk in unsecured funding is the credit risk of the borrower. Therefore, collateral reduces credit risk and funding spread.

[18] See [European Central Bank, 2006, p.37f.]

[19] For risk definitions, see [Schierenbeck, 2003a, p. 6ff.], [Koch and MacDonald, 2000, p. 125ff.], [Heffernan, 1996, p. 165],[Hartmann-Wendels et al., 2007, p. 413], [Zeranski, 2005, p. 49ff.].

[20] See section 3.1.3 for details.

[21] The literature evokes two principal arguments why firms choose short-term funding: (1) Agency Cost (See [Myers, 1977]) and (2) Information Asymmetries (See [Flannery, 1986], [Diamond, 1991], [Kale and Noe, 1990]) By contrast, theory disproves that firms can systematically save funding costs on choosing short-term funding. In reality they run this strategy nonetheless: [Jun and Jen, 2003] find support for market timing. [Graham and Harvey, 2001] asked CFOs how they decide on funding maturity: 36% issue short-term debt if the term structure is steep and 29% issue short-term debt because they expect long-term rates to fall. However, other firms refuse that strategy: for 63%, matching asset to debt maturity was important. 49% prefer long-term debt to avoid refinancing risk. Note that the maturity refers to interest-rate maturity. [Baker et al., 2003] and [Faulkender, 2005] also find strong support that firms try to reduce funding cost by choosing short-term/floating-rate debt if the yield curve steepens and long-term if the yield curve flattens.

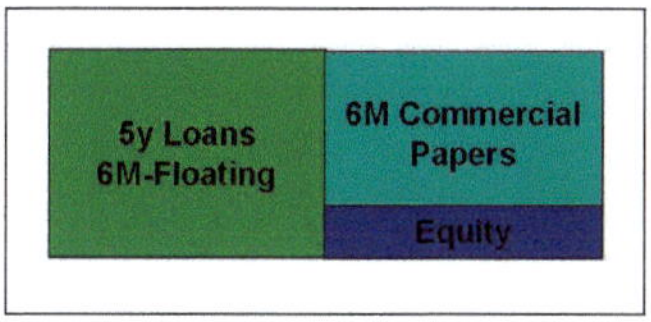

Fig. 3.7 Balance Sheet That Implies a Maturity Mismatch

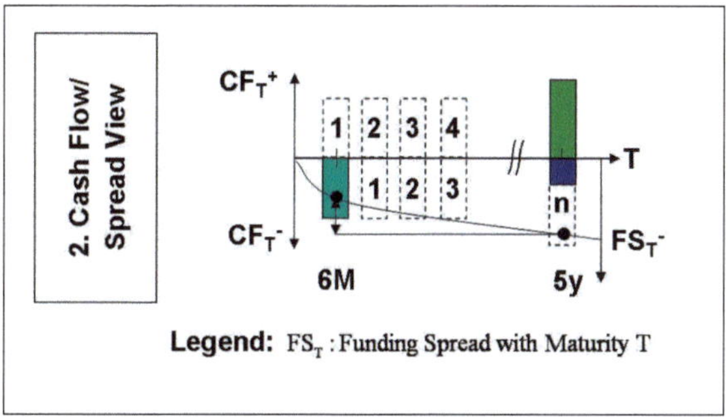

Fig. 3.8 Cash Flow and Funding Spread View

2. Liquidity Option Strategy
   Banks provide liquidity options because they yield an attractive margin.[22]

Both strategies generate a return and imply a liquidity risk.

3.2.1 Maturity Mismatch Strategy

Figure 3.7 shows a balance sheet that is exemplary for a maturity mismatch: a bank issued Commercial Papers with a maturity of six months (6M) and invested them in loans with maturity of five years (5y). Hence, the bank counts on rolling over its commercial papers every 6M. Assets and liabilities have the same interest-rate maturity. Thus, the interest rate position is closed. However, the liquidity position is not closed, as the maturities differ (6M vs. 5y). This is displayed in figure 3.8. Commercial Papers have to be repaid after 6M leading to an outgoing cash flow. This cash flow has to be funded on a rolling basis (dotted boxes). Till loan maturity, the commercial papers will have to be rolled over 9 times.

The benefit of this strategy comes from an upward-sloping funding spread curve: the funding cost for short-term maturities are lower than for longer maturities. From a static perspective, it is favorable to fund rolling short-term at a small funding spread than once long-term at a high funding spread. This strategy has already been known and implemented in banks as 'Riding the Yield Curve' for the interest rate term structure. Here, we

[22] For a definition of liquidity options, please refer to section 3.1.4.

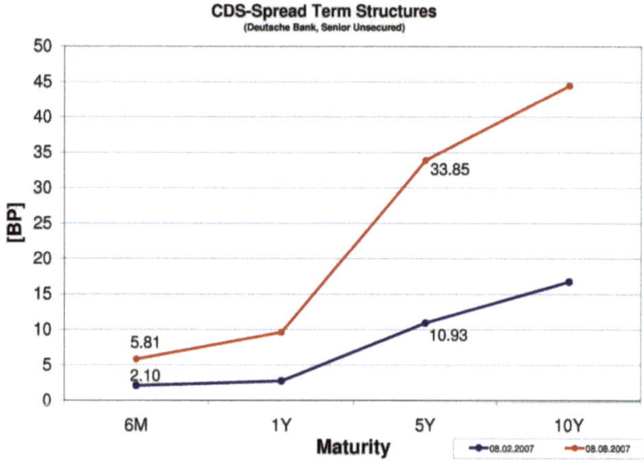

Fig. 3.9 CDS-Term Structure of Deutsche Bank as of 08.02. and of 08.08. 2007 (Source: Markit)

refer to 'Riding the Funding Spread Curve'. However, from a dynamic perspective, the strategy incorporates two types of risk: firstly, funding spreads can rise and, secondly, the funding capacity at the roll-over dates could be insufficient.[23]

Figure 3.9 gives an example for the funding spread risk. It plots the CDS-spreads[24] of Deutsche Bank on February 8, and six months later on August 8, 2007. On February 8, 6M-funding cost 2.10 BP whereas 6M later it already cost 5.81 BP. If the 6M-funding jumps above the original 5Y-funding cost of 10.93, the Maturity Mismatch Strategy turns out to be unfavorable.[25]

As the funding spread is P&L-relevant, this strategy implies a P&L-risk that has to be backed with economic capital. However, this strategy also implies a liquidity risk.

We check the bank liquidity condition (2.4) for our setup:

$$\begin{aligned} \widetilde{FC}_t &\geq CF_t^-, t \in \{0.5, 1.0, 1.5, ..., 4.5\} \\ CF_t^+ &\geq CF_t^-, t \in \{5.0\} \end{aligned} \tag{3.1}$$

Before loans mature, liquidity exclusively relies on external funding. Furthermore, liquidation capacity is zero, as we assumed the loans to be illiquid. As cash flows are deterministic, the only source of liquidity risk is the stochastic of the funding capacity FC_t. The

[23] In rationed markets price and volume might be decoupled.

[24] We use CDS-spreads as proxies for funding spreads. A discussion of the differences between CDS-spreads and funding spreads (e.g. bond spreads), see [Choudhry, 2006].

[25] The success of the Maturity Mismatch Strategy depends on the dynamic of the credit spread curve. If an upward-sloping term structure already anticipates increasing spreads, the strategy was never profitable. On a sample of Corporate bonds with US-banking firms (1994-1999), [Krishnan et al., 2006] find evidence that current credit spread slopes can predict future forward credit spread levels. [Bedendo et al., 2004] confirms that a steep slope predicts increasing credit spreads. Hence, these studies suggest that firms cannot save on funding cost by choosing short-term debt, as the current funding advantage will be absorbed by higher future funding spreads. We are not aware of studies that documented the success of Maturity Mismatch Strategies.

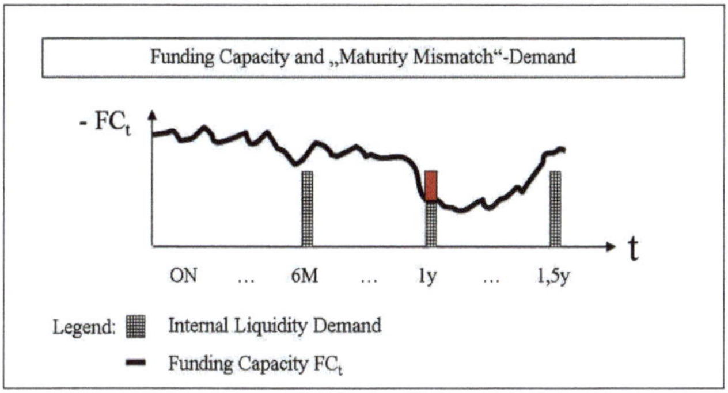

Fig. 3.10 Liquidity Demand and Funding Capacity in Mismatch-Strategy

'tilde' in (3.1) indicates that the funding capacity is stochastic. Figure 3.10 plots funding capacity (continuous line) and internal funding demand (bars every 6M). The funding risk is limited as only particular key dates (0.5,1.0,...) are important. It is not important how the funding capacity evolves between these dates.

An example of materializing funding risk was the cancellation of liquidity backup lines by several banks towards Deutsche Industrie Bank (IKB).[26]

The Maturity Mismatch Strategy is a liquidity strategy because it implies a liquidity risk. Such a risk exclusively results from the stochastic of the funding capacity. The rolling strategy replicates spread floaters. To our knowledge, spread floaters do not exist yet (by contrast with interest rate floaters). If they existed, the spread risk could be decoupled from the liquidity risk. In our example, the bank would fund 5Y with a 6M floating funding spread.

To describe the maturity mismatch strategy, four key variables have to be modelled:

1. Cash Flows
2. Funding Capacity
3. Funding Spread
4. Haircut

The key variables are the variables that a liquidity model has to incorporate. The next section derives the key variables for the Liquidity Option Strategy.

3.2.2 Liquidity Option Strategy

The second liquidity strategy that generates a return as compensation for liquidity risk is the provision of liquidity options. Figure 3.11 shows a balance sheet that is examplary for a pure liquidity option strategy: a bank pools customer deposits and invests them in liquid 5Y-bonds and illiquid 5Y-loans. Loans and bonds still have deterministic cash flows at 5Y. However, deposits can be withdrawn at any date. The corresponding expected cash flow

[26] See [IKB, 2008, p.18].

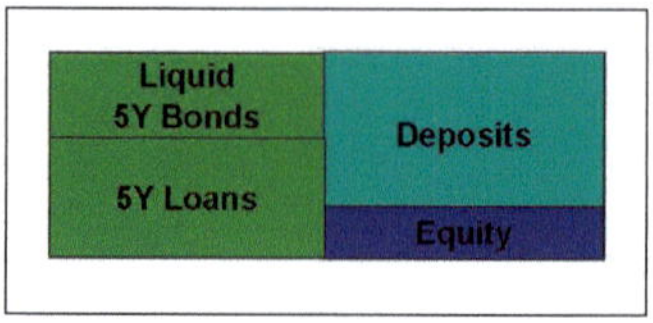

Fig. 3.11 Exemplary Balance Sheet for a Liquidity Option Strategy

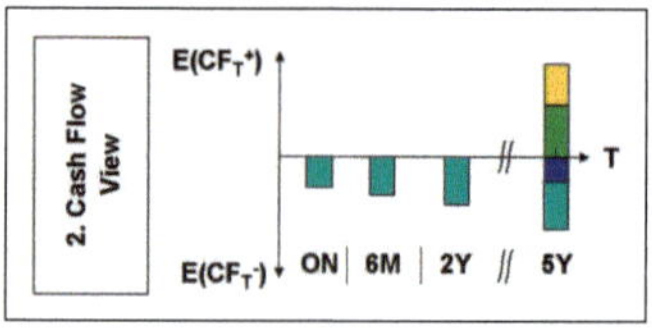

Fig. 3.12 Maturity Ladder

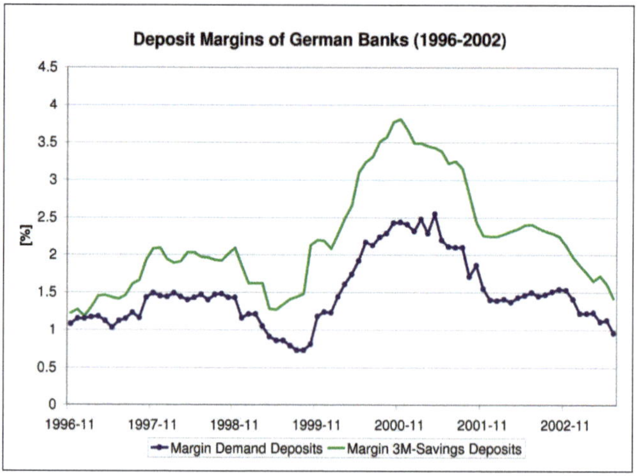

Fig. 3.13 Evolution of 3M-Deposit and Demand Deposit Margins of German Banks (Source: Bundesbank, Own Calculations)

maturity ladder is displayed in figure 3.12. In contrast to the Maturity Mismatch Strategy, the Liquidity Option Strategy involves stochastic cash flows. Therefore, the maturity ladder shows expected cash flows.

Banks provide liquidity options because they yield a comfortable margin. Figure 3.13 shows the average monthly deposit margins of German Banks for the period 11/1996 to 06/2003.[27]

[27] Bundesbank stopped data collection in 2002. The margins are obtained as the difference between the corresponding ON- and 3M-Money Market rates as reported by Frankfurt Banks.

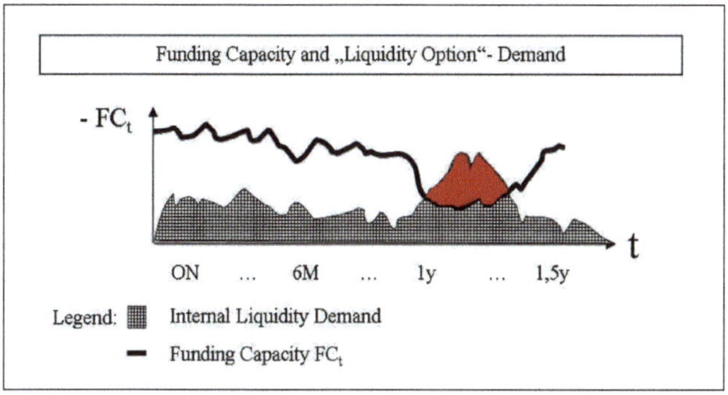

Fig. 3.14 Liquidity Demand and Funding Capacity in Liquidity Option-Strategy

We make two observations: firstly, deposits yield a comfortable margin. Secondly, 3M-saving deposits generate a higher margin than demand deposits.

The attractive margin furthermore results from withdrawal diversification that banks with large liquidity option books benefit from.

Using the liquidity condition (2.4), we check the implications for bank liquidity. For our setup, the condition writes as follows:

$$CF_t^+ + \widetilde{FC}_t + \widetilde{LC}_t \geq \widetilde{CF}_t^-, \forall t \tag{3.2}$$

Stochastic quantities are marked with a 'tilde'. As mentioned above, cash outflows are stochastic. In contrast to the Maturity Mismatch Strategy, outflows can happen every day, not only every six months. Hence, there is a daily liquidity demand that cannot be covered by expected incoming cash flows as loans and bonds have a maturity of 5 years. However, the bank can liquidate bonds. As the liquidation costs are uncertain, the liquidation value L_t is marked with a 'tilde' as well. An alternative to bond liquidation is the raise of external funding. Instead of having a regularly scheduled funding risk, the bank runs a daily funding risk as suggested in figure 3.14. The daily internal liquidity demand meets a daily funding capacity. The funding demand should be lower than the funding capacity. In figure 3.14, the period [1y;1,3y] is critical, as the external funding capacity falls below the internal funding demand.

We cannot generalize that the funding risk for the Option Liquidity Strategy is higher than the one in the Maturity Mismatch Strategy: although the option-strategy implies a daily risk, the amount to be funded is usually smaller. In the Liquidity Mismatch Strategy, funding is only required for key dates, but the amounts to be funded are much higher. As withdrawals have to be cleared every day, the overnight rate is a key variable as well. The overnight rate has an impact on banks' liquidity management for the following reasons:

1. The European Central Bank uses short-term rates and volumes to decide on liquidity interventions[28]
2. Unexpected cash flows usually materialize overnight
   The payment balance of the bank has to be cleared every day. Overnight deposits/loans are essential Money Market instruments.
3. Overnight is the shortest swappable interest rate maturity. It constitutes the 'zero'-point for interest rate management.
   A direct consequence is that interest rate maturity coincides with liquidity maturity for overnight transactions.

Thus, short-term interest rates are relevant for liquidity management. This contrasts with the irrelevance of long-term rates as stated in section 3.1.3. Note that the short-term rate is the risk-free rate. The gross funding costs are obtained as the sum of the short-term rate plus funding spread.

To sum up, modelling the Liquidity Option Strategy requires the following key variables:

- Cash Flows
- Funding Capacity
- Haircut
- Overnight Rate

Compared to the Maturity Mismatch Strategy, the Liquidity Option Strategy requires the overnight rate as an additional variable, but not the funding spread.

[28] ECB-main refinancing operations have a maturity of one week. ECB's longer-term refinancing operations have a maturity of three months. (See [European Central Bank, 2006, p.9]). Liquidity injections within crises can have varying maturities. However, they are often overnight maturities in order to facilitate interbank settlements (The exceptional liquidity tenders in the context of the subprime turmoils in August 2007 were overnight. See [European Central Bank, 2007, p.30ff.]).

Table 3.2 Liquidity Key Variables

Variable	Maturity Mismatch Strategy	Liquidity Option Strategy
Cash Flow (CF)	X	X
Funding Capacity (FC)	X	X
Funding Spread (c)	X	
Haircut (HC)	X	X
Overnight Rate (r_f)		X

3.2.3 Summary

We described the two liquidity strategies run by banks. Firstly, they lend in the long term and fund in the short term to 'Ride the Funding Spread Curve'. We called this strategy Maturity Mismatch Strategy. In a static perspective, they lock in low funding cost. In a dynamic perspective, they bear a funding spread risk at future roll-over dates. Apart from the P&L-funding spread risk, the strategy implies a volume risk.

Secondly, we discussed the Liquidity Option Strategy, which yields a comfortable margin, as funding by (retail) deposits is cheaper than funding at capital markets. However, this strategy implies a liquidity risk due to stochastic withdrawals, and uncertain funding capacity. The overnight rate becomes relevant because unexpected cash flows have to be managed daily.

In both strategies, asset liquidation is relevant as an alternative to external funding.

The strategies are not mutually exclusive. In fact, many banks combine them by granting long-term illiquid loans and funding them with deposits (= liquidity options).

Table 3.2 summarizes which variables are important in the respective strategies: The key variables constitute our framework that is presented in the subsequent section.

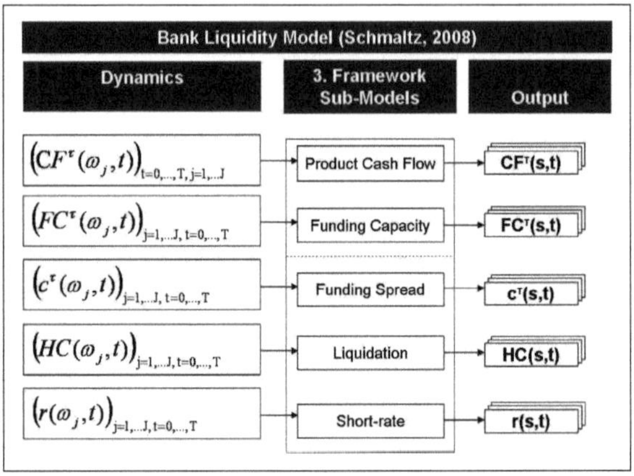

Fig. 3.15 Bank's Liquidity Framework

3.3 Framework

We obtained five key liquidity variables in section 3.2:

1. $CF^{\tau}(\omega_j,t)$
2. $FC^{\tau}(\omega_j,t)$
3. $c^{\tau}(\omega_j,t)$
4. $HC^{\tau}(\omega_j,t)$
5. $r_f(\omega_j,t)$

In order to account for the uncertainty of bank liquidity, all liquidity variables are stochastic processes that describe the evolution of the variables across time. This is indicated by the pair (ω_j,t) where omega j denotes the j-th scenario and t the date. Furthermore, cash flows CF, funding capacity FC, funding spread c and haircut HC have an index τ. τ emphasizes that these variables represent a term structure (vector). The simplest term structure is a distinction between 'short-term' and 'long-term'. Hence, we have short and long-term cash flows, funding capacities, funding spreads and haircuts. All processes are defined on the same probability space (Ω,F_t,P), i.e. on the same set of events Ω, information set F_t and probability measure P.

The key variables as stochastic processes form our liquidity framework that is given in figure 3.15. The sub models generate scenarios s of cash flows $(CF^{\tau}(s,t))$, funding capacities $(FC^{\tau}(s,t))$, funding spreads $(c^{\tau}(s,t))$, haircuts $(HC^{\tau}(s,t))$ and short-rates $(r(s,t))$.

As discussed earlier, the key variables result directly from the two liquidity strategies run by banks. As a result, any internal liquidity model has to account for these key variables.

3. Framework				
Key Variables	**Schmaltz, 2008**	**'Risk Monitors'**	**Cash Mgt Model Schmid, 2000**	**Debt Model D&I,1988[1]**
Cash Flow	x	x	x	x
Funding Capacity	x	x	x	x
Liquidation	x	x	x	x
Funding Spread	x	---	----	----
Interest Rates	x	---	x	x
Stock Prices	---	---	x	---

[1] D&I, 1988: Dempster and Ireland, 1988

Fig. 3.16 Reconciliation of Risk Types and Liquidity Condition

3.4 Comparison with Literature

Within this section we study whether our key variables are in line with other sources.

We distinguish three sources: 'risk monitors'[29], the cash management model presented by Schmid (2000)[30] and the debt management model published by Dempster and Ireland (1988)[31]. Figure 3.16 compares the key variables of the different sources. Recall the liquidity condition (2.4) from page 19:

$$CF_t^+ + FC_t + LC_t \geq CF_t^-$$

Being:

$$CF_t^{+/-} : \text{Product Cash Flows}$$
$$FC_t : \text{Funding Capacity}$$
$$LC_t : \text{Liquidation Capacity}$$

The liquidity risk is that the condition is not met. Thus, the variables of the liquidity condition are sufficient to model the risk side.

Risk monitors only require these variables as figure 3.16 suggests.[32]

---

[29] Risk monitors are sources that are exclusively interested in liquidity risk, like (a) regulators, (b) rating agencies, and (c) textbooks. We use (a) Regulators: MaRisk: [Bundesanstalt für Finanzdienstleistungsaufsicht, 2005, BTR3], IIF: [IIF, 2007, p.27,31], BCBS: [BCBS, 2008, p.10,No 25], (b) Rating agencies: Fitch: [Fitch, 2007, p.15], (c) Textbooks: [Schierenbeck, 2003a, p. 6ff.], [Koch and MacDonald, 2000, p. 125ff.], [Heffernan, 1996, p. 165], [Hartmann-Wendels et al., 2007, p. 413], [Zeranski, 2005, p. 49ff.].

[30] See section 1.2.2.1.

[31] See section 1.2.2.2.

[32] Textbooks split liquidity risk into different sub-risks (e.g. call risk for liquidity options). However, their sub-risks can be reconciled with the liquidity condition.

Models of optimal liquidity management need to describe the return as well. All variables that risk monitors do not model are variables that are P&-L relevant. These are funding spread, interest rates and stock prices.

We model the funding spread as driving factor for debt maturity (Maturity Mismatch Strategy). Dempster and Ireland (1988) and Schmid (2000) do not model the funding spread. Obviously, they consider fixed-rate instruments where interest-rate and debt maturity coincide. Interest rates are key variables in all three models. However, we only model the short-rate whereas Schmid (2000) and Dempster (1988) also model long-term interest rates.[33] Schmid (2000) also models stock prices, as its investment instruments also include stocks. We do not model stocks, as a bank liquidity manager is unlikely to invest in stocks, which is done by the proprietory trading desks instead. Dempster and Ireland (1988) do not model stocks since their model focuses on funding.

We can conclude that there is a broad consensus with respect to cash flows, funding capacity and liquidation. The set of return variables is more heterogeneous. It depends on the managing department's set of instruments.

3.5 Summary

The objective of the chapter was the identification of key variables to describe bank liquidity.

In a preparatory step we introduced concepts that are important in liquidity modelling.

Later, we derived liquidity key variables upon the liquidity strategies run by banks. To reduce the funding cost, banks run a maturity mismatch between assets and funding: they lend in the long term and fund in the short term. This reduces funding costs from a static perspective. From a dynamic perspective, it introduces funding spread and rollover risk. The key variables to describe the mismatch and its implications are cash flows, funding capacity, funding spread and haircut. The maturity mismatch strategy operates on deterministic product cash flows.

Stochastic product cash flows are introduced by liquidity options which are bank-specific and part of the liquidity options strategy. Banks sell liquidity options because they yield an attractive margin. The key variables to model the liquidity option strategy are the same variables as the mismatch strategy, minus the funding spread plus the short-term interest rate. These key variables constitute the liquidity framework for banks. A complete bank liquidity model needs to incorporate cash flows, funding capacity and spread, haircut and short-rate. These variables are sufficient to describe the liquidity situation in bank. The framework is not a model but rather a family of models. Within the framework, liquidity models are derived by specifying the stochastic processes for the key variables.

We reconciled our framework with risk monitors, the cash management model presented by Schmid (2000), and the debt management model of Dempster and Ireland (1988). All sources model cash flows, funding capacity and liquidation. The modelling of other variables depends on the organisational setup. We argued that a liquidity model for banks has to consider funding spread and short-rate.

---

[33] See section 3.1.3 for the detailed argument as to why we do not model long-term interest rates.

Chapter 4
Liquidity Model

The step from the generic framework to a concrete liquidity model is taken by assuming specific processes for the liquidity variables. In chapter 3 we saw that a complete liquidity model needs the following sub-models:

- Cash Flow Model
- Funding Model
- Liquidation Model
- Short-rate Model

This chapter proposes one analytical internal liquidity model for banks. Our model goes beyond regulatory requirements for the following reasons:[1]

1. Regulators are mainly focused on the variables of the liquidity condition (2.4), but not on the cost involved.[2]
   Our model incorporates both liquidity variables and their P&L-impact.
2. Regulators require quantitative models but do not specify them.
   Our model, in contrast, is quantitative.
3. Regulators require liquidity to be assessed in different scenarios (business-as-usual, stress) but do not require one integrated model.
   Our model is stochastic and accounts for different scenarios.

This chapter is organized as follows: for each sub-model we discuss regulatory requirements, study determining factors and motivate the modelling approach that we choose. The complete set of sub-models forms our bank liquidity model.

4.1 Time Scale

Our liquidity model is defined on a discrete time scale:

$$t = 0 < t_1, \ldots, t_k, \ldots t_K$$

---

[1] The requirements below are based on [BCBS, 2008, p.11 and p.14].

[2] See also the comparison with the existing literature in section 3.4.

The time scale is equidistant:

$$\Delta t_k = \Delta t$$

If not stated differently, Δt refers to one day. Daily variables have a time index t_k.

Apart from daily variables, we also have quarterly variables. The quarterly time scale is defined as:

$$q = 0 < q_1, \ldots, q_k, \ldots q_K$$

The quarterly time scale is equidistant:

$$\Delta q_k = \Delta q = 90\Delta t$$

Hence, quarterly variables have a q_k-index. The length of one quarter is 90 Δt.

The two time scales with different granularities are necessary in order to model both daily and quarterly variables.

4.2 Cash Flow Model

4.2.1 Requirements

The requirements are based on the recent publications of regulators and industry sources.[3] A cash flow model should project all future cash flows from assets, liabilities and off-balance sheet items, as figure 4.1 suggests. The aggregated cash flow is obtained as the sum of asset, liability and off-balance sheet products. The cash flow model should provide prospective, dynamic cash flow forecasts and include behavioral components of counterparties. With respect to deposits, banks should distinguish between retail and wholesale deposits as retail deposits are likely to be more stable. With respect to contingent cash flows, the bank should analyze their triggers. Common triggers entail changes in economic variables, credit rating downgrades, country risk or specific market disruptions. Furthermore, it is stated that banks should not assume normally distributed cash flows, as large cash outflows are more probable than suggested by the normal distribution.[4] This requirement is in line with the existence of triggering products and justifies stress tests.

In short, a cash flow model should:

- model cash flows from all products
- incorporate future business
- distinguish sub-products within a product category
- incorporate a behavioral and discontinuous element (triggers)

The next section proposes a cash flow process that satisfies these requirements.

---

[3] See [BCBS, 2008, Principle 5 and Explanations] and similar, but less granular, [IIF, 2007, Recommendation 14].

[4] See [Zeranski, 2005, p.102ff.].

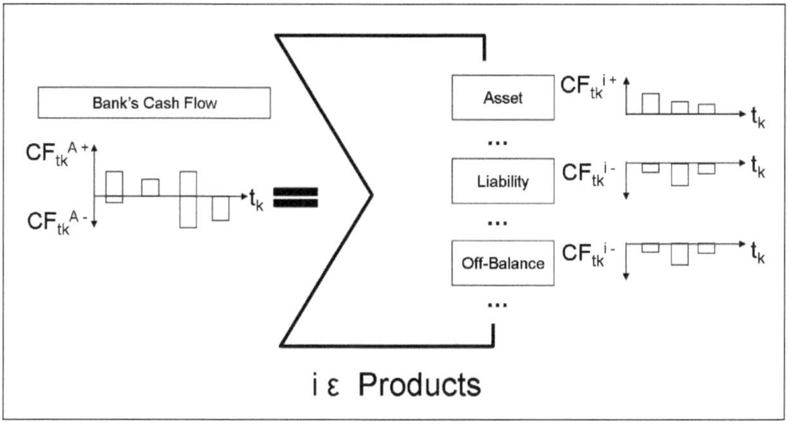

Fig. 4.1 Cash Flow Aggregation

4.2.2 Product Cash Flows

4.2.2.1 Cash Flow Assumption

Within this section, we derive a cash flow model that is able to describe all product cash flows. It is obvious that such a model must be of a very general form. Variables on the product level have a superscript i. We assume that the bank holds d products: $i = 0, 1, 2, \ldots, d$. The product cash flow is the cash flow for a product group, not for a single customer. We believe that a bank cannot incorporate customer-specific characteristics because, firstly, it is unlikely that the bank has such granular information and, secondly, it would make the analysis too complex. The modelling on the product level assumes that each product can be described by a representative customer.

The first step towards a cash flow model is the classification of products.

The literature proposes the classification of Fiedler and Bier.[5]

Fiedler distinguishes three types of cash flows:

1. Fixed (determined) cash flows
   Fixed cash flows are contractually determined in amount and time.
2. Variable cash flows
   Variable cash flows are indexed to market variables - options, floaters or currency deals are examples.
3. Hypothetical cash flows
   Hypothetical cash flows result from new business.

A product can generate more than one type of cash flow. For instance, a standard floater generates a variable interest-rate and a deterministic principal cash flow.

[5] For the classification of Fiedler, see [Fiedler, 2000, p.448] in combination with [Fiedler, 2007, p.180]. The classification of Bier is cited in [Bartetzky, 2008, p.15].

Bier distinguishes:

1. Deterministic Cash Flows (e.g. Standard Loans)
2. Stochastic Cash Flows (e.g. Loan Commitments, Structured Products)
3. Behavioral Cash Flows (e.g. Demand/Term/Savings Deposits)
4. Semi-autodetermined Cash Flows (e.g. Proprietory Trading)
5. Autodetermined Cash Flows (e.g. drawing of obtained Credit Lines)

An ideal classification scheme trades-off economic complexity and modelling simplicity. Therefore, one must also consider how the different categories are modelled.

In both classification schemes, deterministic cash flows have their own category. Bier's classification contains semi-autodetermined and autodetermined cash flows. Fiedler's classification only knows autonomuous, i.e. customer-driven cash flows. Autodetermined cash flows can be summarized as deterministic cash flows.[6] The idea behind the categories 'semi-autodetermined/autodetermined' is that of liquidity actions: it is the bank that decides these cash flows. Therefore, they can be used to generate extra liquidity.

Stochastic cash flows are assigned to different groups. Fiedler labels uncertain cash flows from existing business as 'variable', and uncertain cash flows from new business as 'hypothetical'. Bier groups uncertain cash flows in 'stochastic' and 'behavioral'. As behavior is stochastic, too, the distinction between stochastic and behavior is not without ambiguity. The idea behind Bier's classification is the distinction between liabilities with liquidity options ('Behavioral') versus assets/off-balance sheet items with liquidity options ('Stochastic').

Similar to Bier, our classification scheme takes customer behavior as a reference point. We assume that customer behavior is driven by three factors:

1. Contractual terms
   Contractual terms rule out customer behavior. After contract origination, customers' needs and preferences do not affect the product cash flow.
2. Liquidity Needs
   Customers decide on withdrawals and deposits with respect to their individual liquidity needs. This driver determines cash flows of all existing products with liquidity options and of future funding.
3. Confidence
   Customers only keep their funds if they are confident they will get them back. Also, customers only confer new funds to banks that satisfy a minimum confidence. This driver is at work in all existing liabilities with liquidity options and in future business.

There are suitable mathematical concepts that model each factor. The mapping between factors and mathematical concepts is given in figure 4.2. Our starting points are the three determinants for customer behavior: 1. Contract, 2. Liquidity Needs, 3. Confidence. The liquidity factor is split into a planned (expected) and unplanned (unexpected) component. The former component goes into the deterministic, the latter into the 'Stochastic\Liquidity' category. 'Contract' directly goes into the 'Deterministic', 'Confidence' directly into the 'Stochstic\Confidence' category. Finally, each category is modelled with a particular mathematical term:

[6] The reason for this is that the bank cannot 'surprise' itself with autodetermined cash flows.

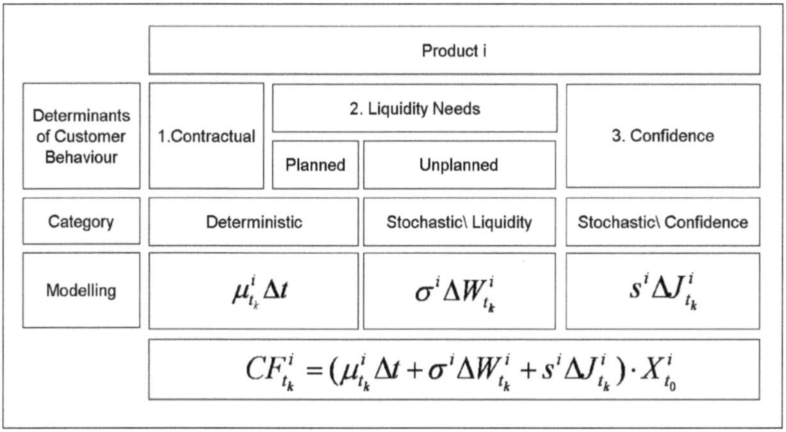

Fig. 4.2 Mapping of Customer Behavior and Cash Flow Components

1. Deterministic
   The deterministic category is modelled with a deterministic drift term:

$$\mu^i_{t_k} \cdot \Delta t$$
$$\mu^i_{t_k} \in R$$

The drift $\mu^i_{t_k}$ is time-dependent. The drift vector $(\mu^i_0, \mu^i_1, ..., \mu^i_{t_k})$ represents expected cash flows as of t_0. If i is a product with contractual cash flows, the vector represents contractual cash flows. If i is a product with liquidity options, it represents expected cash flows. If i is future business, it models planned business.
The drift has the following properties:

$$E[\mu^i_{t_k} \cdot \Delta t] = \mu^i_{t_k} \cdot \Delta t$$
$$Var[\mu^i_{t_k} \cdot \Delta t] = 0$$

2. Stochastic\Liquidity
   The 'Stochastic\Liquidity' category is modelled with Brownian increments:[7]

$$\sigma^i \cdot \Delta W^i_{t_k}$$
$$\sigma^i \geq 0$$

$W^i_{t_k}$ is a Wiener Process that is defined by the probability space $(\Omega, F, (F_{t_k})_{k \in N}, P)$. $(F_{t_k})_{k \in N}$ denotes the information set that is increasing in time. $\Delta W^i_{t_k}$ are independent increments that are F_{t_k}-measurable. We assume σ^i to be constant, but product-specific. Forecast cash flows are contained in the drift term. Forecast errors due to unexpected

[7] For Brownian Motion see [Shreve, 2004, p.93ff.].

liquidity needs are modelled by the Brownian component. Hence, the parameter σ^i measures the forecast quality for product i. Unexpected liquidity needs are liquidity shocks that customers are exposed to. They can offload that risk at the bank by holding liquidity options. The Brownian Component is normally distributed. The first two moments are:

$$E[\sigma^i \cdot \Delta W^i_{t_k}] = 0 \tag{4.1}$$

$$Var[\sigma^i \cdot \Delta W^i_{t_k}] = (\sigma^i)^2 \cdot \Delta t \tag{4.2}$$

(4.1) states that the forecast error is unbiased. (4.2) states that the forecast error increases in the forecast horizon.

3. Stochastic\Confidence
The 'Stochastic\Confidence' term is modelled by a jump component:[8]

$$s^i \Delta J^i_{t_k}$$
$$s^i \geq 0$$

$J^i_{t_k}$ is defined on the same probability space as the Brownian component. In contrast to continuous Brownian increments, jumps are discontinuous increments characterized by the number of jumps per finite time interval and jump size. The number of jumps is described by a counting model and the jump sizes by a jump size model. If the number of jumps is infinite, the process is a Lévy-process with infinite activity.[9] Lévy-processes with a finite number of jumps can be modelled via poisson processes. If the jump size is random (i.i.d.) and independent on the number of jumps, the process is a Compound Poisson Process. If the jump size is standardized to one, it is a pure poisson process. A pure poisson process counts the number of jumps.
In our application, a jump represents the loss of confidence. As such a loss of confidence is a rare event, we only need a finite number of jumps suggesting a poisson process. As the jump component should allow for different scenarios (e.g. bank-specific vs. market-wide), the jump size should be stochastic, suggesting a Compound Poisson Process. The Compound Poisson Process is defined by (4.3):

$$J_{t_k} = \sum_{j=1}^{N_{t_k}} Y_j \tag{4.3}$$
$$Y_j \leq 0$$

N_{t_k} is the counting model (Poisson-distributed). It takes values in $\{0,1,2,...,\}$. Y_j is the jump size model. Y_j is the jth jump of random size. We only model confidence-driven outflows. Therefore, jumps are negative. The jump increments (cash flows) of product i are:

[8] See [Shreve, 2004, p.468ff.].

[9] See [Cont and Tankov, 2004, p.103].

$$s^i \cdot \Delta J^i_{t_k} = s^i \cdot (J^i_{t_k+\Delta t} - J^i_{t_k}) \tag{4.4}$$

$$\underbrace{=}_{\text{stationarity}} s^i \cdot \Delta J^i_{t_k} \tag{4.5}$$

$$= s^i \cdot \sum_{j=1}^{\Delta N^i_{t_k}} Y^i_j \tag{4.6}$$

Note that both counting and jump size model are product-specific at this stage. In the following, we derive the statistical properties of the jump component. The expected number of jumps per Δt is:[10]

$$E[N^i(\Delta t)] = \lambda^i \cdot \Delta t$$

The variance of the number of jumps in Δt is:

$$Var[N^i(\Delta t)] = \lambda^i \cdot \Delta t$$

Hence, the number of jumps per time unit is described by lambda. Given that the expected jump size is $E[Y^i] = \vartheta^i_1$ and its variance $Var[Y^i] = \vartheta^i_2$, it holds:[11]

$$E[\Delta J^i_{t_k}] = \vartheta^i_1 \cdot \lambda^i \cdot \Delta t$$
$$Var[\Delta J^i_{t_k}] = (\vartheta^i_2 + (\vartheta^i_1)^2) \cdot \lambda^i \cdot \Delta t$$

To sum up, we obtain the following properties for the confidence-driven cash flow of product i:

$$E[s^i \cdot \Delta J^i_{t_k}] = s^i \vartheta^i_1 \lambda^i \Delta t$$
$$Var[s^i \cdot \Delta J^i_{t_k}] = (s^i)^2 (\vartheta^i_2 + (\vartheta^i_1)^2) \cdot \lambda^i \Delta t$$

The jump sensitivities s^i are product-specific. $s^i > 1$ models products whose investors are particularly nervous. $s^i < 1$ models products whose investors are particularly resistant. $s^i = 1$ means that investors of product group i behave like the representative investor.[12] The representative investor is described by the jump size model Y_j.

Finally, the cash flow of product i writes as follows:

$$CF^i_{t_k} = (\mu^i_{t_k} \cdot \Delta t + \sigma^i \Delta W^i_{t_k} + s^i \cdot \Delta J^i_{t_k}) \cdot X^i_{t_0} \tag{4.7}$$

(4.7) suggests that the parameters are normalized to one unit initial product volume. The product cash flow is obtained by scaling with the initial amount $X^i_{t_0}$. (4.7) is a jump-diffusion process. As cash flows are not scaled to the current amount $X^i_{t_k}$ but to the initial amount $X^i_{t_0}$, products can be overdrawn. Examples are saving accounts that can become negative or loans that can become positive.

[10] See [Shreve, 2004, p.466f.].

[11] See [McNeil et al., 2005, p.474].

[12] The representative investor is the average across all products.

An alternative cash flow assumption that avoids that problem is (4.8):

$$CF_{t_k}^i = (\mu_{t_k}^i \cdot \Delta t + \sigma^i \Delta W_{t_k}^i + s^i \cdot \Delta J_{t_k}^i) \cdot X_{t_k}^i \tag{4.8}$$

(4.8) is a geometric jump-diffusion process. The advantage to have cash flows relative to the current inventory goes together with two disadvantages: firstly, cash flows are not quoted in monetary units, but as percentages. Secondly, aggregation is multiplicative instead of additive. Thus, the aggregated cash flow results as the product of (relative) product cash flows. As the multiplication of 'cash flows' is not intuitive, we prefer (4.7). A model based on (4.8) is subject to further research.

Drift, Brownian, and Jump-component are independent as they model different economic factors.[13]

The product cash flow has the following properties:

$$\begin{aligned} E[CF_{t_k}^i] &= (\mu_{t_k}^i + s^i \vartheta_1^i \lambda^i) \cdot \Delta t \cdot X_{t_0}^i \\ Var[CF_{t_k}^i] &= ((\sigma^i)^2 + (s^i)^2 (\vartheta_2^i + (\vartheta_1^i)^2) \lambda^i) \cdot \Delta t \cdot (X_{t_0}^i)^2 \end{aligned} \tag{4.9}$$

A dynamic cash flow model must incorporate future business. In contrast to existing products, future business does not have contractual cash flows, as it has not been contracted yet. Thus, the category 'Deterministic Cash Flows' represents planned business. Deviations of future business are planning errors of the business lines. This concerns all products, not only products with liquidity options. Analogous to existing products, future business can deviate from planning due to unexpected liquidity needs or due to a loss of confidence. In contrast to existing products, this concerns prospective customers, not current customers. Therefore, future business has the same cash flow structure as liquidity options and can be easily incorporated by an additional product j.

Ultimately, we want to reconcile our classification with those of Fiedler and Bier. Figure 4.3a maps the classification scheme proposed by Bier to ours. The deterministic components match directly. Products of Bier's stochastic category are modelled with a drift and a Brownian term. Products of his behavioral category are modelled by drift, Brownian and jump-component in our setup. We model semi-autodetermined and autodetermined positions as deterministic cash flows.

Figure 4.3b maps the classification scheme proposed by Fiedler to the one we developed. Deterministic cash flows are modelled by the drift term in our setup. His floating category refers to cash flows that are indexed to market variables. Our classification is based on customer behavior. Therefore, his floating category does not have a direct equivalent in our setup. However, there is an indirect link. If we split up his floating category into 'cash flows indexed to non-liquidity market variables' and 'cash flows indexed to liquidity market variables', our setup indirectly covers the second group if customer behavior is correlated with liquidity market variables. Cash flows of that type are modelled with the drift (planned) and Brownian (unplanned) component in our setup. The first group, 'cash flows indexed to non-liquidity market variables', contains cash flows that are driven by factors that belong to other risk types (e.g. interest rates, currency). We assumed that

[13] Drift: Contract & Planned Liquidity, Brownian: Unplanned Liquidity, Jump: Confidence.

Bier		Schmaltz/ Categories		
		Deterministic	Stochastic\ Liquidity	Stochastic\ Confidence
Category	Products	$\mu^i_{t_k}\Delta t$	$\sigma^i \Delta W^i_{t_k}$	$s^i \Delta J^i_{t_k}$
Deterministic	Products with Fixed Terms	X		
Stochastic	Assets/ Off-Balance Sheet items with Liquidity Options	X	X	
Behavioural	Liqabilities with Liquidity Options	X	X	X
Semi-autodetermined	Proprietory Trading	X		
Autodetermined	Obtained Credit Lines Equity	X		

Fig. 4.3a Category Mapping Bier/ Schmaltz

Fiedler		Schmaltz/ Categories		
		Deterministic	Stochastic\ Liquidity	Stochastic\ Confidence
Category	Products	$\mu^i_{t_k}\Delta t$	$\sigma^i \Delta W^i_{t_k}$	$s^i \Delta J^i_{t_k}$
Deterministic	Products with Fixed Terms	X		
Floating	Non-Liquidity Market Variables			
	Liquidity Market Variables	X	X	
Hypothetical	New Business	X	X	X

Fig. 4.3b Category Mapping Fiedler/ Schmaltz

these risk types are managed in other books so that the positions are value and liquidity closed from the liquidity manager's point of view.

Hypothetical cash flows refer to new business that we model with a drift for planned new business plus a Brownian component for unplanned new business.

4.2.2.2 Generic Product

The cash flow is modelled by a very general process. The use of a general process ensures that any product can be modelled. (4.7) can be thought of as a generic product that nests all other products. As a consequence, not every product has every modelling component. Some are set to zero for certain products. This idea is illustrated by figure 4.4. Figure 4.4 shows how term deposits, credit lines and saving deposits are modelled. Term deposits only have a drift term, credit lines have a drift and a Brownian term, saving deposits have a drift, Brownian and jump term.

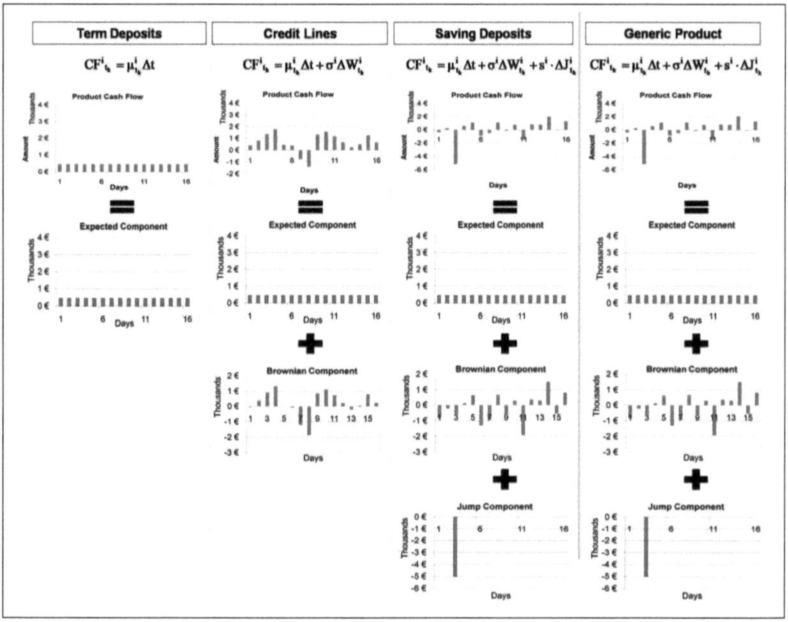

Fig. 4.4 Interpretation of Cash Flow Assumption as a Generic Product

4.2.2.3 Model Horizon

This section discusses the model horizon. There are four arguments to restrict the model horizon:

1. Cumulated Forecast Error Increases In Time
   Based on (4.9), it holds:

$$\begin{aligned}\lim_{k\to\infty} Var(\sum_{j=0}^{k} CF^i_{t_j}) &= \lim_{k\to\infty} Var(\sum_{j=0}^{k}(\mu^i_{t_k}\Delta t + \sigma^i \Delta W^i_{t_k} + s^i \Delta J^i_{t_k})X^i_{t_0}) \\ &= \lim_{k\to\infty} \sum_{j=0}^{k} (\sigma^i)^2 + (s^i)^2(\vartheta^i_2 + (\vartheta^i_1)^2)\lambda^i) \cdot \Delta t \cdot (X^i_{t_0})^2) \\ &= \lim_{k\to\infty} k \cdot (\sigma^i)^2 + (s^i)^2(\vartheta^i_2 + (\vartheta^i_1)^2)\lambda^i) \cdot \Delta t \cdot (X^i_{t_0})^2) \\ &= \infty\end{aligned} \tag{4.10}$$

   The cumulated cash flow refers to the cumulated changes in inventory. (4.10) suggests that the forecast uncertainty related to inventories far in the future is very high. Cash flow forecasts based on such high inventory error are not reasonable. In order to have a finite forecast error, the model horizon should be finite.

2. Unexpected New Business With Deterministic Components
   New business might unexpectedly occur. However, it might expectedly mature. Take the example of a 5y term deposit that has been unexpectedly contracted: once it is contracted, its cash flow is not stochastic anymore. Neglecting the information of the fixed maturity ignores a possibility to reduce uncertainty. In order to account for this information, the model horizon should be finite.
3. Managerial Action
   Our model incorporates neither strategic changes – like a change of the business model - nor changes of the institutional framework. It is likely that the management reacts with a change of business model if new business does not occur as expected. Furthermore, it has to react if the framework changes. In order to account for these feedback effects the model horizon has to be limited and a model with adjusted parameters has to be set up.
4. Restricted Products
   Section A.1 shows that a limited model horizon is particularly recommended if products are restricted. In fact, the majority of products are restricted: deposits (liabilities) cannot have a negative balance and loans (assets) cannot have a positive balance. This restriction introduces path-dependence, which means that observed cash flow deviations contain information for future cash flows. Using such information reduces cash flow uncertainty. The information can be used by applying conditional expectations. However, we apply unconditional expectations to ensure deterministic ones. The implied model error increases with the time that information is not used. Hence, limiting the model horizon is a way to limit the model error due to the use of unconditional expectations for restricted products.

We conclude that the model horizon should be limited to reduce the cumulated forecast error, to incorporate information about new business, to allow for managerial feedback effects and to apply unconditional expectations on restricted products.

4.2.3 Aggregation

Liquidity management is performed on aggregate variables.[14] Thus, product cash flows (4.7) have to be aggregated. We denote aggregate variables with a superscript A.

Although deterministic components can be easily aggregated by summation, stochastic components require assumptions about the dependence structure. This section discusses dependence structures and determines the aggregate cash flow $CF_{t_k}^A$ with its parameters $(\mu_{t_k}^A, \sigma^A, s^A)$.

[14] See section 2.2.

The set of cash flows from d products can be written in matrix form as follows:

$$\begin{pmatrix} CF^1_{t_k} \\ CF^2_{t_k} \\ \dots \\ CF^d_{t_k} \end{pmatrix} = \begin{pmatrix} \mu^1_{t_k} \\ \mu^2_{t_k} \\ \dots \\ \mu^d_{t_k} \end{pmatrix} \cdot \Delta t + \begin{pmatrix} \sigma^1 \Delta W^1_{t_k} \\ \sigma^2 \Delta W^2_{t_k} \\ \dots \\ \sigma^d \Delta W^d_{t_k} \end{pmatrix} + \begin{pmatrix} s^1 \Delta J^1_{t_k} \\ s^2 \Delta J^2_{t_k} \\ \dots \\ s^d \Delta J^d_{t_k} \end{pmatrix} \tag{4.11}$$

The aggregated cash flow is obtained by:

$$\begin{aligned} CF^A_{t_k} &= \begin{pmatrix} 1 \\ 1 \\ \dots \\ 1 \end{pmatrix}^T \cdot \begin{pmatrix} CF^1_{t_k} \\ CF^2_{t_k} \\ \dots \\ CF^d_{t_k} \end{pmatrix} \\ &= (\sum_{i=1}^{d} \mu^i_{t_k}) \cdot \Delta t + \sum_{i=1}^{d} \sigma^i \Delta W^i_{t_k} + s^i \Delta J^i_{t_k} \\ &= \mu^A_{t_k} \cdot \Delta t + \sigma^A \Delta W^A_{t_k} + s^A \Delta J^A_{t_k} \end{aligned}$$

The aggregate cash flow is again a Lévy-process as the summation preserves the process structure.[15] In particular, the aggregate cash flow has a drift, a Brownian and a jump component.

After having determined the structure of $CF^A_{t_k}$, we have to express its parameters $(\mu^A_{t_k}, \sigma^A, s^A)$ by the product parameters $(\mu^i_{t_k}, \sigma^i, s^i)$.

For the parameters (σ^A, s^A) we need to make additional assumptions concerning the dependence structure between products. In the following, we describe several dependence structures and determine which structure is preferable for liquidity management.

- Brownian Component
  With respect to the granularity of the stochastic source, several configurations are possible:
  - Product-specific Factor $\sigma^i \Delta W^i_{t_k} = \sigma^{i,p} \cdot \Delta W^{i,p}_{t_k}$
    A product-specific factor models product-inherent uncertainty. The economic interpretation is that customers use certain products for certain unexpected liquidity needs.[16] Product-specific factors have the highest granularity and introduce inter-product diversification.[17]
  - Systematic Factor $\sigma^i \Delta W^i_{t_k} = \sigma^{i,m} \cdot \Delta W^m_{t_k}$
    A systematic factor has the lowest granularity. The economic interpretation of a systematic factor is that all customers are surprised by a liquidity shock and they use all products (proportionally) to compensate for the shock. This implies that liquidity-motivated cash flows are perfectly correlated and cannot be diversified.
  - Factor approach $\sigma^i \Delta W^i_{t_k} = \sigma^{i,p} \Delta W^{i,p}_{t_k} + \sum_{k=1}^{K} \sigma^{i,k} \Delta W^k_{t_k}$

[15] See [Cont and Tankov, 2004, p.105f.].

[16] E.g. customers use product x if they receive a tax bill and product y if they are surprised by a garage bill.

[17] For further reading, please refer to [Süchtig and Paul, 1998, p.601].

A factor approach combines product-specific and systematic factors: it assumes a product-specific (idiosyncratic) factor and k-systematic factors. All factors are independent. This approach is frequently used in financial modelling.[18]

Certainly, the approaches are institute-specific and depend on the length and granularity of available cash flow time series as well as the number of products and the heterogeneity of customers.

We choose a factor model with one common factor and unsystematic risk for each product. Such a dependence structure is economically motivated by the fact that customers might be exposed to common liquidity shocks.[19] Product-specific liquidity factors account for the fact that different products attract different customers. Also, this dependence structure is the simplest one that can separate common and idiosyncratic factors and that can be easily extended to multiple systematic factors.

The one-factor Brownian model is as follows:

$$\sigma^i \Delta W_{t_k}^i := \sigma^{i,p} \Delta W_{t_k}^{i,p} + \sigma^{i,m} \Delta W_{t_k}^m \tag{4.12}$$

being:

$\sigma^{i,p}$: Exposure of product i to product-specific liquidity shock

$\Delta W_{t_k}^{i,p}$: Product-specific liquidity shock

$\sigma^{i,m}$: Exposure of product i to systematic liquidity shock

$\Delta W_{t_k}^m$: Systematic liquidity shock

The product-specific liquidity shock is modelled by $\Delta W_{t_k}^{i,p}$. The systematic liquidity shock is denoted $\Delta W_{t_k}^m$. Note that the product-specific shock has a product-index i whereas the systematic liquidity shock is not product-indexed.

After having determined the factor structure, we specify their interaction.

As common in factor models, we assume the systematic factor to be independent on product-specific factors:

$$\rho(\Delta W_{t_k}^{i,p}, \Delta W_{t_k}^m) = 0, \forall i = 1, ..., d$$

This independence is delineated by construction, as the factor approach separates the stochastic sources.

We assume product-specific factors also to be independent:

$$\rho(\Delta W_{t_k}^{i,p}, \Delta W_{t_k}^{j,p}) = 0, \forall i = 1, ..., d, j = 1, ..., d, i \neq j$$

In particular, this excludes product clustering. Product clustering means that some products are related. An example might be saving deposits and current accounts: if deposit transactions are done via the current account, their cash flows are perfectly negatively correlated. In contrast, if customers withdraw funds from demand deposits and over-

[18] Factor models are used in interest rate modelling (see [Novosyolov and Satchkov, 2008] for a recent study and literature review), portfolio credit risk models (see [Martin et al., 2006, p.129ff.]) or asset allocation (e.g. APT, For a survey see [Shanken, 1992] and a more recent paper [Chiu and Xu, 2004].).

[19] Examples of common liquidity shocks are shocks in petrol prices or taxes.

draft facilities to compensate large liquidity shocks, products exhibit a perfect positive correlation. Assuming independence can be understood as the assumption that product clustering offsets on the aggregate level.

- Jump Component
  In contrast to liquidity needs, it is unreasonable to model product-specific losses of confidence. A loss of confidence is widely publicised across the media, and thus it is very likely that it affects all customers. This implies that the jump dynamic is the same for all products:

$$\Delta J^i_{t_k} := \Delta J_{t_k}$$

The factor s^i introduces product-sensitivity. As stated above, s^i can be used to account for the different sensitivity of wholesale versus retail depositors.
Nevertheless, there is a need to model several scenarios (e.g. bank-specific or market-wide crises). The following approaches are possible:

- Stochastic Jump Size
  The jump size describes the severity of the scenario. This refers to a single Compound Poisson Process. In order to distinguish bank-specific (bs) and market-wide (mw) crises, a binomial jump size model is sufficient.

$$\Delta J_{t_k} = \sum_{j=1}^{N(\Delta t)} Y_j \tag{4.13}$$

$$Y_j = \begin{cases} y^{\text{bs}} & , P[Y_j = y^{\text{bs}}] = p^{bs} \\ y^{\text{mw}} & , P[Y_j = y^{\text{mw}}] = 1 - p^{bs} \end{cases} \quad \text{Being:}$$

y^{bs} : Jump size of banks-specific crisis
y^{mw} : Jump size of market-wide crisis
p^{bs} : Probability of bank-specific crisis

- Multiple Jump Processes
  Bank-specific and market-wide crises can also be modelled using two jump processes:

$$\Delta J_{t_k} = \sum_{j=1}^{N(\Delta t)} Y_j^1 + \sum_{j=1}^{M(\Delta t)} Y_j^2 \tag{4.14}$$

Being:
$N(t)$: Poisson-Process, bank-specific crisis
$M(t)$: Poisson-Process, industry-wide crisis
Y^1 : Jump Size Model, bank-specific crisis
Y^2 : Jump Size Model, industry-wide crisis

The advantage of (4.14) compared to (4.13) is that it models bank and industry-crises separately. This allows us to model the different degrees of severity for each crisis.

The disadvantage is that it does not exclude the possibility that both crises occur at the same time. Furthermore, two Compound Poisson Processes substantially increase model complexity. Therefore, we choose 4.13.

Hence, the product cash flow (4.7) extended by the chosen dependence structure is formulated as follows:

$$CF_{t_k}^i = (\mu_{t_k}^i \cdot \Delta t + \sigma^{i,p} \Delta W_{t_k}^{i,p} + \sigma^{i,m} \Delta W_{t_k}^m + s^i \cdot \Delta J_{t_k}) \cdot X_{t_0}^i \tag{4.15}$$

For such a particular dependence structure, the set of product cash flows is:

$$\begin{pmatrix} CF_{t_k}^1 \\ CF_{t_k}^2 \\ \dots \\ CF_{t_k}^d \end{pmatrix} = \begin{pmatrix} \mu_{t_k}^1 \\ \mu_{t_k}^2 \\ \dots \\ \mu_{t_k}^d \end{pmatrix} \cdot \Delta t + \begin{pmatrix} \sigma^{1,p} & 0 & \dots & 0 \\ 0 & \sigma^{2,p} & \dots & 0 \\ \dots & \dots & \dots & \dots \\ 0 & 0 & \dots & \sigma^{d,p} \end{pmatrix} \cdot \begin{pmatrix} \Delta W_{t_k}^{1,p} \\ \Delta W_{t_k}^{2,p} \\ \dots \\ \Delta W_{t_k}^{d,p} \end{pmatrix} \tag{4.16}$$

$$+ \begin{pmatrix} \sigma^{1,m} \\ \sigma^{2,m} \\ \dots \\ \sigma^{d,m} \end{pmatrix} \cdot \Delta W_{t_k}^m + \begin{pmatrix} s^1 \\ s^2 \\ \dots \\ s^d \end{pmatrix} \cdot \sum_{j=1}^{N(\Delta t)} Y_j \tag{4.17}$$

The aggregated cash flow is obtained by:

$$\begin{aligned} CF_{t_k}^A &= \begin{pmatrix} 1 \\ 1 \\ \dots \\ 1 \end{pmatrix}^T \cdot \begin{pmatrix} CF_{t_k}^1 \\ CF_{t_k}^2 \\ \dots \\ CF_{t_k}^d \end{pmatrix} \\ &= (\sum_{i=1}^d \mu_{t_k}^i) \cdot \Delta t + (\sum_{i=1}^d \sigma^{i,p} \Delta W_{t_k}^{i,p}) + (\sum_{i=1}^d \sigma^{i,m}) \cdot \Delta W_{t_k}^m + (\sum_{i=1}^d s^i) \cdot \sum_{j=1}^{N(\Delta t)} Y_j \\ &= \mu_{t_k}^A \cdot \Delta t + \sigma^A \Delta W_{t_k}^A + s^A \cdot \Delta J_{t_k} \end{aligned} \tag{4.18}$$

Aggregated parameters are based on product parameters:

$$\mu_{t_k}^A = \sum_{i=1}^d \mu_{t_k}^i$$

$$\sigma^A = \sqrt{\sum_{i=1}^d (\sigma^{i,p})^2 + (\sum_{i=1}^d \sigma^{i,m})^2}$$

$$s^A = \sum_{i=1}^d s^i$$

The statistical properties of (4.18) are:

$$E[CF^A_{t_k}] = (\mu^A_{t_k} + s^A \cdot \lambda \cdot \vartheta_1) \cdot \Delta t$$

$$= (\sum_{i=1}^{d} \mu^i_{t_k} + \lambda \cdot \vartheta_1 \cdot \sum_{i=1}^{d} s^i) \cdot \Delta t \quad (4.19)$$

$$Var[CF^A_{t_k}] = \sum_{i=1}^{d} (\sigma^{i,p})^2 \Delta t \quad (4.20)$$

$$+ (\sum_{i=1}^{d} \sigma^{i,m})^2 \cdot \Delta t \quad (4.21)$$

$$+ \lambda [\vartheta_2 + (\vartheta_1)^2] \cdot (\sum_{i=1}^{d} s^i)^2 \cdot \Delta t \quad (4.22)$$

Being:

$\vartheta_1 = p^{bs} \cdot y^{\mathrm{bs}} + (1-p) \cdot y^{\mathrm{mw}}$

$\vartheta_2 = p^{bs} \cdot (1-p^{bs}) \cdot (y^{\mathrm{bs}} - y^{\mathrm{mw}})^2$

y^{bs} : Jump size, bank-specific crisis

y^{mw} : Jump size, market-wide crisis

p^{bs} : Probability, bank-specific crisis

(4.19) suggests that drift and jump component contribute to expected cash flows. (4.20) ... (4.22) show how the aggregate variance can be expressed by the product-level parameters.

4.3 Funding Model

4.3.1 Requirements

The funding model describes the evolution of funding volumes and funding spread. The aggregated funding capacity is obtained as the sum of capacity estimates across investors, as figure 4.5 suggests. Banks only observe the used fraction of funding capacity. There is no indication of the size of unused capacity. Therefore, funding capacity is unobservable and there is no sound quantitative estimation methodology.[20] Regulators provide rather qualitative guidelines on how to estimate funding capacity.[21] However, they consider funding diversification an important step to reduce funding capacity volatility. Regulators believe that the funding capacity can be stabilized by diversifying across investors, products, market places, and currencies. In order to limit the roll-over risk, funding should also be diversified across maturities. Banks should consider correlation between funding

[20] In section 4.3.3 we discuss three complementary methods to estimate funding capacity.

[21] The following arguments are based on [IIF, 2007, Recommendation 16 and 17]. Banks should employ a dedicated desk to strengthen investor relations. They should identify the main factors that affect investors' willigness to lend. This is to say that banks should identify investor's investment policy and rules.

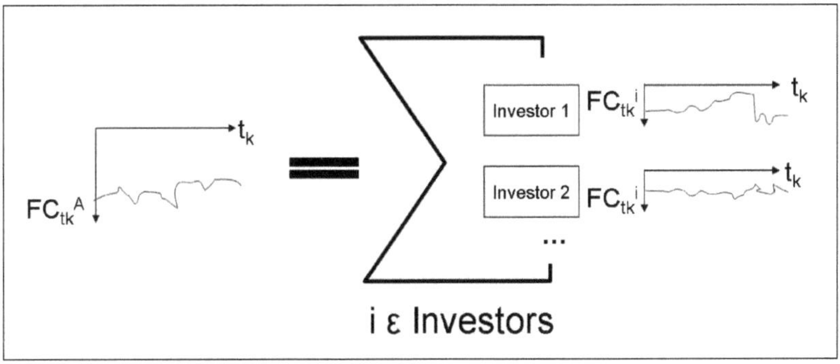

Fig. 4.5 Aggregated Funding Capacity

sources and market conditions.[22] In any case, the funding model should be stochastic as regulators require scenario-specific funding capacities. Our funding model should also account for a funding crisis where external funding is unavailable. This scenario is a widely tested stress scenario.[23]

In contrast to funding capacity, the funding spread is not a regulatory issue.

4.3.2 Funding Model

The first step towards a funding model is the classification of funding in a 'funding matrix'. Our classification is given in figure 4.6. The funding matrix classifies sources of potential funding. The dimensions are [investor x instrument] as suggested in the previous section.

With respect to investors, many sources stress the distinction between retail and wholesale investors. However, the funding of retail customers is a product and part of planned business. In our model it is already captured by future business in the cash flow model. Therefore, our funding model has to account for Wholesale Funding only.

With regard to instruments, the first distinction is debt versus equity. Both generate a cash inflow at issuance. In fact, only their future cash flows differ: debt matures and pays profit-independent coupons whereas equity does not mature and pays profit-dependent dividends. As they have the same liquidity impact at issuance, we do not explicitly distinguish between them in the funding model.

Debt can further be classified according to its maturity, collateralization, priority (junior vs. senior), interest-rate scheme (floating vs. fixed-rate), currency (foreign vs. domestic) and optionalities (plain vanilla vs. structured bonds).[24] We assume that priority, interest-rate scheme, currency and optionalities are of secondary interest for liquidity manage-

[22] See [BCBS, 2008, Principle 7].

[23] Standard & Poor's use the survival time without external funding for the liquidity assessment in their rating methodology. See [CEBS, 2008, p.75].

[24] See [Brealey and Myers, 2003, p. 701ff.] for details on the characteristics.

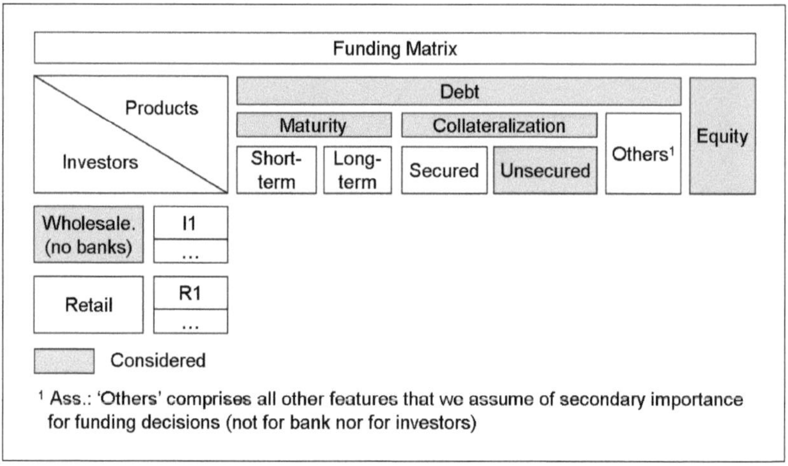

Fig. 4.6 Funding Classification Based on [Brealey and Myers, 2003, p. 701ff.]

ment.[25] Our model that describes funding capacity does not distinguish between funding capacity for secured and unsecured funding. The reason is that secured funding also absorbs funding capacity to fund the collateral.

As suggested by regulators, our funding model distinguishes short-term and long-term funding.[26] The motivation for this is threefold:

1. Short and long-term funding involves different agents on both the investor's and the bank's behalf.
   Short-term funds are traded on the money/interbank market whereas long-term funds are issued and traded on the fixed-income market. Money and fixed-income markets differ in traders, instruments and investment policies.[27]
2. Short and long-term funds have different ratings.
   Different ratings are an indication that short and long-term funds are not perfect substitutes.
3. Time-to-funding
   The time between initiation and effective funding is shorter for short-term than for long-term funds. Short-term funds are acquired by telephone whereas long-term issues usually require a formal issuance process.

Our funding model is given in table 4.1. It describes both funding capacity (*FC*) and Funding Spread (*c*). The index 'st' refers to short-term, 'lt' refers to long-term.

[25] The 'secondary interest' results from the assumption that the bank would agree to any of these characteristics if it needs additional funds. We assume the liquidity needs to be higher than the importance of these features.

[26] See section 4.3.1.

[27] [Choudhry, 2007] provides an introduction to money and fixed-income market on page 47 and page 133, respectively.

Table 4.1 Funding Model

Variable	Normal $\Delta J_t^A = 0$ $\sigma^A \cdot \Delta W_t^A \leq L$	Distressed $\Delta J_t^A = 0$ $\sigma^A \cdot \Delta W_t^A > L$	Crisis $\Delta J_t^A > 0$
FC_{st}	$FC_{st}^{fund.}$	$FC_{st}^{fund.}$	0
FC_{lt}	$FC_{lt}^{fund.}$	0	0
c_{st}	c_{st}^{fund}	$c_{st}^{\text{distressed}}$	∞
c_{lt}	c_{lt}^{fund}	∞	∞

The variables in table 4.1 have the following meaning:

$$FC_{(.)}^{fund.} : \text{Fundamental capacity}$$
$$c_{(.)}^{\text{fund}} : \text{Fundamental credit spread}$$
$$c_{(.)}^{\text{distressed}} : \text{Distressed credit spread}$$

Columns in table 4.1 refer to scenarios, rows to funding variables. In particular, the model distinguishes three funding scenarios: normal funding, distressed funding and funding crisis. Funding scenarios are linked to cash flows: a funding crisis occurs if jumps occur. The link 'externalises' the distinction between Brownian deviations and jumps.[28] Without that link, it is difficult to assess whether a jump or large Brownian deviations occur.

The funding crisis is characterized by zero funding capacities and infinite spreads. Hence, the only way to generate liquidity is asset liquidation.[29] In times without jumps, normal and distressed funding are possible. The distinction is linked to Brownian deviations: if the deviations exceed a boundary L, the bank faces distressed funding. In this case, long-term funds are not available. Short-term funds are only available at elevated funding spreads. As long-term funds vanish quicker, they are less robust than short-term funds. In times of normal funding, all variables are at their fundamental values.

To sum up, our funding model has the following characteristics:

1. Funding is linked to Brownian Deviations and Confidence
2. Short-term funding is more robust than long-term funding
3. Three funding scenarios are distinguished: Usual Funding/Distressed Funding/Funding Crisis

As funding capacity is an unobservable quantity we discuss estimation approaches in the next section.

[28] This assumption implies that a jump is the only reason that external funding is unavailable.

[29] This scenario addresses regulators' requirement to consider a scenario in which external funding is unavailable.

4.3.3 Calibration

The funding capacity of the liquidity model is stochastic, but can only take two values: fundamental capacity and zero. To estimate the fundamental funding capacity, it can be split up into the used fraction (observable) and the unused fraction (unobservable). The used fraction corresponds to the current funding volume. To determine the fundamental funding capacity, one has to estimate the unobservable fraction.

We propose three complementary methods to estimate the funding capacity:

1. Limit Testing
   If the funding line is used to the limit (limit testing), funding capacity becomes observable. In fact, limit testing implies that funds might be borrowed beyond funding needs. Regulators require the periodic testing of funding limits as it allows to monitor the evolution of funding capacity.[30]
2. Pricing Policies
   If counterparties offer volume-dependent spreads, a proxy of the stable part is the amount up to which the bank can fund at the lowest credit spread. Volumes that can only be tapped by paying elevated spreads, might not always be available but subject to the liquidity situation of the counterparty.
3. Bank's Investment Policy
   Banks act on both sides of the funding desk as borrowers and investors. Assuming that counterparties use similar investment rules as the bank does, their own investment rules could provide some insight into the factors that determine available funding.

Interpolating observations into the future is critical. For this reason, it is almost impossible to anticipate how counterparties will react in different scenarios. Based on this argument, it might be reasonable to assume that external funds are unavailable. This is what we assume in our model: in the occurrence of jumps, funding is not available at all. In distressed markets, long-term funding is not available.

The second component of the funding model is the funding spread. As it is an observable quantity, its calibration is less sophisticated. The fundamental spread can be proxied by the average spread and the distressed spread can be proxied by a spread quantile.

4.4 Liquidation Model

4.4.1 Requirements

In contrast to funding capacity, regulators provide detailed recommendations with regard to the liquidation model.[31] As stated in section 2.1, asset liquidity is described by the liquidation cost (haircut) and the time-to-liquidity. Regulators require that the bank esti-

[30] See [BCBS, 2008, Principle 7].

[31] In the following we refer to [IIF, 2007, Recommendation 25] and [BCBS, 2008, Principle 9].

mates both quantities for assets that are considered to be liquidated. With regard to the haircut[32] estimation regulators require:

1. Scenario Dependency
   Haircuts reflect bank's own liquidity conditions and those of counterparties. As the conditions might change, haircuts are scenario-dependent.
2. Liquidation Channels
   Potential liquidation channels are sale and secured funding. The latter is split up into the channels Central Bank pledging, repoing and securitization. Haircut models differ across liquidation channels. The same asset might have different haircuts if liquidated via different channels.
3. Asset groups
   For a given liquidation channel, haircuts differ upon security-specific characteristics like rating, market price availability, maturity, type of security or issuer type. Hence, within a liquidity channel, haircuts are defined for asset groups.
4. Models
   Regulators recommend basing the haircut estimation on prior experience, best-practice assumptions, liquidation scenarios, adjusted market or credit risk models, and market liquidity models.

Finally, banks should be able to calculate the liquidation value of their assets in a timely manner.

4.4.2 Liquidation Model

Figure 4.7 illustrates the main ideas of a liquidation model.

The liquidation model calculates the liquidation capacity (See (2) in figure 4.7) of the asset side of the accounting balance (1). The liquidation capacity LC_t is the sum of the liquidation values L_t^i of m assets:[33]

$$LC_t = \sum_{i=1}^{m} L_t^i$$

Assets can be liquidated by either selling or repoing. The liquidation value of asset i is obtained as its present value[34] reduced by a sale haircut or its market price reduced by a repo haircut:

[32] For a definition of haircuts, see section 2.1.

[33] The liquidation value defines equation (2.1) on page 16.

[34] More generally, it could be any other model-based value.

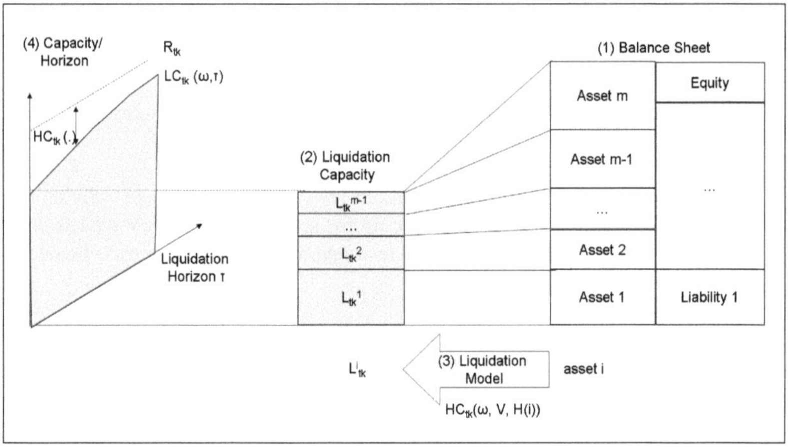

Fig. 4.7 Liquidation Model

Sale:

$$P_t^i = PV_t \cdot (1 - HC^R(i))$$

PV_t : Present Value

P_t : Market Price

Repo:

$$L_t^i = P_t \cdot (1 - HC^S(i))$$

Generic:

$$L_t^i = R_t \cdot (1 - HC(i))$$

R_t : Reference Value: either Present Value (Sale) or Market Price (Repo)

We use the reference value R_t to account for both sale and repo.

The sale haircut measures market illiquidity. Based on the present value, it estimates the market price. The repo haircut protects the lender from future price deterioration of asset i.

The liquidation model (3) assigns haircuts to assets. Haircuts are a function of liquidation channel[35], asset characteristics H(i), scenario ω and transaction volume V:

$$HC(\omega, V, H(i)) = f(\omega, V, H(i))$$

The dependence on the transaction volume reflects the limited capacity of channels to absorb large volumes. Not all assets are liquidated overnight. In fact, a liquidation strategy $(v_{t_k})_{t_k=1,\ldots,\tau}$ is used to determine the volumes liquidated per day (v_{t_k}). The liquidation horizon is τ. It can be used as proxy for the speed of liquidation: a large τ indicates a slow

[35] For easier notation, we do not index the haircut for different liquidation channels.

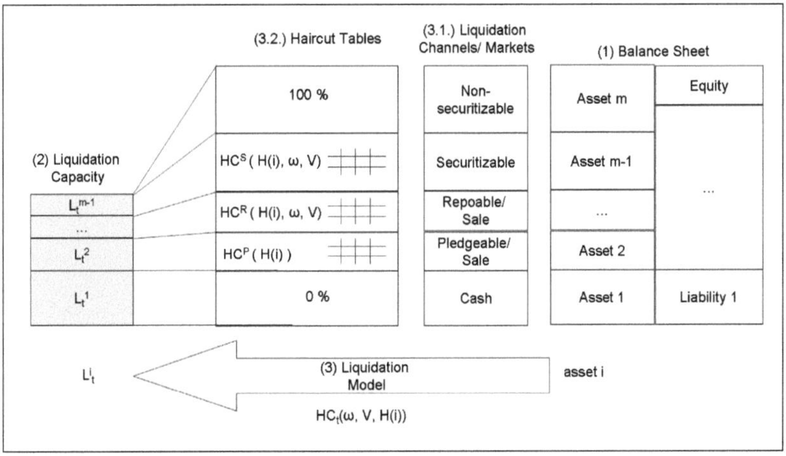

Fig. 4.8 Liquidation Model Insight

liquidation whereas a small τ indicates an accelerated liquidation. As the haircut might be volume-sensitive, there is an inverse relation between liquidation horizon and haircut: the larger the liquidation horizon, the smaller the haircut. This implies that the liquidation value converges towards the reference value as suggested by the capacity-horizon graph (4) in figure 4.7.

Therefore, the liquidation capacity also depends on the scenario ω and liquidation horizon τ:

$$LC_t(\omega,\tau) = \sum_{i=1}^{m} R_t^i \cdot (1 - HC(\omega, V(\tau), H(i)))$$

Within the liquidation model, the model has to account for different liquidation channels. This can be seen in column (3.1.) in figure 4.8. The main liquidation channels are repo and asset sale. Repo splits up in bilateral and central bank repo. Asset sale splits up in individual asset sales and securitization (portfolio asset sale). For each channel, eligibility criteria exist that define the assets that can be liquidated through it. Eligibility criteria are fixed for central bank repoing[36] and are subject to negotiations for other channels. The channels are not disjointed, however, as assets can be eligible for more than one channel.[37] For each channel, haircut tables assign haircuts depending on channel and security-specific characteristics (3.2.). Official haircut tables exist for central bank repoing. For other channels, they have to be estimated. Central bank haircuts are constant while all others might differ according to market circumstances and transaction volume.

[36] For central bank repoing, see [European Central Bank, 2006, p.34ff.].

[37] An example are government bonds that are eligible for repoing and sale.

Although repo and sale follow the haircut concept, haircuts and their determining factors are different due to the underlying transaction.[38]

The economic drivers of both haircuts are summarized in table 4.2. Repo and sale have

Table 4.2 Haircut-Determining Factors

Criterion	Sale	Repo
Factors	Market Setup Asset Information Structure	Credit Risk Market Price Risk

two different economic drivers: a repo is a secured loan[39] whereas the sale is a spot deal without future transactions. The repo haircut protects the lender from price deterioration during the loan's lifetime. The sale haircut accounts for market illiquidity. It translates model values of perfectly liquid markets to prices of imperfectly liquid markets. Both haircuts serve as protection, but their factors are different: the repo haircut is credit and market-risk sensitive whereas the sale haircut is driven by market and informational factors.

Currently, no market standards have been established to estimate haircuts.

With respect to repo haircuts, the haircuts of the Eurosystem (ECB repoing)[40] serve as a benchmark for bilateral repos. ECB repo distinguishes marketable and non-marketable assets. Marketable ones are grouped into four liquidity categories according to issuer and asset type. The categories are credit risk indicators. Within each group, haircuts differ according to the residual maturity and coupon structure (market risk indicators). Non-marketable assets have an overall markup for credit risk with respect to the lowest category of marketable assets. Furthermore, non-marketable individual claims have maturity-dependent haircuts. Portfolios of claims (mortgage-backed securities) have a global haircut of 20%.

As to sale haircuts, market liquidity models can be used. These models explain the average market liquidity of an asset as well as the phenomenon of varying market liquidity.[41] Although attractive from an academic view point, they are rarely used in the banking industry. If used at all, they are used for pricing rather than liquidity management.[42]

As we are unaware of a model for sale haircuts, we propose a simple one that can be implemented easily. Let us recall the calculation of the liquidation value for an asset sale for a particular scenario:

---

38 Regulators stress that both haircuts are different. See [IIF, 2007, p.31].

39 See section 3.1.5 .

40 See [European Central Bank, 2006, p.49ff.].

41 Early market liquidity models explained bid-ask spreads (see [Grossman and Miller, 1988], [Stoll, 1978], [Glosten and Milgrom, 1985]). Recent market liquidity models focus on explaining the volatility of market liquidity (see [Chowdhry and Nanda, 1998], [Brunnermeier and Pedersen,]). Empirical papers show that market illiquidity is priced (see [Longstaff et al., 2005], [Frank De Jong and Joost Driessen, 2005]) and how much an adequate market illiquidity premium is (See [Pástor and Stambaugh, 2003], [Acharya and Pedersen, 2005].).

42 See section 2.1.

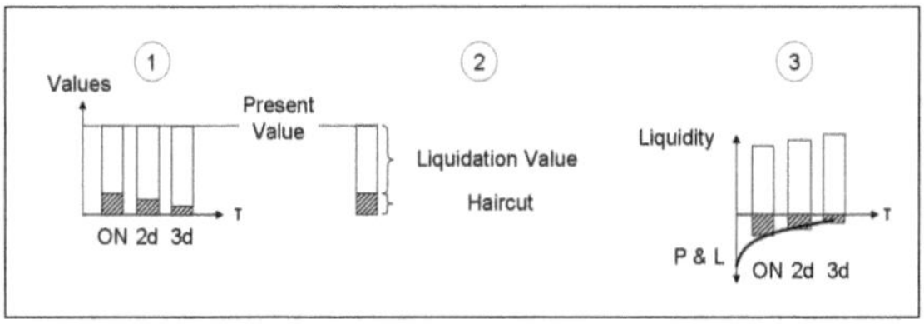

Fig. 4.9 Decomposition of Present Value in Liquidity- and P&L-Fraction

$$
\begin{aligned}
L_t &= (1 - HC^S(\tau)) \cdot PV_t \\
L_t &: \text{Liquidation Value} \\
PV_t &: \text{Present Value} \\
HC^S &: \text{Sale Haircut} \\
\tau &: \text{Liquidation Horizon}
\end{aligned}
$$

Another way of interpreting the haircut is that it cuts the present value in a liquidity and a profit& loss-part as suggested by (4.23):

$$PV_t = HC^S(\tau) \cdot PV_t + (1 - HC^S(\tau)) \cdot PV_t \tag{4.23}$$

$$PV_t = \underbrace{PV_t \cdot HC^S(\tau)}_{Profit\&Loss} + \underbrace{L_t}_{Liquidity} \tag{4.24}$$

This is displayed in figure 4.9. (1) states that the present value is split up into liquidation value and haircut. The haircut decreases in the liquidation horizon τ. (3) stresses that two levels, the cash flow and the P&L-levels, are involved. The longer the time horizon, the higher the part of present value that is recovered as liquidity.

It is convenient to model the haircut with a functional form as indicated in (3). The functional form has the advantage of describing a term structure of haircuts with only two parameters. We propose the exponential function given by (4.25):

$$HC_{t_k} = HC^{ON} \cdot e^{-\eta \cdot t_k} \tag{4.25}$$

Being:

HC^{ON} : Haircut for Overnight

η : Speed of Haircut Improvement

We choose an exponential form to account for the non-linearity in liquidation cost. The haircut function uses two parameters: the overnight haircut HC^{ON} and eta. The overnight haircut is the starting point of the liquidation function. It can be interpreted as market depth.[43] The shape of the haircut function is determined by η. It measures the speed of haircut improvement, i.e. the speed at which buying orders flow into the market. It can be interpreted as market resiliency.[44]

[43] See section 2.1.

[44] See section 2.1.

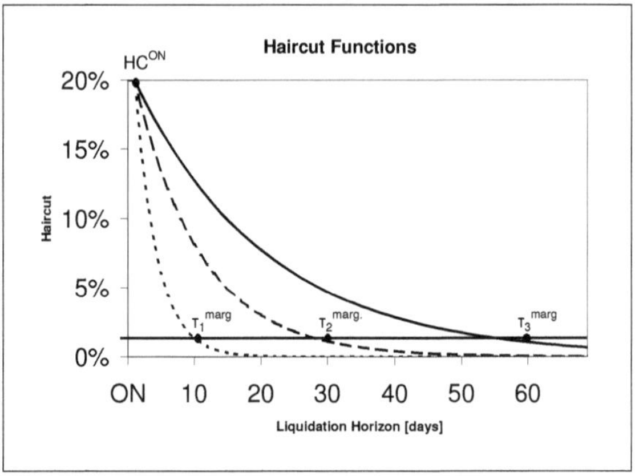

Fig. 4.10 Haircut Functions for Different Liquidation Horizons

However, eta is a somewhat artificial quantity. A more natural parameter is the time $\tau^{\text{marg.}}$ till the haircut has reached a marginal level of a. This way, the haircut function can be parametrized with the overnight haircut HC^{ON} and the (marginal) liquidation horizon $\tau^{\text{marg.}}$. Eta follows as:

$$\eta = -\frac{\ln \frac{a}{HC^{ON}}}{\tau^{\text{marg.}}}$$

Figure 4.10 plots a set of haircut functions that share the same overnight haircut ($HC^{ON} = 20\%$) but have different marginal liquidation horizons ($\tau^{\text{marg.}} = (60|30|10)$). The marginal haircut a is 1%.

In fact, figure 4.10 offers two interpretations, namely the haircut functions of three different assets or three haircut scenarios for the same asset.

If the first interpretation holds, the liquidation of asset 1 is favorable if market liquidity is the only decision criterion: asset 1 has the lowest haircut function. If haircut functions intersected, a shift from one asset to another, depending on the liquidation horizon, would be required. As no intersections occur in our example, asset 1 is always liquidated first.

The second interpretation stresses the dependence of haircuts on market circumstances. Imbalances between supply and demand might widen haircuts. In order to account for these variations, one could abandon the assumption of constant parameters and introduce stochastic overnight haircuts and marginal liquidation horizons.

A binomial haircut model distinguishing normal and distressed markets is given by (4.26):

$$(HC^{ON}, \tau^{\text{marg.}}) = \begin{cases} (10\%, 5), & P[\text{'normal'}] = 0.9 \\ (20\%, 10), & P[\text{'distressed'}] = 0.1 \end{cases} \tag{4.26}$$

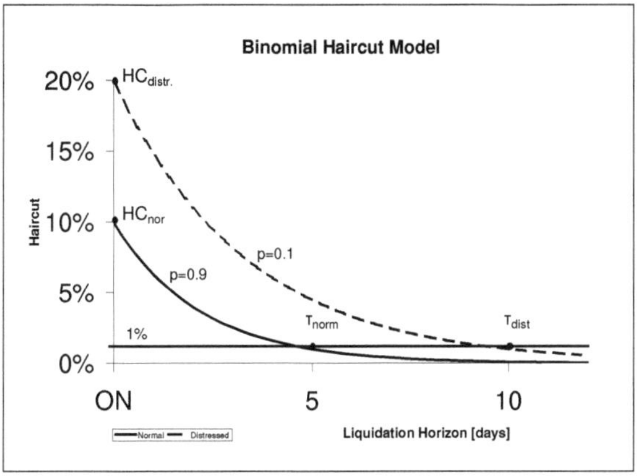

Fig. 4.11 Numerical Example of a Binomial Haircut Model

The corresponding haircut functions are displayed in figure 4.11. Research has shown that investors are compensated for higher market liquidity volatility.[45] Instruments with high and stable market liquidity are usually low yield instruments. Hence, an optimal asset reserve balances expected liquidation costs (haircut) to the higher yield.

The liquidation model is important for the optimal management of confidence crises. As we do not detail this aspect, we chose a basic haircut model as defined by (4.27):

$$HC = \begin{cases} 0, & \text{Liquid Assets} \\ 1, & \text{Illiquid Assets} \end{cases} \tag{4.27}$$

(4.27) does not distinguish between sale and repo haircuts. Furthermore, it only accounts for two asset groups and does not incorporate varying market circumstances.

4.5 Interest Rate Model

Similar to the credit spread, regulators do not require the modelling of interest rates. Section 3.2.2 stated that the overnight rate is a key liquidity variable as deviations have to be cleared every day.

In contrast to cash flow, funding and liquidation models, interest rate models ('IR'-models) are not specific for liquidity management, but are widely used in instrument pricing and market risk analyses. Prices and risk measures are very sensitive to the model assumptions. By contrast, liquidity models are not very sensitive to the chosen IR-model since rates play a minor role.

45 Empirical studies are available for stock and bond markets. See for stock markets: [Pástor and Stambaugh, 2003], [Gibson and Mougeot, 2004] and [Acharya and Pedersen, 2005]. See for bond markets: [Buraschi and Menini, 2002], [Longstaff et al., 2005] and [Frank De Jong and Joost Driessen, 2005].

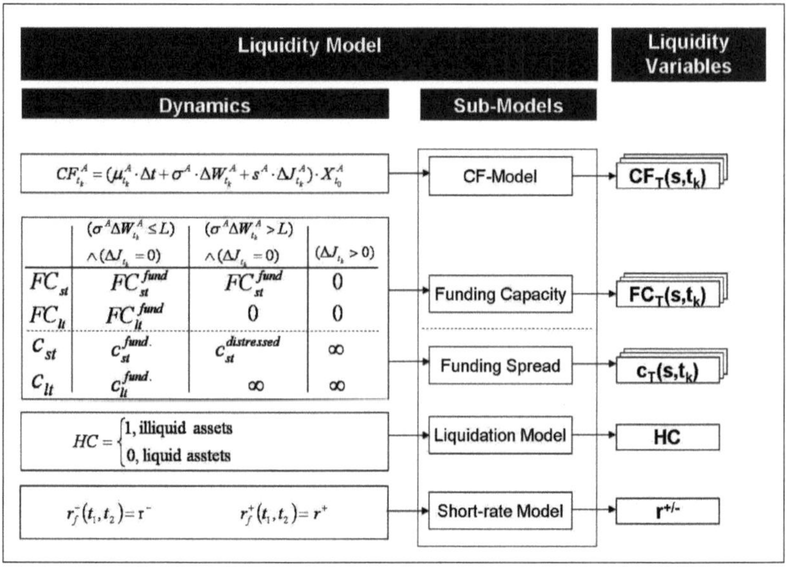

Fig. 4.12 Bank Liquidity Model

Whereas other authors set interest rates to zero, we model interest rates. However, we opt for constant risk-free rates:

$$r_f^-(t_1,t_2) = r^-$$
$$r_f^+(t_1,t_2) = r^+$$

Further specifications concerning the short-rate are provided in chapter 6.3. More complex models do not add substantial insight to liquidity management.

4.6 Bank Liquidity Model

The sub models discussed in the previous sections form our liquidity model. The model is given in figure 4.12. Note that the model describes bank liquidity, meaning that cash flow and funding capacity are aggregated variables. Our liquidity model consists of four sub-models:

1. Cash Flow Model
2. Funding Model (Capacity and Spread)
3. Liquidation Model
4. Short-rate Model

Our modelling focus is clearly on the cash flow model. We describe cash flows as a jump-diffusion process.

1. The components (Drift/Brownian/Jump) directly correspond to customer behavior (Contractual/Liquidity/Confidence).
2. The process assumption is that it generally covers all products.
3. The structure ensures that the aggregated cash flow has the same components (Drift/Brownian/Jump).

Our funding model distinguishes long and short-term funding, and three funding scenarios, namely normal and distressed funding as well as funding crisis. The funding stochastic is directly linked to the cash flow stochastic; therefore, funding crises materialize if jumps (loss of confidence) occur. Funding is distressed if the systematic liquidity shock is beyond a threshold L and there are no jumps. Without these and large systematic shocks, funding is assumed to be normal, characterised by fundamental spreads and fundamental funding capacities. If markets are distressed, long-term funding vanishes and short-term funding is only available at elevated cost. This assumption incorporates the observation that short-term funding is still available although long-term funding no longer is. In a funding crisis, external funds are unavailable.

Liquidation and the short-rate model are kept very simple. Thus the liquidation model is a binary haircut model that classifies assets as perfectly liquid (haircut = 0) and perfectly illiquid (haircut = 0). The short-rate model assumes constant risk-free rates for both funding and investment.

4.7 Summary

Based on the liquidity framework, this chapter suggests a particular liquidity model. For each liquidity variable, we discussed requirements, modelling approaches and particularities. By specifying the process for each key variable, we obtain the bank liquidity model.

The cash flow model is defined on the product level and derived from customer behavior. Cash flows are deterministic or stochastic whereby stochastic cash flows can be refined in liquidity and confidence-driven. Deterministic cash flows encompass contractual and planned cash flows. They are described by a drift. The drift varies across time. Cash flow shocks that are liquidity-driven are modelled by a Brownian component. It can be interpreted as the forecast error of customers' liquidity needs. The Brownian exposure is measured in standard deviations and remains constant. Cash flow shocks that are confidence-driven are modelled by a jump component. The jump exposure is measured by a constant scaling factor. Brownian and jump component are assumed to be independent. The reconciliation of our cash flow model with classifications in the literature suggests that our model covers all types of cash flows. We suggested that the model horizon should be limited to reduce the inherent modelling error due to simplifying assumptions. As liquidity management is performed on the bank level, product cash flows have to be aggregated. The aggregation process requires additional assumptions about the dependence structure between products. With respect to the Brownian component, we propose a one-factor model. A one-factor model consists of one systematic factor and product-specific unsystematic risk. With respect to the jump component, we assume that confidence is a systematic factor.

The funding scenarios are linked to the cash flow model: a crisis is triggered by a cash flow jump. Distressed funding is triggered if Brownian deviations are beyond a critical boundary L. We stressed that the calibration of the funding model encounters serious difficulties, as the funding capacity is an unobservable quantity. We propose to use limit testing, pricing policies and the banks' own investment policies to gather information about factors that funding capacity is sensitive to. The funding spread is observable and can be calibrated by using time series.

The liquidation model describes haircuts. They depend on liquidation channel, scenario, volume and asset characteristics. Liquidation channels are repo and sale. 'Scenario' refers to the fact that haircuts might not be constant but depend on market circumstances. Volume is a direct function of the liquidation horizon. Asset characteristics subsume further attributes that lead to different haircuts. We discuss an exponential liquidation model that can be extended to incorporate several scenarios. The model that we chose is of a simple structure: it only distinguishes perfectly liquid and perfectly illiquid assets. It assigns constant haricuts to either group.

The interest rate model describes the evolution of interest rates. Also, we choose a simple binary model for funding rates. Investment rates are constant.

The sub-models form the bank liquidity model that underlies the management process discussed within the next section.

Chapter 5
Liquidity Management

This section consists of two parts: first, we split the product cash flow and transfer the components to different departments (Cash Flow Transfer Model). In this manner, the transfer permits us to separate the management of cash flow and spread risk. A separate management is desirable as both risks have different characteristics and require different instruments. Furthermore, separate management reduces complexity. In the second part, we derive prices at which the components are transferred (Transfer Pricing). The transfer prices are based on the cost that the management of the components implies. In the dichotomy 'controlling' versus 'management', this section is more controlling-oriented. However, it is titled 'Liquidity Management' as it describes the management process. Particularly, it discusses where which cash flow component is managed.

5.1 Cash Flow Transfer

5.1.1 Basic Transfer Model

We propose to split up the cash flow and to separately manage cash flow components.

This separation has the following advantages:

1. Risk and Performance Separation
   Separating deterministic and stochastic components leads to a separation of illiquidity and spread risk. As spread risk is based on deterministic, and illiquidity risk on stochastic cash flows, we separate deterministic (drift $\mu_{t_k}^A \Delta t$) and stochastic components (Browian component $\sigma^A \Delta W_{t_k}^A$ and Jump component $s^A \Delta J_{t_k}^A$). The deterministic component is transferred to one department, the stochastic components to another. The separation conforms with the literature that distinguishes liquidity and liquidity risk.[1] Our deterministic component refers to liquidity, our stochastic components in turn refer to liquidity risk. In contrast to the literature, we do not only distinguish, but also manage them separately.
2. Local Optimization
   The separation allows for local (department-wise) optimization. Local optimization is less complex than a global optimization.

[1] [Leistenschneider, 2008] distinguishes transfer prices for structural liquidity risk and contingency liquidity risk.

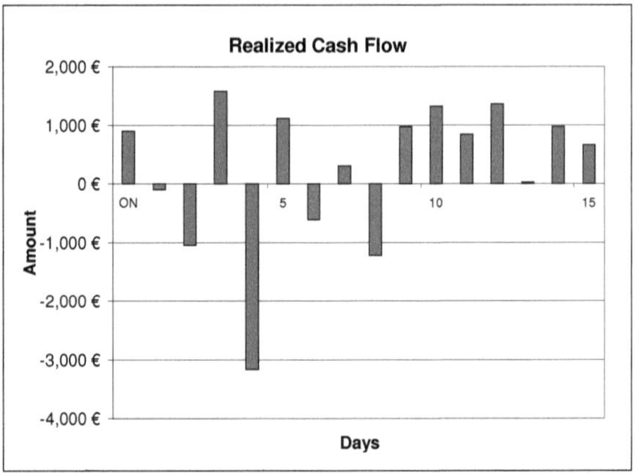

Fig. 5.1a Jump-Diffusion Cash Flow

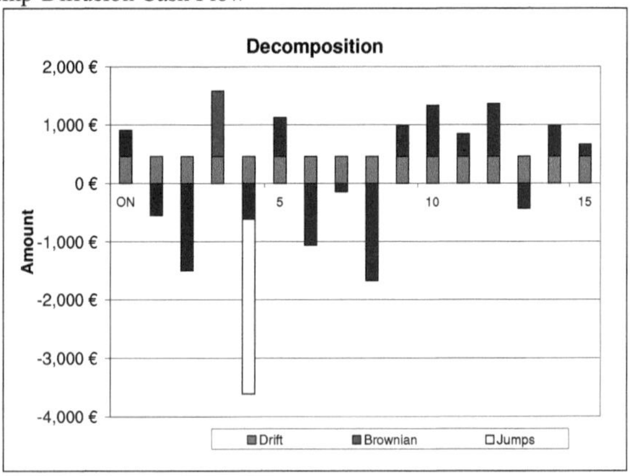

Fig. 5.1b Decomposed Cash Flow

Figures 5.1a and 5.1b demonstrate the decomposition of a realized cash flow: figure 5.1a shows the gross cash flow. Figure 5.1b is the same cash flow decomposed into deterministic, Brownian and jump-component.

Deterministic and stochastic portfolios should be managed in different departments. With respect to the deterministic portfolio, we propose the Origination Desk (in the following Origination/OD). With respect to the stochastic portfolio, we propose the Money Market Desk (in the following Money Market/MMD).[2]

Origination is responsible for short and long-term funding via securities. It issues short-term commercial papers and long-term bonds. We assume that Origination issues on an

[2] The exact name of the security issuing department and the short-term liquidity department might vary across banks. However, we believe that such a separation exists in large banks. [Witt, 1994, p.44] proposes an organisational structure that has a Money Market desk and a fixed-income desk. The separation according to maturity is evident.

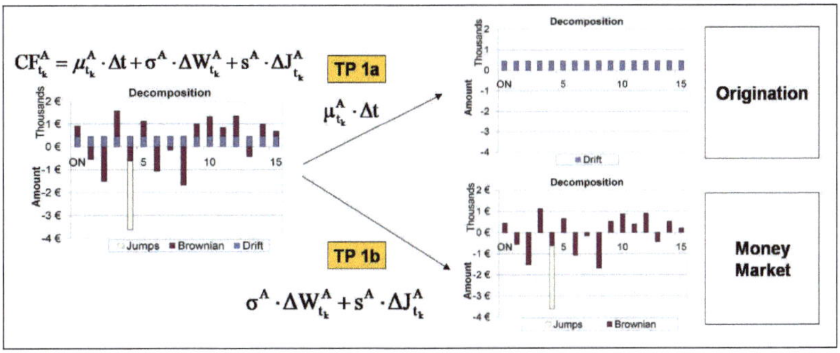

Fig. 5.2 Basic Transfer Model

unsecured basis. Money Market operates on the interbank and central bank market, using short-term deposits and loans. Money Market uses secured and unsecured funding. Both departments differ with respect to the markets that they operate in and their instruments.

We choose Origination for the deterministic and Money Market for the stochastic component for the following reasons:

1. Stochastic Cash Flows materialize overnight
   Stochastic cash flows are deviations from expected cash flows. They materialize overnight and require short-term management. The department that manages overnight and short-term cash flows is the Money Market, using Money Market instruments that have a maximal maturity of one year.
2. Maturity Mismatch strategy involves long-term cash flows.
   The mismatch involves long-term cash flows, as it is the gap between short and long-term maturities.[3] Adjusting the mismatch requires the use of long-term issues. The department that is responsible for issues is Origination, using fixed-income instruments that usually have a maturity beyond 3M.

Figure 5.2 summarizes this concept. We separate deterministic and stochastic cash flow components. The deterministic component is transferred to Origination, which optimizes the maturity profile μ_t^A by using capital market instruments. It operates on deterministic cash flows and bears a spread risk (Maturity Mismatch-Strategy). The stochastic component is transferred to the Money Market, which optimizes the liquidity reserve by using Money Market instruments. It operates on stochastic cash flows and bears an illiquidity risk (Liquidity Option-Strategy).

Each component is transferred at a transfer price. The transfer prices are specified in section 5.2.

[3] Deterministic cash flows can be long-term. Stochastic cash flows can only be short-term because realized deviations are only known the day that they emerge.

However, this basic transfer model exhibits several drawbacks:

1. Origination still bears an illiquidity risk
   The Maturity Mismatch strategy assumes that short-term maturities can be rolled over. If the roll-over is not possible, the bank can run into illiquidity. Our objective is that Origination only bears spread risk.
2. Very short-term deterministic cash flows in Origination
   Currently, all deterministic cash flows are allocated to Origination. However, Origination is not able to manage very short-term cash flows since it does not have the required Money Market instruments. Our objective is that Origination does not manage very short-term deterministic cash flows.
3. Money Market has to manage loss of confidence
   Currently, Money Market has bought both stochastic components, namely the liquidity and the confidence-driven component. The liquidity-driven component can be managed with standard Money Market instruments. The degree of liquidity distress is reflected in the prices. By contrast, in a loss of confidence instruments are not available any longer.[4] Hence, Money Market is not prepared to manage such a crisis. We propose that the jump component is transferred to Risk Controlling (RC). Risk Controlling monitors and balances the jump exposure.

The basic transfer model of figure 5.2 does not ensure risk separation. To overcome the drawbacks 1-3, we have to extend the model. These extensions are discussed in the next section.

5.1.2 Extended Transfer Model

This section extends the basic transfer model of the previous section. Beginning with a particular case, we successively generalize. We start with a bank that has only deterministic quarterly product cash flows. In a second step, we relax the assumption of quarterly cash flows and allow for daily deterministic cash flows. In a third step, we also relax the assumption of deterministic product cash flows and allow for stochastic product cash flows.

Deterministic Quarterly Product Cash Flows

This section addresses two issues: firstly, that Origination might bear an illiquidity risk although all product cash flows are perfectly deterministic; secondly, that Money Market has to manage a loss of confidence although it cannot do so by assumption. As clarified above, Money Market uses Money Market instruments. However, we previously assumed that Money Market instruments are not available in a loss of confidence.

Both issues can be analyzed in a minimalistic setup where the bank has only deterministic quarterly product cash flows. An example is a bank that only runs a mismatch strat-

[4] For instance, unsecured funding is not available in a confidence crisis.

egy.[5] Long-term and short-term leg of the strategy are based on contractual cash flows. Moreover, we assume that the product cash flows exactly match quarter beginnings. For this reason, we replace the general time index t_k by the particular (quarterly) index q_k.

Let us denote the long-term leg as '1' and short-term leg as '2'. For convenience, we assume that the product volumes are '+1' (long-term leg) and '-1' (short-term leg). The aggregate deterministic product cash flow is:

$$CF_{q_k}^{1+2} = \mu_{q_k}^{1+2} \cdot \Delta q$$

The stochastic cash flow components are zero as we assume only deterministic product cash flows. The deterministic cash flow is transferred to Origination. Nothing is transferred to Money Market.

If Origination decides in favor of a Mismatch strategy, future (roll-over) business must be modelled. The cash flow from planned roll-over business '3' presents itself as follows:

$$CF_{q_k}^{3} = \mu_{q_k}^{3} \cdot \Delta q + \sigma^{3} \cdot \Delta W_{q_k}^{3} + s^{3} \cdot \Delta J_{q_k}^{3}$$

Although cash flows of all existing deals are deterministic, stochastic is introduced by planned roll-overs. This is because the roll-overs are uncertain: investors might refuse to roll over for liquidity reasons ($\sigma^3 \cdot \Delta W_{q_k}^3$) or for confidence reasons ($s^3 \cdot \Delta J_{q_k}^3$). If the roll-over fails, the bank becomes illiquid. Note that the stochastic components result from the Origination strategy, but not from product cash flows. Therefore, cash flow '3' is in Origination. The aggregated cash flow in Origination is as follows:

$$\begin{aligned} CF_{q_k}^{OD} &= \mu_{q_k}^{1+2+3} \cdot \Delta q + \sigma^{3} \cdot \Delta W_{q_k}^{3} + s^{3} \cdot \Delta J_{q_k}^{3} \\ &= \mu_{q_k}^{OD} \cdot \Delta q + \sigma^{OD} \cdot \Delta W_{q_k}^{OD} + s^{OD} \cdot \Delta J_{q_k}^{OD} \end{aligned}$$

As stated at the beginning, we do not want Origination to bear cash flow risk. Cash flow risk should be managed by Money Market instead. Thus, the cash flow risk has to be transferred to it. The transfer is realized with a liquidity backup line that costs the sum of Brownian and Jump risk transfer prices $TP^B(\sigma^{OD}) + TP^J(s^{OD})$. The backup line is a liquidity option with maturity T and exercise frequency q. Figure 5.3 summarizes these ideas. It displays the cash flow maturity ladder of Origination (top) and of Money Market (bottom). The contractual cash flows in Origination are marked. The cash flows of planned business are left white. In '1', a contractual cash outflow has to be covered by an uncertain cash inflow from roll-over. The backup line in '1' is plotted around the roll-over cash flow with a dotted line. The dotted line indicates that backup cash flows are state-dependent. The dotted line around the planned cash flow in '1' works like a protection. Now, planned business is ensured. All cash flows in Origination are deterministic. If the roll-over is successful, the funds come from the capital market; otherwise, they come from Money Market. In either case they do come. Hence, the backup line transfers the cash flow risk to the Money Market.

The volume that has to be backed at each quarter is the cumulated roll-over exposure, which is the negative part of the sum of contractual cash flows as (5.1) suggests:

[5] The Liquidity Mismatch Strategy is introduced in section 3.2.1.

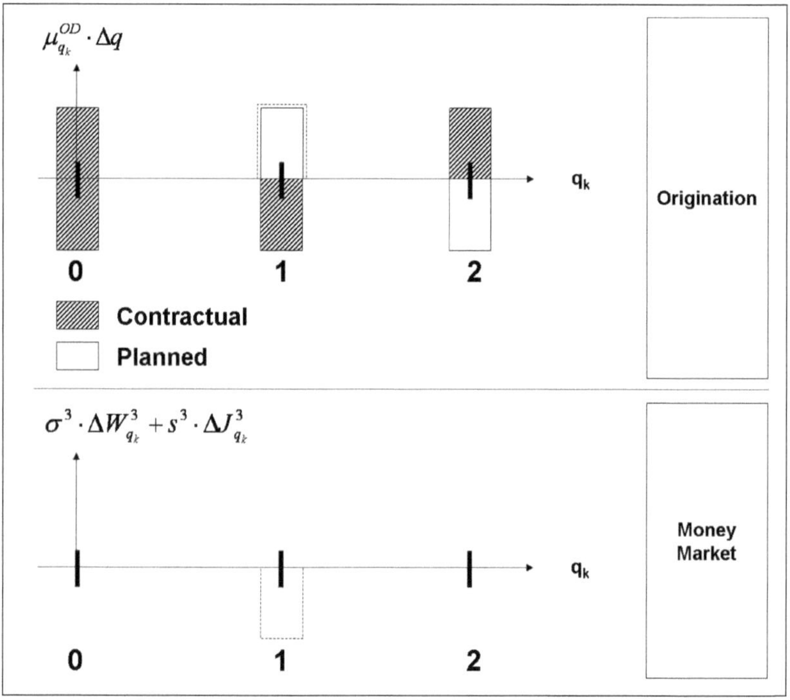

Fig. 5.3 Deterministic Quarterly Product Cash Flows

$$V_{t_k} = -\min\left(\sum_{i=1}^{k} CF_{t_i}^{\text{Contractual}}, 0\right) \tag{5.1}$$

Being:

V_{t_k} : Cumulated Balance of Contractual Cash Flows

The cumulated amount incorporates past roll-over volumes. In case of roll-overs continuously failing, the exposure from each roll-over date accumulates. This is why we need the cumulated sum.

As Origination solely wants to transfer the volume risk but not the spread risk, the backup line only guarantees the volume. Origination pays the spread at which Money Market procures funds in the market.

Hence, the transfer price does not reflect spread protection, but volume protection. The backup line immunizes Origination against cash flow risk that is introduced by the strategic mismatch decision. The spread risk remains in Origination.

Currently, both stochastic components are in the Money-Market portfolio. As motivated at the beginning, Money Market cannot manage a loss of confidence, as Money

Market instruments are unavailable. Due to this, we have to transfer the jump component to another department. We propose Risk Controlling (RC) to be in charge of jump risk. The jump component models a loss of confidence. A loss of confidence is an aggregate event that challenges the existence of the bank, which is why bank-wide decisions are required. A single department cannot deal with such an event. Hence, Money Market does not manage jump risk. Instead, a crisis committee is established that manages the loss of confidence. It uses all liquid assets beyond those that are held by Money Market to generate extra liquidity. In contrast to the reserve that Money Market runs (central reserve), the decentrally located assets are called 'decentral reserve'. Furthermore, the reserve run by Money Market is primarily used for liquidity purposes. By contrast, decentral assets are bought for operating business (hedging, trading). The fact that they are liquid is an 'add on'. In a loss of confidence, decentral departments renounce their ownership in favor of the crisis committee that liquidates them. To compensate asset holders for any cost related to the loss of ownership, they are compensated upfront with a premium. The premium is the transfer price for jump risk. The transfer price is charged to those departments and products that expose the bank to jump risk.[6]

The task of Risk Controlling is the balancing of collateral and jump risk exposure.[7] Risk Controlling buys the right to draw on collateral in a loss of confidence. This is an internal collateral backup line. The price for the backup line is the transfer price for jump risk.

Let us summarize these ideas in figure 5.4. To ensure the inflow from planned business, Origination buys protection against Brownian and jump risk from Money Market in the form of a backup line. The double protection is illustrated by the two dotted lines. As Money Market cannot manage a loss of confidence itself, it buys protection against jump risk from Risk Controlling. Its jump risk exposure (to Origination) and jump risk protection (from Risk Controlling) net.

Finally, Origination is left with deterministic cash flows, Money Market with Brownian exposure and Risk Controlling with jump risk exposure:

$$\begin{aligned} CF_{q_k}^{OD} &= \mu_{q_k}^{A} \cdot \Delta q \\ CF_{q_k}^{MMD} &= \sigma^{A} \cdot \Delta W_{q_k}^{A} \\ CF_{q_k}^{RC} &= s^{A} \cdot \Delta J_{q_k}^{A} \end{aligned}$$

To save one process, the jump component is directly transferred to Risk Controlling without passing by Money Market. Thus, Origination buys two backup lines: one against Brownian risk from Money Market, and one against jump risk from Risk Controlling. For the Brownian backup line it pays the Brownian transfer price while paying the jump transfer price for the jump backup line.

---

6 Departments can expose the bank to jump risk by (a) the strategies that they choose and (b) the products that they sell. A strategy example is the Maturity Mismatch strategy chosen by Origination. A product example are saving deposits.

7 This is discussed in section 6.4.

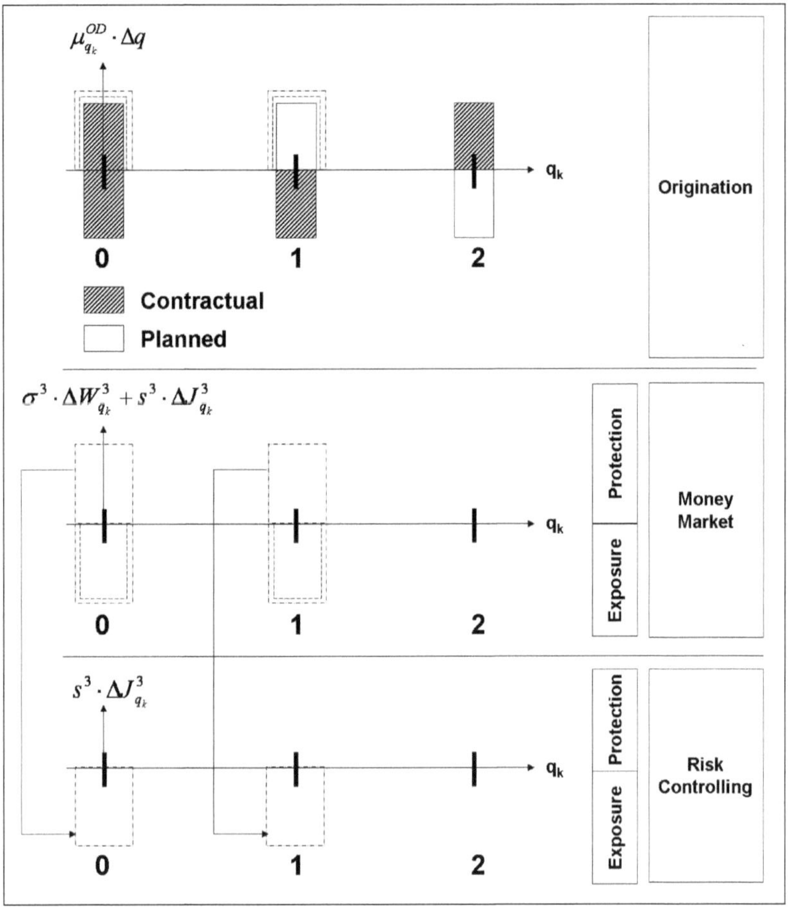

Fig. 5.4 Transfer of Jump Component

Deterministic Daily Product Cash Flows

This section addresses the issue that Origination receives all deterministic cash flows, even those of very short-term maturity. These cash flows are managed with Money Market instruments. However, not Origination but Money Market has access to Money Market instruments. Therefore, cash flows of a short term have to be transferred to Money Market.

In order to discuss this issue, we generalize the model by relaxing the assumption of quarterly cash flows and by admitting daily deterministic product cash flows. We switch from the quarterly index to the general (daily) time index t_k.

The aggregated daily cash flow is formulated as below:

$$CF_{t_k}^A = \mu_{t_k}^A \cdot \Delta t$$

The deterministic cash flow is transferred to Origination.

For spread management, a quarterly granularity is sufficient for the following reasons:

- Performance is insensitive to daily granularity
  The performance of Origination depends on the spread slope. The slope between consecutive days is approximately zero. As a result, issues of Origination do not try to match future days exactly.
- Forecast precision is decreasing in forecast horizon
  A daily forecast for future time periods is of artificial precision, as some components (e.g. planned business) cannot be forecast with a daily granularity.

Due to this, future deterministic cash flows can be projected to quarter beginnings for the purpose of spread management.[8] The projection is realized with discount factors. Note that the projection is only for valuation purposes. Cash flows are not physically moved to quarters.

The quarterly projected cash flow is the sum of all intra-quarter cash flows projected to a quarter's beginning:

$$\hat{CF}_{q_k} = \sum_{i=k\Delta q}^{(k+1)\Delta q-1} CF_{t_i} \cdot \frac{DF(0,t_i)}{DF(0,q_k)} \tag{5.2}$$

Being:

Δq : Quarter Length

(5.2) projects all intra-quarter cash flows of quarter q to q's beginning as figure 5.5 suggests. The quarter begins at $k \cdot \Delta q$ and ends one day before the new quarter starts at $(k+1) \cdot \Delta q - 1$. The 'hat' indicates that the projected cash flow is not the sum of nominal cash flows but the sum of forward values of cash flows. In the particular case of the first quarter, the projected value equals the present value.

After this preparatory step, Origination again operates on quarterly cash flows. The quarterly granularity for deterministic cash flows is not sufficient for the next quarter as the liquidity condition (2.4) has to be fulfilled every day. As a consequence, deterministic cash flows of the next quarter have to be managed on a daily basis. Such very short-term cash flows are managed with Money Market instruments. As only Money Market has access to those, the deterministic cash flows of the next quarter have to be transferred to it. The transfer of the first quarter is displayed in figure 5.6. Figure 5.6 consists of three blocks: the original daily cash flow, the deterministic cash flow in Origination and the deterministic cash flow in Money Market.

Note that the time scale in Money Market is exactly the next quarter as it only manages the deterministic cash flows of that quarter.

[8] A more conservative approach is an asymmetric cash flow projection: incoming cash flows are projected to quarter ends. Outgoing cash flows are projected to quarter beginnings.

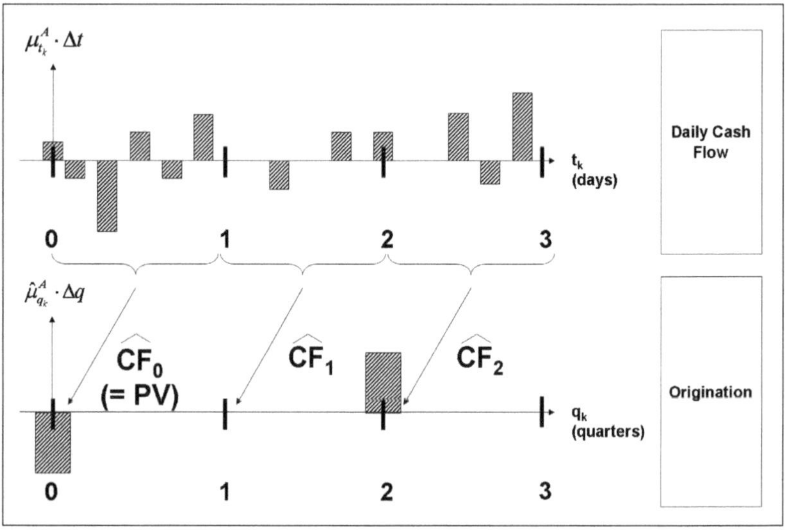

Fig. 5.5 Intra-Quarter Projecting

The first step is the projection of original daily cash flows to quarters in Origination (see (1) in figure 5.6). The quartered cash flow of the first quarter equals the present value. In our example, the present value is negative, i.e. outgoing cash flows dominate the first quarter. As compensation for the transfer, Origination has to pay the PV to Money Market (see (2)). Money Market now owns the cash flows of the first quarter and the transfer price (PV). The sum of both (net present value) is zero, i.e. the deal is fair. Money Market obtains the present value as cash to cover future outgoing cash flows.

Origination pays the present value by new issues (see (3)). Here, the result of the last section comes into play: we do not want Origination to bear funding risk. Hence, the funding risk of new issues is transferred to Money Market via backup lines. The previous section stated that backup lines are bought for every quarter with cumulated negative projected cash flow. In particular, there exists a backup line for the next quarter in case of a negative value. If new issues fail, Origination draws the backup line, which results in Money Market having to buy the first quarter without receiving the present value as compensation. Thus, Money Market funds the first quarter and all following quarters (drawing of future backup lines) till Origination has market access again.

Figure 5.7 depicts the complete setup with backup lines and first quarter transfer: in a first step, deterministic daily product cash flows are transferred to Origination. In Origination they are projected to the quarter's beginnings. For quarters with negative projected cash flows, liquidity backup lines are bought from Money Market against Brownian risk, and from Risk Controlling against a loss of confidence. As Origination cannot manage daily cash flows of the next quarter, they are transferred to Money Market instead. The price for the first quarter is the present value. If it is negative, Origination has to pay.

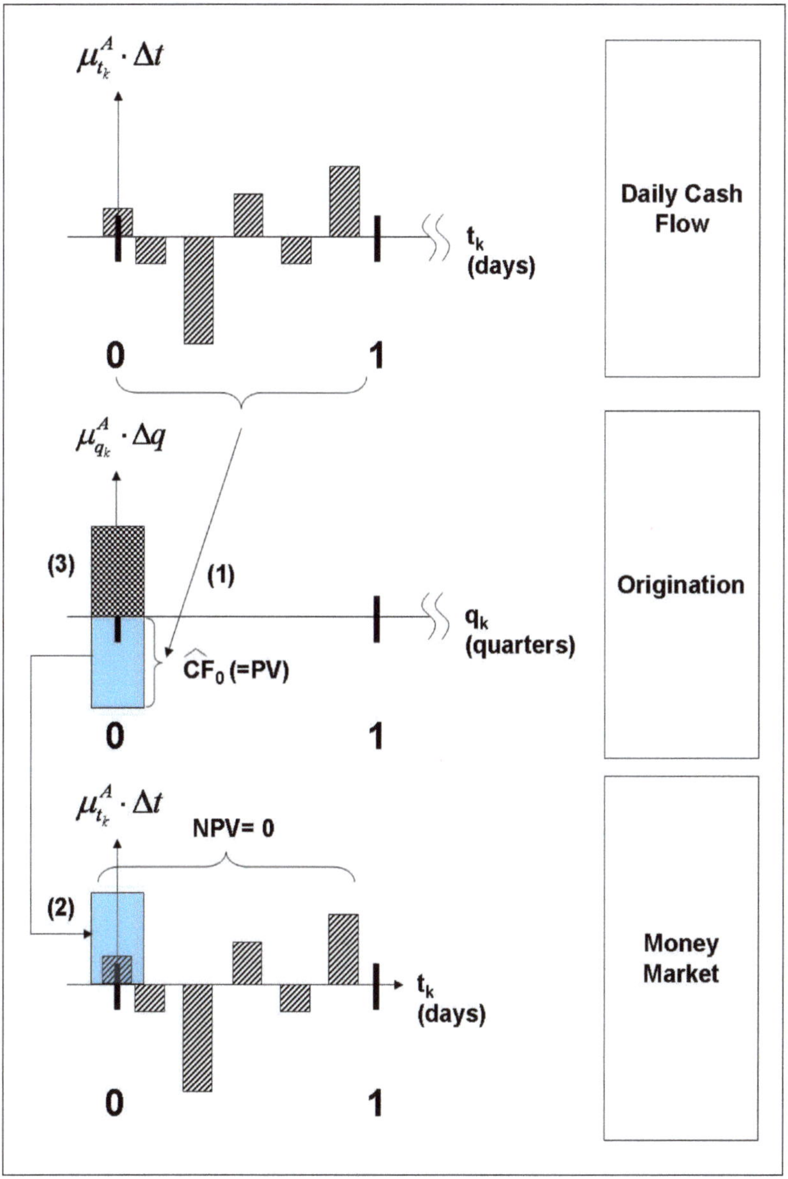

Fig. 5.6 Transfer of Next Quarter

Otherwise, it obtains the present value. Origination funds a negative present value by its current issue. If the issue fails, it draws on one of the backup lines. It repays the backup lines as soon as it can place issues in the market again.

If the present value is negative, Origination invests it at the desired maturity.

Origination manages all deterministic quartered cash flows:[9]

$$\hat{CF}_{q_k}^{OD} = \hat{\mu}_{q_k}^{A} \cdot \Delta q, \forall q_k$$

Money Market manages two portfolios: one with deterministic daily cash flows of the next quarter and one with Brownian cash flows from all quarters:

$$CF_{t_k}^{MMD,det.} = \mu_{t_k}^{A} \cdot \Delta t, t_k = 0, \ldots, \Delta q - 1$$
$$CF_{q_k}^{MMD,stoch.} = \sigma^{A} \cdot \Delta W_{q_k}^{A}, k = 0, \ldots, Q$$

Whether both portfolios are managed together or separately is discussed in the optimization section.

RC is in charge of the jump component of all quarters:

$$CF_{q_k}^{RC} = s^{A} \cdot \Delta J_{q_k}^{A}, k = 0, \ldots, Q$$

The stochastics so far result from uncertainty of planned roll-overs, but not from existing products. The next section introduces stochastic product cash flows.

Stochastic Product Cash Flows

In the previous section, we introduced daily deterministic cash flows. Within this section, we allow for daily stochastic cash flows. Daily stochastic cash flows result from the Liquidity Option strategy. With respect to Origination, nothing changes as Origination operates on deterministic product cash flows. The only changes affect the stochastic portfolios of Money Market and Risk Controlling: there are daily exposures due to liquidity options as well as quarterly exposures due to the Mismatch Strategy. Hence, the exposure varies across time:

$$\sigma_{t_k}^{A}$$
$$s_{t_k}^{A}$$

Furthermore, Brownian and jump cash flows can occur every day. Figure 5.8 illustrates our ideas. It shows the relevant stochastic portfolios of Money Market and Risk Controlling. The dotted lines reflect the Brownian (Money Market) and jump risk (Risk Controlling) exposures. Note that the Brownian exposure is symmetric (positive and negative cash flows), whereas the jump exposure is asymmetric (negative cash flows only). The inter-quarterly exposures are exposures from liquidity options. We assume the volume of liquidity options to be constant.

---

[9] It also manages the quartered cash flow of the first quarter by transferring it to Money Market.

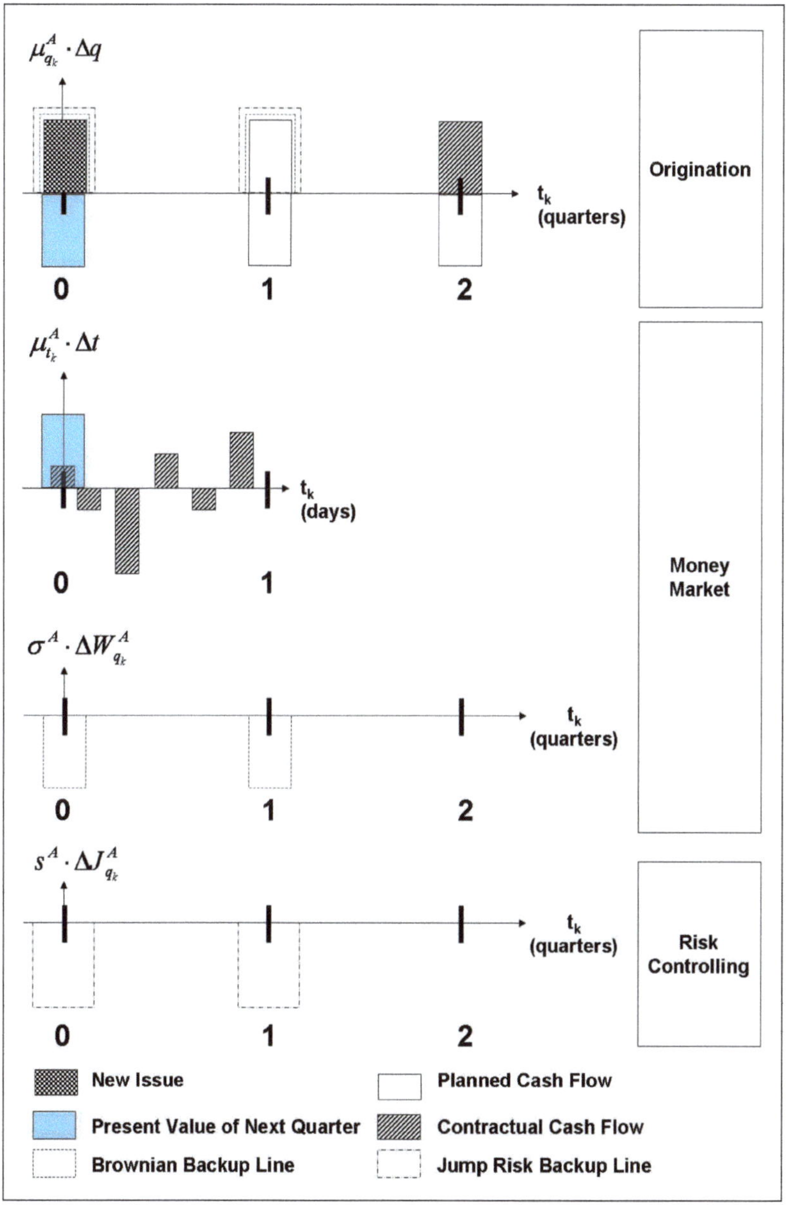

Fig. 5.7 Complete Transfer Model for Deterministic Product Cash Flows

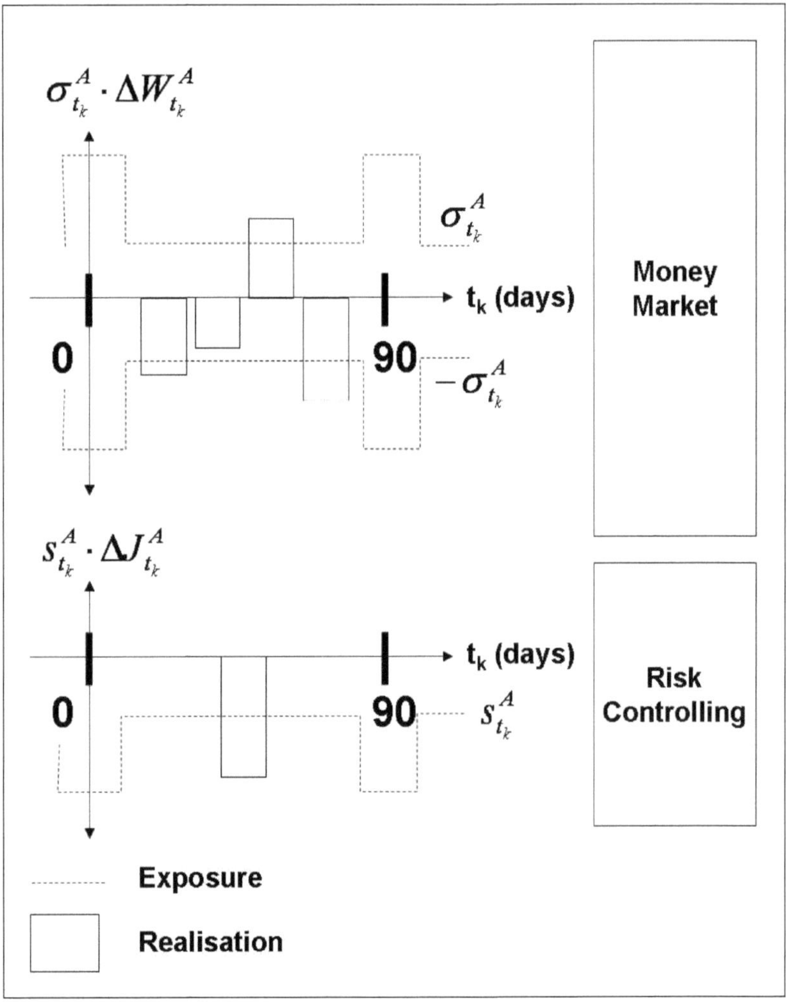

Fig. 5.8 Money Market with Daily Stochastic Cash Flows

At a quarter's beginnings, funding exposures come on top, leading to peaks. Money Market manages two portfolios of which one has deterministic daily cash flows of the next quarter and another has Brownian cash flows from all time points:

$$CF_{t_k}^{MMD,det.} = \mu_{t_k}^A \cdot \Delta t, k = 0, ..., \Delta q - 1$$
$$CF_{t_k}^{MMD,stoch.} = \sigma_{t_k}^A \cdot \Delta W_{t_k}^A, k = 0, ..., T$$

Risk Controlling is in charge of the jump component of all time points:

$$CF_{t_k}^{RC} = s_{t_k}^A \cdot \Delta J_{t_k}^A, k = 0, ..., T$$

5.1.3 Model Horizon

This section discusses the model horizon that refers to the time point where the model ends and a new model with adjusted parameters begins. The model horizon is different from the consideration period that describes the points in time that are considered by the model. The model horizon is either shorter than the consideration period or equal to it. In a model with terminal wealth, model horizon and consideration period coincide. In a present value model, the model horizon is usually shorter than the consideration period. The model horizon of a present value model can be one day. However, as the present value considers future cash flows, the consideration period is well beyond that day. Within this section, we discuss model horizons for both Money Market- and Origination model. For this purpose, we need a dynamic perspective that describes the processes at the beginning, during and at the end of a quarter. For the horizon decision, we distinguish between the theoretical and the practical level. On the former, unrestricted products exist. In practice, nonethteless, products are restricted. We begin with the theoretical level.

Unrestricted Products

Figure 5.9 describes the dynamic of the liquidity model. It analyzes the management in Origination and Money Market at several points in time. The starting point is an expected balance consisting of loans, deposits and equity. The quarterly expected cash flows are given in (a \0). 'a' refers to the Origination-model, '0' to the point in time. New loans and deposits are expected for the next quarter. We assume loans and deposits to be unrestricted in amount and time. They can be drawn and repaid whenever customers wish to do so. The expected cash flows of the first quarter are transferred to Money Market and displayed as $E[\hat{\mu}_{t_k}^A \cdot \Delta t]$ in (b \0). The diagram sequence $\sigma^A \cdot \Delta W_{t_k}^A$ (b \0-1) plots the Brownian deviations. At quarter's beginning (b \0), there are no Brownian deviations. During the quarter, Brownian deviations materialize. As stated in section A.1, the deviations are pure deviations with respect to the current expected daily cash flows $E[\hat{\mu}_t^A \cdot \Delta t]$. This is indicated by the dotted line. They do not provide information about future cash flow deviations. In particular, they do not give a reason to adjust expectations regarding future cash flows.

At the end of the first quarter, the Brownian Money Market account exhibits an almost certain balance, because Brownian shocks are only zero on average. We propose to limit Money Markets horizon to one quarter and to set up a new Money Market model (model c) that is characterised by new deterministic daily cash flows (as transferred from Origination) and a new initial balance. The initial balance results from the previous period. The proposition to limit the Money Markets horizon to one quarter is based on two arguments: firstly, the daily granularity makes the Money Markets model very complex.

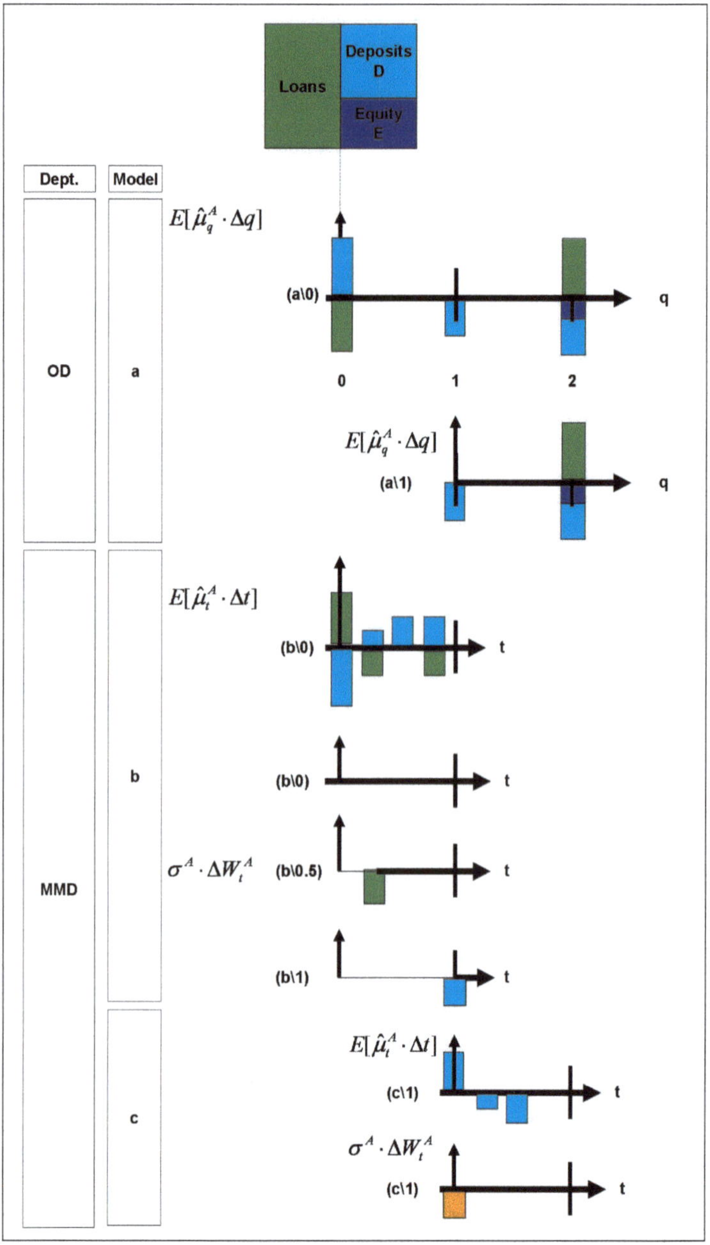

Fig. 5.9 Unrestricted Products: Expected versus Realized Cash Flows

Secondly, information regarding deterministic cash flows in the far future are not of interest to Money Market because it does not have appropriate long-term instruments to integrate this information in its strategy.

In contrast to Money Market, Origination operates on the same model, i.e. on the same expected cash flows. The only change for Origination is the funding spread. Hence, we have several Money Market models that operate within a long-run Origination model.

Restricted Products

With respect to the unrestricted setup, we make two adjustments. First, we assume that the loans of figure 5.9 are non-revolving: amounts that are repaid cannot be drawn again. Then, we assume that they have been completely drawn.[10] Thus, all further cash flows are repayments. Figure 5.10 is identical to figure 5.9 with the exception of the Brownian shock: the unexpected high inflow of loans are anticipated future payments (see $a\backslash 0$ in figure 5.10). Therefore, expected cash flows can be reduced by the Brownian amount. This interpretation of Brownian shocks is only possible because the loans are non-revolving. As Origination should be immunized against cash flow risk, expectations cannot be adjusted in our model. Before adjusting expectations, the model has to be terminated, expectations updated, and a new model with new expectations has to be set up. In order to reduce the model error, we propose to limit the model horizon. How much the horizon should be reduced depends on the product structure: a bank with many non-revolving products should choose a shorter horizon than a bank with many revolving products.

In the following, we choose two quarters as Origination's model horizon.

The shift from unrestricted to restricted products does not have an impact on Money Market, as its horizon is even shorter.

5.2 Transfer Pricing

Transfer prices are internal prices for services and goods transferred between departments.[11]

There are several arguments supporting the establishment of liquidity transfer pricing:

1. Regulatory requirements[12]
   Regulators require liquidity cost and benefits to be considered in product pricing. Each product is to be charged for the liquidity that it uses and rewarded for the liquidity that it provides. Products with liquidity risk have to be charged for the cost to back this risk.
2. Awareness of Liquidity as Costly Input Factor
   Internal pricing of liquidity leads to the awareness that liquidity is not a free resource: liquidity is limited and costly. It is an input factor that enters the (loan) production

[10] Also, we assume that they are funded temporarily with Money Market loans and are now replaced by the retail saving deposits.

[11] [Schmalenbach, 1908] was the first to apply the concept of internal prices as a coordination mechanism of large companies. He argues that large companies are too complex to be coordinated by individuals only; additional coordination mechanisms are necessary. An introduction to internal transfer prices provides [Horváth, 1996, p.564ff.].

[12] See principle 4 in [BCBS, 2008].

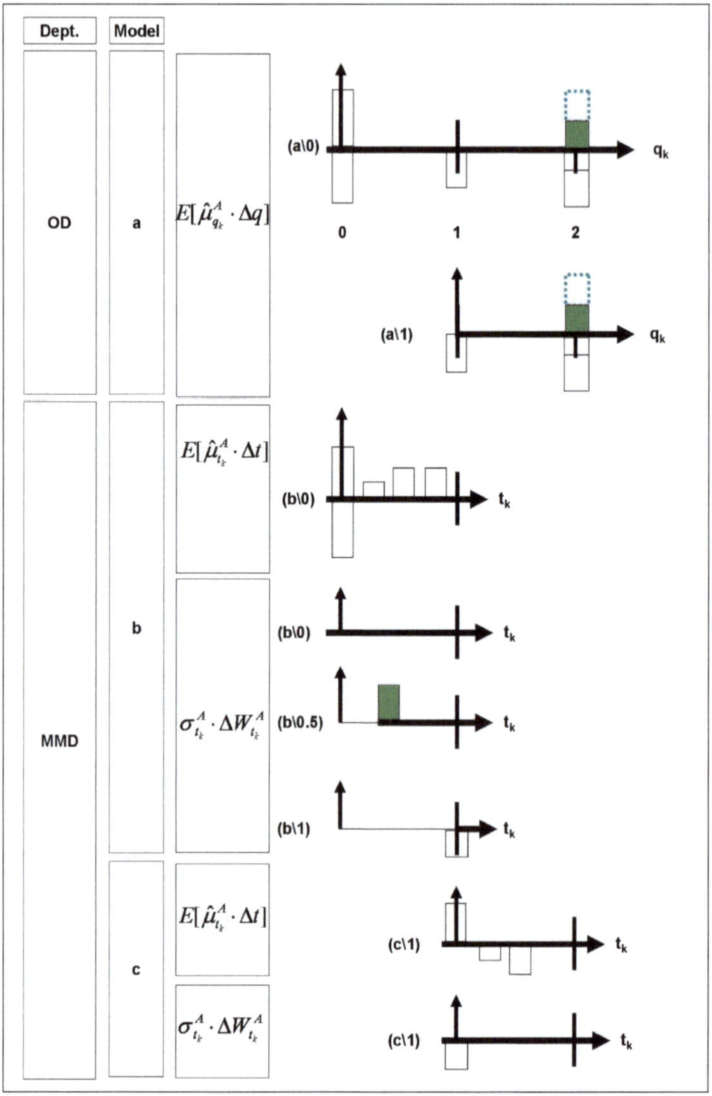

Fig. 5.10 Restricted Products: Expected versus Realized Cash Flows

function of a bank. Like other input factors, liquidity costs have to be incorporated in the final (loan) price.[13] This is important as products can be profitable before, but unprofitable after liquidity cost.

3. Awareness of Liquidity Risk
Since banks have to back risk with economic capital, risk taking has become costly in banks.[14] Although illiquidity risk does not have to be backed with economic capital, it does not mean that liquidity risk taking is for free.[15] The pricing of liquidity risk creates an awareness of that type of risk. Furthermore, it provides a mechanism to align exposure and risk taking capacity.
4. Performance Measurement
We transfer cash flow components that have to be managed. The prices reflect the cost of static management, i.e. a management without a department. The task of the departments is that actual costs realized by dynamic management should be lower than static costs (transfer prices). Due to this, transfer prices constitute the benchmark that the relative performance of the managing departments is measured against.

The literature agrees on the necessity of liquidity transfer pricing.[16] However, the sources postulate general requirements, but do not specify how to determine transfer prices.

The literature distinguishes transfer prices for liquidity and liquidity risk.[17] Transfer prices for liquidity refer to transfer prices for our deterministic cash flow component. Transfer prices for liquidity risk refer to our Brownian and jump component.

Apart from the parameters of the cash flow process, a poduct is described by its maturity T, volume X_{t_0} and number of exposure dates n_2. The number of exposure dates is necessary to distinguish liquidity options of different exercise frequencies.[18] Exposures remain constant across exposure dates.[19] Product i is described by the parameter set $(\mu^i_{t_k}, \sigma^{i,p}, \sigma^{i,m}, s^i, n^i_2, T^i, X^i_{t_0})$. The objective of this section is the derivation of the transfer price of product i:

$$\begin{aligned}TP^i(\mu^i_{t_0},\dots,\mu^i_{t_T},\sigma^{i,p},\sigma^{i,m},s^i,n^i_2,T^i,X^i_{t_0}) = (&TP^D(\mu^i_{t_k})\\ &+TP^B(\sigma^{i,p},\sigma^{i,m},n^i_2,T^i)\\ &+TP^J(s^i,n^i_2,T^i))\cdot X^i_{t_0}\end{aligned}$$

Being:

$TP^D(.)$: Transfer Price 'Deterministic Component'

$TP^B(.)$: Transfer Price 'Brownian Component'

$TP^J(.)$: Transfer Price 'Jump Component'

---

[13] The production costs constitute a lower price boundary. Thus, it is important to consider them in pricing. See [Hoitsch and Lingnau, 2007, p.267f.] and [Jórasz, 2003, p.273f.].

[14] For German Banks see [Bundesanstalt für Finanzdienstleistungsaufsicht, 2006a, Paragraph 2].

[15] It is backed with counterbalancing capacity. See section 2.2.

[16] See [BCBS, 2008, Principle 4], [Akmann et al., 2005], [Leistenschneider, 2008], [Neu, 2007, p.35].

[17] [Leistenschneider, 2008] distinguishes transfer prices for structural liquidity risk and contingency liquidity risk.

[18] Liquidity options can be of daily, quarterly or annual exposure.

[19] The time-dependent exposures of the previous section resulted from the juxtaposition of daily and quarterly time scales. However, the quarterly exposure was constant on the quarterly, the daily exposure constant on the daily time scale.

The transfer prices for each cash flow component are normalized to one unit product volume. The final transfer price is obtained as the sum of the normalized transfer prices times volume.

In the following we describe our pricing approach for the deterministic, Brownian and Jump component and compare them with those in the literature.

5.2.1 Transfer Price for Deterministic Cash Flows

The deterministic component is:

$$\mu^i_{t_k} \cdot \Delta t$$

We determine the transfer price $TP^D(\mu^i_{t_0},...,\mu^i_{t_T})$.

The literature agrees on the transfer price for deterministic cash flows.[20] It is defined as the difference between a funding and an interest rate curve:

$$TP^D(\mu_{t_k}) := (r(0,t_k) - r_s(0,t_k)) \cdot \mu_{t_k} \cdot \Delta t \tag{5.3}$$

Being:

$r(0,t_k)$: Funding Curve

$r_s(0,t_k)$: Interest Rate Curve

The difference $r(0,t_k) - r_s(0,t_k)$ is the funding spread.[21]

No consensus exists as to which market curve to choose as funding or interest rate curve.

Funding curves may be instrument-specific.[22] In fact, a bank might face different funding curves for the same maturity. Some authors suggest to use the senior debt curve.[23]

The interest rate curve separates interest and funding cost. Theory suggests that an appropriate curve is the risk-free interest rate curve.[24] By using it, the funding spread is the default premium. In practice, risk-free instruments do not exist. Triple-A bonds can be used as proxies, but they are not perfectly liquid. Therefore, the rate curve of more liquid instruments - interest rate swaps - is used in practice.[25] The reasons for swaps as interest rate benchmark are threefold: firstly, swaps are used for interest rate management.

[20] See [Leistenschneider, 2008, p.174] and [Neu et al., 2007]. However, [Reichardt, 2006] discusses whether customers should be charged bank's funding spread or their individual funding spread. He agrees that funding costs have to be considered in product pricing. He disputes whether bank's funding spread is the correct liquidity cost. Further, he argues that the funding spread reflects the credit quality of the existing loan portfolio. Therefore, new customers are not charged for their individual funding cost, but for portfolio funding costs: a customer with a better rating than the bank's would pay a lower credit spread than the bank. [Reichardt, 2006] proposes that customers are charged their individual funding spread minus a diversification discount or plus a mark-up for correlation with the existing loan portfolio. Banks that charge customers for their individual credit risk and for bank's credit risk (liquidity transfer price) charge the customer twice.

[21] [Schierenbeck, 2003b, p.231] calls it 'Standing Margin'.

[22] The differences in rates might be caused by different degrees of market liquidity, collateral or seniority.

[23] See [Neu et al., 2007].

[24] See [Schierenbeck, 2003b, p.231].

[25] See [Neu et al., 2007] and [Akmann et al., 2005].

Secondly, they are (unfunded) derivatives with minimal liquidity impact.[26] Thirdly, the resulting funding spread equals the asset-swap spread that is traded.

The definition of the demarcation line between interest and liquidity is a pure controlling issue. The bank pays the funding rates no matter how they are internally split up. Different definitions of demarcation lines shift cost/benefit between interest rate and liquidity department. The curve definitions are bank-specific and should account for the dominant funding channel.

We adopt (5.3) as transfer price for deterministic cash flows. Hence:

$$\begin{aligned} TP^D(\mu^i_{t_k}) :=& (r(0,t_k) - r_s(0,t_k)) \cdot \mu^i_{t_k} \cdot \Delta t \\ r(0,t_k) :& \text{ Funding Curve} \\ r_s(0,t_k) :& \text{ Swap Curve} \end{aligned}$$

As a product has a whole term structure $\mu^i = (\mu^i_{t_0}, ..., \mu^i_{t_k})$ of deterministic cash flows, the product transfer price is obtained as the sum across all $\mu^i_{t_k}$:

$$TP^D(\mu^i_{t_0}, ..., \mu^i_{t_k}) = \sum_{j=0}^{T} (r(0,t_j) - r_s(0,t_j))\Delta t \cdot \mu^i_{t_j} \cdot (t_j - t_0) \tag{5.4}$$

Note that (5.4) is normalized to one unit product volume.

5.2.2 Transfer Price for the Brownian Component

The Brownian component is:

$$\sigma^{i,p} \cdot \Delta W^{i,p}_{t_k} + \sigma^{i,m} \cdot \Delta W^m_{t_k}$$

We determine the transfer price $TP^B(\sigma^{i,p}, \sigma^{i,m}, n^i_2, T^i)$.

Transfer prices of stochastic components have not been discussed extensively yet.[27] Authors agree that transfer prices for stochastic cash flows have to be based on reserve costs.

Our transfer price for Brownian cash flow risk derives from the reserve that Money Market holds. We discuss the following steps:

1. Determination of required funding capacity $FC(\sigma^A)$ to back aggregate Brownian exposure σ^A
2. Determination of cost implied by required funding capacity $FC(\sigma^A)$
3. Brownian Transfer Prices for Product i
4. Transfer Prices for Arbitrary Maturities and Exercise Frequencies
5. Product Examples

---

26 In fact, the liquidity impact of interest rate swaps are the netted interest rate payments.

27 To our knowledge, the only reference for a pricing model for stochastic cash flows is [Neu et al., 2007].

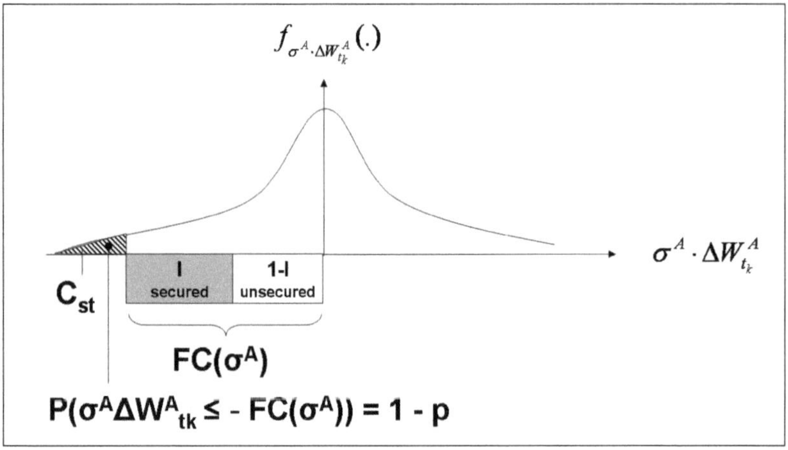

Fig. 5.11 Model of Required Funding Capacity

1. Determination of required funding capacity $FC(\sigma^A)$ to back aggregate Brownian exposure σ^A

In a first step, we determine the funding capacity that is necessary to back Brownian deviations at the confidence level p.

Figure 5.11 illustrates our setup. It plots the density function of aggregated Brownian deviations. To ensure p given a Brownian risk quantity of σ^A requires a funding capacity $FC(\sigma^A)$. The required funding capacity must be below the short-term unsecured funding capacity C_{st}.[28] At this stage, we introduce an additional degree of freedom in the form of the parameter l: we assume that the bank can decide to keep the whole funding capacity unsecured or to back a fraction l with a reserve (secured).[29] The advantage of secured funding is that the funding spread is rather stable, as it refers to the credit quality of the reserve (collateral).[30] The disadvantage, however, is the reserve cost. By contrast, unsecured funding does not imply current cost, but funding might only be possible at a distressed spread in the future.

[28] The short-term funding capacity has been defined in the funding model in section 4.3.2. The required funding capacity must be below the short-term capacity because funding is needed to set up the reserve.

[29] Secured funding is executed as repo. Repo has been introduced in section 3.1.5.

[30] Note that our funding model does not assume a volume risk for short-term funds given Brownian shocks.

Given that setup, the required funding capacity to cover σ^A units Brownian deviation during Δt at a confidence level p is:

$$
\begin{aligned}
P(\sigma^A \cdot \Delta W_{t_k}^A \leq -FC(\sigma^A)) &= 1-p \\
\Phi(\frac{\Delta W_{t_k}^A}{\sqrt{\Delta t}} \leq -\frac{FC(\sigma^A)}{\sigma^A \cdot \sqrt{\Delta t}}) &= 1-p \\
FC(\sigma^A) &= -\sqrt{\Delta t} \cdot \Phi^{-1}(1-p) \cdot \sigma^A \qquad (5.5)
\end{aligned}
$$

Being:

$$\Phi^{-1}(1-p): \text{(1-p)-Quantile of Standard Normal Distribution} \qquad (5.6)$$

(5.5) states that σ^A units of Brownian standard deviation have to be backed with funding capacity of $-\sqrt{\Delta t} \cdot \Phi^{-1}(1-p) \cdot \sigma^A$ given the confidence level p. The function FC(.) translates the risk quantity σ^A into a risk buffer FC(σ^A).

Note that the required funding capacity is linear in the risk quantity:

$$
\begin{aligned}
FC(\sigma^A) &= -\sqrt{\Delta t} \cdot \Phi^{-1}(1-p) \cdot \sigma^A \\
&= FC(1) \cdot \sigma^A \qquad (5.7)
\end{aligned}
$$

Being:

$$FC(1) = -\sqrt{\Delta t} \cdot \Phi^{-1}(1-p)$$

The Brownian risk taking capacity is limited by the short-term funding capacity C_{st}. Hence, there is a maximal (aggregated) Brownian standard deviation:

$$
\begin{aligned}
C_{st} = FC(\overline{\sigma^A}) &= -\sqrt{\Delta t} \cdot \Phi^{-1}(1-p) \cdot \overline{\sigma^A} \\
\overline{\sigma^A} &= -\frac{C_{st}}{\sqrt{\Delta t} \cdot \Phi^{-1}(1-p)}
\end{aligned}
$$

Brownian risk beyond the short-term funding capacity has to imply infinite transfer prices. So, there is a non-linearity in the Brownian transfer price with respect to σ^A. In the following, we assume $\sigma^A \leq \overline{\sigma^A}$.

2. Determination of cost implied by required funding capacity $FC(\sigma^A)$

The required funding capacity is split up in secured (l) and unsecured (1-l) funding:

$$FC(\sigma^A) = \underbrace{l \cdot FC(\sigma^A)}_{\text{Secured}} + \underbrace{(1-l) \cdot FC(\sigma^A)}_{\text{Unsecured}}$$

The transfer of Brownian cash flow risk implies the cost for the funding capacity. The transfer price must be based on these costs. The link between funding capacity and cost is established by a cost function. We assume that the secured fraction implies reserve cost.[31]

[31] We do not specify the cost function. [Leistenschneider, 2008, p.177] states that the reserve cost can be proxied by the spread between unsecured interbank funding and secured AAA-repos.

For the unsecured fraction, we do not assume cost. In contrast to secured funding that requires a liquidity reserve, unsecured funding does not tie any resources. We assume the cost function $c^R()$ to be linear in the reserve amount. Hence, the transfer price to take σ^A Brownian standard deviations $TP^B(\sigma^A)$ amounts to:

$$\begin{aligned} TP^B(\sigma^A) &= c^R(l \cdot FC(1) \cdot \sigma^A) + c^U((1-l) \cdot FC(1)) \cdot \sigma^A \\ &= c^R(l \cdot FC(1) \cdot \sigma^A) + 0 \\ &= c^R(-l \cdot \sqrt{\Delta t} \cdot \Phi^{-1}(1-p)) \cdot \sigma^A \end{aligned}$$

Being:

c^R : Cost Function, Secured Funding

c^U : Cost Function, Unsecured Funding

3. Brownian Transfer Prices for Product i

After having determined the transfer price for the aggregate Brownian exposure, we have to disaggregate the transfer price to products. The disaggregation has to account for diversification effects.[32] In the following we determine transfer prices $TP^B(\sigma^{m,i}, \sigma^{p,i}, n_2^i, T^i)$.

From section 4.2.3 we know that the aggregate Brownian deviation σ^A results from individual deviations as follows:

$$\sigma^A = \sqrt{\sum_{i=1}^{d} (\sigma^{i,p})^2 + (\sum_{i=1}^{d} \sigma^{i,m})^2} \tag{5.8}$$

Similar to the allocation of (aggregate) economic capital for P&L-risk, we have to allocate funding capacity for Brownian cash flow risk.[33]

Diversification implies that the sum of product funding capacities overestimates the aggregate funding capacity:

$$\sum_{i=1}^{d} FC(\sigma^{p,i}, \sigma^{m,i}) \geq FC(\sigma^A)$$

Our objective is the adjustment of individual risk quantities $(\sigma^{p,i}, \sigma^{m,i})$ so that:

$$FC(\sigma^A) = \sum_{i=1}^{d} FC(\sigma^{p,i,adj}) + \sum_{i=1}^{d} FC(\sigma^{m,i,adj}) \leq \sum_{i=1}^{d} FC(\sigma^{p,i}) + \sum_{i=1}^{d} FC(\sigma^{m,i})$$

---

[32] Products have two Brownian deviations: one for market-wide liquidity risk ($\sigma^{m,i}$) and one for product-specific liquidity risk ($\sigma^{p,i}$). We assumed that product-specific factors are independent from each other and independent from the systematic factor. See section 4.2.2 for details.

[33] This analogy also demonstrates the difference between liquidity risk and P&L-risks: liquidity risk is backed with funding capacity (Reserve and unsecured funding) whereas P&L-risks are backed with economic capital. However, in order to establish a risk-based performance measurement, it is necessary to allocate (and charge) liquidity risk buffers to risk originators (products).

Note the following property:

$$FC(\sigma^A) = \sum_{i=1}^{d} FC(\sigma^{p,i,adj}) + \sum_{i=1}^{d} FC(\sigma^{m,i,adj})$$

$$\Leftrightarrow$$

$$FC(1) \cdot \sigma^A = FC(1) \cdot \sum_{i=1}^{d} \sigma^{p,i,adj} + FC(1) \cdot \sum_{i=1}^{d} \sigma^{m,i,adj}$$

$$\sigma^A = \sum_{i=1}^{d} \sigma^{p,i,adj} + \sum_{i=1}^{d} \sigma^{m,i,adj}$$

Therefore, the allocation of aggregated funding capacity $FC(\sigma^A)$ is equivalent to the allocation of aggregate standard deviation σ^A.[34] This is a direct consequence of the linearity of funding capacity with respect to risk quantity. As transfer prices are also linear to risk quantities, we could base the allocation algorithm on transfer prices as well.

We use funding capacity to stress the analogy to the allocation of economic capital and standard deviation to shorten the exposition.

Existing literature proposes five approaches for the allocation of economic capital/VaR:[35]

1. Stand-alone Approach
   The 'Stand-alone' approach neglects diversification effects and is not additive. Applied to our context, one would calculate the funding capacity per product as if the bank only held this product ('Stand-alone').
2. Marginal Approach
   The 'Marginal approach' considers diversification, but is not additive. Applied to our context, the marginal funding capacity required for product i is the difference of aggregate funding capacity with and without product i.
3. Adjustment Approach
   The adjustment approach is additive, considers diversification and has an analogy to the allocation of overhead cost. Applied to our context, we calculate the funding capacity for each aggregation level and introduce adjustment factors that make them additive to the next level. The adjustment factors proportionally allocate the aggregate funding capacity. The proportional allocation is the analogy to overhead cost.
4. Incremental Approach
   The incremental approach extends the adjustment approach by using correlation-weighted adjustment factors. The approach is additive and considers diversification effects. However, the approach requires the estimation of a correlation matrix that might not be available.

[34] The allocation of an aggregate quantity to individual units has been discussed extensively in the controlling literature for overhead cost. For a definition of overhead cost, see [Jórasz, 2003, p.57f.] and [Freidank, 2008, p.95]. For the allocation of overhead cost, see [Jórasz, 2003, p.112ff.], [Freidank, 2008, 142ff.] and [Horváth, 1996, p.253ff.]. The allocation of aggregate funding capacity is comparable to the allocation of overhead cost. The difference is that we have to consider diversification effects. This refers to economies of scale in the overhead cost context.

[35] See [Schierenbeck, 2003a, p.519ff.].

5. Cost Gap Approach
   Applied to our context, the cost gap approach allocates the difference between the sum of marginal funding capacity and aggregate funding capacity. The allocation is based on game theory arguments.

None of the approaches is always preferable.[36] 'Stand-alone' and 'Marginal' approach can be discarded, as they are not additive. From the range of 'Adjustment', 'Incremental' and 'Cost Gap' approaches, we choose the adjustment approach for two reasons:

1. The method is particularly favorable if the number of allocation levels is small.
   As we only have two diversification levels (product/market, product/product), the method is most suitable for our setup.
2. Further assumptions
   The adjustment approach does not require further assumptions. The incremental approach needs the correlation matrix that might not be available. The cost gap approach requires the calculation of marginal funding capacities.

Thus, we choose the adjustment approach to allocate $FC(\sigma^A)$ to products. Our risk factor yet to be adjusted is the standard deviation. The adjustment factors measure the diversification effect in percentage.

We need two adjustment factors: one for the diversification between product-specific and systematic factor and a second for the diversification among products.

We start deriving the adjustment factors for product/systematic diversification.

Using (5.8) and the linearity of the funding capacity function, the aggregated funding capacity expressed with product exposures is formulated as follows:

$$FC(\sigma^A) = \Phi^{-1}(1-p) \cdot \sqrt{\Delta t} \cdot \sqrt{\sum_{i=1}^{d} (\sigma^{i,p})^2 + (\sum_{i=1}^{d} \sigma^{i,m})^2}$$

The superscripts 'p' and 'm' are used to distinguish between unsystematic and systematic Brownian risk on the product level. We refine the notation and introduce the superscripts 'P' and 'M' to distinguish unsystematic Brownian risk across all products.

If we had only product-specific Brownian risk, the required funding capacity would be:

$$\begin{aligned} FC^P &= \Phi^{-1}(1-p) \cdot \sqrt{\Delta t} \cdot \sqrt{\sum_{i=1}^{d} (\sigma^{i,p})^2 + 0} \\ &= \Phi^{-1}(1-p) \cdot \sqrt{\Delta t} \cdot \sigma^P \end{aligned}$$

Being:

σ^P : Unsystematic Brownian Risk across all Products

[36] See [Schierenbeck, 2003a, p.536ff.] for a detailled discussion.

If we had only systematic Brownian risk, the required funding capacity would be:

$$
\begin{aligned}
FC^M &= \Phi^{-1}(1\%) \cdot \sqrt{\Delta t} \cdot \sqrt{0 + (\sum_{i=1}^{d} \sigma^{i,m})^2} \\
&= \Phi^{-1}(1\%) \cdot \sqrt{\Delta t} \cdot \sum_{i=1}^{d} \sigma^{i,m} \\
&= \Phi^{-1}(1\%) \cdot \sqrt{\Delta t} \cdot \sigma^M
\end{aligned}
$$

Being:

σ^M : Systematic Brownian Risk across all Products

Under perfect correlation, the required funding capacities were additive:

$$FC(\sigma^P + \sigma^M) = FC(\sigma^P) + FC(\sigma^M)$$

The diversification effect can be measured as percentage by taking the relation 'actual funding capacity' to 'funding capacity under perfect correlation':

$$
\begin{aligned}
\gamma &= \frac{FC(\sigma^A)}{FC(\sigma^P) + FC(\sigma^M)} \\
&= \frac{\sigma^A FC(1)}{\sigma^P FC(1) + \sigma^M FC(1)} \\
&= \frac{\sigma^A}{\sigma^P + \sigma^M}
\end{aligned}
$$

Gamma measures the diversification effect between product-specific and systematic factor. The product-only and market-only deviations are adjusted for gamma:

$$
\begin{aligned}
\sigma^{P,adj.} &= \gamma \cdot \sigma^P \\
\sigma^{M,adj.} &= \gamma \cdot \sigma^M
\end{aligned}
$$

Note that the funding capacities after adjusting for diversification effects add to the aggregate funding capacity:

$$
\begin{aligned}
FC(\sigma^{P,adj.}) + FC(\sigma^{M,adj.}) &= FC(\gamma \cdot \sigma^P) + FC(\gamma \cdot \sigma^M) \\
&= FC(\frac{\sigma^A}{\sigma^P + \sigma^M} \cdot \sigma^P) + FC(\frac{\sigma^A}{\sigma^P + \sigma^M} \cdot \sigma^M) \\
&= FC(\sigma^A) \cdot (\frac{\sigma^P}{\sigma^P + \sigma^M} + \frac{\sigma^M}{\sigma^P + \sigma^M}) \\
&= FC(\sigma^A)
\end{aligned}
$$

After allocating funding capacity to product and market-wide risk factors, we have to allocate them to product i. Note the following relation for the market-wide factor:

$$\begin{aligned}
FC(\sigma^{M,adj.}) &= FC(\gamma \cdot \sigma^{M}) \\
&= FC(\gamma \cdot \sum_{i=1}^{d} \sigma^{m,i}) \\
&= FC(\sum_{i=1}^{d} \gamma \cdot \sigma^{m,i}) \\
&= \sum_{i=1}^{d} FC(\gamma \cdot \sigma^{m,i}) \\
&= \sum_{i=1}^{d} FC(\sigma^{m,i,adj.})
\end{aligned}$$

Hence:

$$\sigma^{m,i,adj.} = \gamma \cdot \sigma^{m,i}$$

Note the following relation for the unsystematic factor:

$$\begin{aligned}
FC(\sigma^{P,adj.}) &= FC(\gamma \cdot \sigma^{P}) \\
&= FC(\gamma \cdot \sqrt{\sum_{i=1}^{d} (\sigma^{p,i})^2}) \\
&\leq FC(\gamma \cdot \sum_{i=1}^{d} \sigma^{p,i})
\end{aligned}$$

The allocation of the product-specific factor requires the incorporation of inter-product diversification. The second adjustment factor γ^p comes into play:

$$\gamma^p := \frac{\sigma^P}{\sum_{i=1}^{d} \sigma^{i,p}}$$

$$\Leftrightarrow$$

$$\sigma^P = \gamma^p \cdot \sum_{i=1}^{d} \sigma^{i,p}$$

Therefore, we obtain the following formula:

$$
\begin{aligned}
FC(\sigma^{P,adj.}) &= FC(\gamma \cdot \sigma^{P}) \\
&= FC(\gamma \cdot \sqrt{\sum_{i=1}^{d} (\sigma^{p,i})^2}) \\
&= FC(\gamma \cdot \gamma^{p} \cdot \sum_{i=1}^{d} \sigma^{p,i}) \\
&= FC(\sum_{i=1}^{d} \gamma \cdot \gamma^{p} \cdot \sigma^{p,i}) \\
&= \sum_{i=1}^{d} FC(\gamma \cdot \gamma^{p} \cdot \sigma^{p,i}) \\
&= \sum_{i=1}^{d} FC(\sigma^{p,i,2\text{ x adj.}})
\end{aligned}
$$

Hence:

$$
\sigma^{p,i,2xadj.} = \gamma \cdot \gamma^{p} \sigma^{p,i}
$$

Finally, we obtain:

$$
\begin{aligned}
FC(\sigma^{A}) &= FC(\sigma^{P,adj.}) + FC(\sigma^{M,adj.}) \\
&= \sum_{i=1}^{d} FC(\sigma^{p,i,2xadj.}) + \sum_{i=1}^{d} FC(\sigma^{m,i,adj.}) \\
&= \sum_{i=1}^{d} FC(\gamma \cdot \gamma^{p} \cdot \sigma^{p,i}) + \sum_{i=1}^{d} FC(\gamma \cdot \sigma^{m,i}) \\
&= \sum_{i=1}^{d} FC(1) \cdot \gamma \cdot (\gamma^{p} \cdot \sigma^{p,i} + \sigma^{m,i})
\end{aligned}
\tag{5.9}
$$

(5.9) shows that the adjustment factors ensure additivity. The required funding capacity for a product with $(\sigma^{p,i}, \sigma^{m,i})$ is:

$$
FC(\sigma^{p,i}, \sigma^{m,i}) = -\Phi^{-1}(1-p) \cdot \sqrt{\Delta t} \cdot \gamma \cdot (\sigma^{m,i} + \gamma^{p} \sigma^{p,i})
$$

Finally, the transfer price of a product with Brownian exposure of $\sigma^{m,i}$ and $\sigma^{p,i}$ at a confidence level p, with a reserve intensity l is formulated as follows:

$$\begin{aligned} TP^{B}(\sigma^{p,i},\sigma^{m,i}) =& c^{R}(FC(\sigma^{p,i},\sigma^{m,i}),k) \\ =& c^{R}(-l\cdot\Phi^{-1}(1-p)\cdot\sqrt{\Delta t})\cdot\gamma\cdot(\sigma^{m,i}+\gamma^{p}\sigma^{p,i}) \end{aligned} \tag{5.10}$$

Being:

$$\gamma = \frac{\sigma^{A}}{\sigma^{M}+\sigma^{P}}$$

$$\gamma^{p} = \frac{\sigma^{P}}{\sum_{i=1}^{d}\sigma^{p,i}}$$

$$\sigma^{M} = \sum_{i=1}^{d}\sigma^{m,i}$$

$$\sigma^{P} = \sqrt{\sum_{i=1}^{d}(\sigma^{p,i})^{2}}$$

Note that the transfer price is stated for one unit product volume and a period of Δt.

Banks that hold many homogeneous products can diversify away product-specific Brownian risk and only price systematic liquidity risk. This result is known from asset pricing and is recovered in our pricing approach. In the following, we derive this result.

For a homogeneous product portfolio, the product-specific exposures can be approximated by a common exposure:

$$\begin{aligned} \sigma^{p,i} &= \sigma^{p} \\ \sigma^{m,i} &= \sigma^{m} \end{aligned} \tag{5.11}$$

Section B.1 in the appendix shows that we get, for large portfolios ($d \rightarrow \infty$):

$$\lim_{d\rightarrow\infty}\gamma = 1$$

$$\lim_{d\rightarrow\infty}\gamma^{p} = 0$$

Applying this result to (5.10) yields:

$$\begin{aligned} \lim_{d\rightarrow\infty} TP^{B}(\sigma^{p},\sigma^{m}) =& c^{R}(-l\cdot\Phi^{-1}(1-p)\cdot\sqrt{\Delta t})\cdot\gamma\cdot(\sigma^{m,i}+\gamma^{p}\sigma^{p,i}) \\ =& c^{R}(-l\cdot\Phi^{-1}(1-p)\cdot\sqrt{\Delta t})\cdot 1\cdot(\sigma^{m,i}+0\cdot\sigma^{p,i}) \\ =& TP(\sigma^{m}) \end{aligned}$$

Hence, for large homogeneous portfolios only the systematic liquidity factor is internally priced.

4. Transfer Prices for Arbitrary Maturities and Exercise Frequencies

Before we can determine the transfer price for products, we have to specify how product maturity and number of exercise dates enter the calculation. Clearly, a quarterly backup line with a maturity of one year has to have a transfer price different from a daily backup line of one year. Maturity and exercise frequencies have to be taken into account.

Note that our time unit is Δt. Hence, all time quantities have to be interpreted as multiples of Δt. Recall the following relation:

$$\begin{aligned} Var(\sum_{j=1}^{n} \Delta W_{t_j}) &= \sum_{j=1}^{n} Var(\Delta W_{t_j}) \\ &= \sum_{j=1}^{n} \Delta t \\ &= n\Delta t \\ &= Var(W_{t_n} - W_{t_0}) \\ &= Var(\Delta W_{t_n}) \end{aligned} \quad (5.12)$$

(5.12) describes the evolution of the variance across time. It states that the sum of n shocks in $[t_0, t_n]$ and one shock in $[t_0, t_n]$ have the same variance and, therefore, the same quantile. Furthermore, the variance grows linearily in time. Consequently, the quantile grows with factor $\sqrt{n}$.

In case of a **constant** quantile, the transfer price is:

$$TP^B(\ldots, n \cdot \Delta t) = n \cdot TP^B(\ldots, \Delta t) \quad (5.13)$$

A constant quantile means that the reserve to be held is constant. The reserve costs are calculated per Δt.[37] Hence, reserve cost and transfer price for the product's lifetime is linear in the maturity.

Obviously, the time that determines the quantile in (5.12) and the time that determines the transfer price in (5.13) are two different concepts.

The time that enters (5.12) is the time between two shocks, which we denote n_1. One can interpret this as one liquidity option. The time that enters (5.13) is the number of exposure dates/liquidity options. There are $\frac{T}{n_1} := n_2$ liquidity options or exposure dates during the product's lifetime.

One has to decompose maturity T in the period without exercises (=n_1) times the number of exercise dates (=n_2):

$$T := n_1 \cdot n_2$$

Thus, a liquidity option is decomposed in a sequence of liquidity options for each exposure day.

The two extrema are: daily options ($n_1 = 1, n_2 = T$) and options that can only be exercised once ($n_1 = T, n_2 = 1$).

---

[37] Note that reserve costs are expressed as rates.

n_1 enters with square root. n_2 enters linearily. The transfer price for a shock period of one Δt is given by (5.10). The transfer price of $n_1 \cdot \Delta t$ writes:

$$TP^B(...,n_1 \cdot \Delta t) = \sqrt{n_1} \cdot TP^B(...,\Delta t)$$

Being:

$$TP^B(...,\Delta t) : \text{Transfer Price (5.10)}$$

The transfer price for the product maturity is n_2 times the n_1-price:

$$\begin{aligned} TP^B(T,n_1) &= TP^B(n_1 \cdot \Delta t) \cdot n_2 \\ &= \sqrt{n_1} \cdot TP^B(\Delta t) \cdot n_2 \\ &= \sqrt{n_1} \cdot TP^B(\Delta t) \cdot \frac{T}{n_1} \\ &= \frac{T}{\sqrt{n_1}} \cdot TP^B(\Delta t) \end{aligned} \tag{5.14}$$

It is more convenient to express (5.14) in terms of n_2, the number of exercise dates:

$$TP^B(...,T,n_2) = \frac{T}{\sqrt{n_1}} \cdot TP^B(...,\Delta t) \tag{5.15}$$

$$= \frac{T}{\sqrt{\frac{T}{n_2}}} \cdot TP^B(...,\Delta t) \tag{5.16}$$

$$= \sqrt{T} \cdot \sqrt{n_2} \cdot TP^B(...,\Delta t) \tag{5.17}$$

Therefore, an option with maturity T $[\Delta t]$ that can be exercised once $(n_2 = 1)$ yields a transfer price of:

$$\begin{aligned} TP^B(T,1) &= \sqrt{T} \cdot \sqrt{1} \cdot TP^B(\Delta t) \\ &= \sqrt{T} \cdot TP^B(\Delta t) \end{aligned}$$

An option with maturity T $[\Delta t]$ that can be exercised T times $(n_2 = T)$ yields a transfer price of:

$$\begin{aligned} TP^B(T,T) &= \sqrt{T} \cdot \sqrt{T} \cdot TP^B(\Delta t) \\ &= T \cdot TP^B(\Delta t) \\ &> \sqrt{T} \cdot TP^B(\Delta t) = TP^B(T,1) \end{aligned}$$

The higher number of exposure days of the second option is priced.

Refining (5.10) for the maturity T^i and the number of exercise dates n_2^i yields:

$$TP^B(\sigma^{p,i},\sigma^{m,i},T^i,n_2^i) = c^R(-l \cdot \Phi^{-1}(1-p) \cdot \sqrt{\Delta t}) \cdot \gamma \cdot (\sigma^{m,i} + \gamma^p \sigma^{p,i}) \cdot \sqrt{T^i} \cdot \sqrt{n_2^i} \tag{5.18}$$

$TP^B(\sigma^{p,i}, \sigma^{m,i}, T^i, n_2^i)$ is the transfer price per Δt for a product with Brownian exposure of $\sigma^{p,i}$ and $\sigma^{m,i}$ with maturity T^i and number of exposure dates n_2^i. Note that (5.18) is for one unit product volume.

5. Product Examples

Brownian Transfer Price of a Roll-over Liquidity Backup Line

We are given a liquidity backup line of maturity T $[\Delta t]$ and an amount BL [€]. The backup line can be drawn at every quarter, i.e. $\frac{T}{q}$ times. The length of a quarter is q Δt. Backup lines have a product-specific Brownian risk per unit notional of $\sigma^{p,BL}$ and a systematic Brownian risk per unit notional of $\sigma^{m,BL}$. The diversification benefits product/market and product/product are reflected by γ and γ^p, respectively.

Based on (5.18), the Brownian transfer price yields:

$$
\begin{aligned}
TP^{B,BL} =& TP^B(\sigma^{p,i}, \sigma^{m,i}, T, \frac{T}{q}) \cdot BL \\
=& c^R(-l \cdot \Phi^{-1}(1-p) \cdot \sqrt{\Delta t}) \cdot \gamma \cdot (\sigma^{m,i} + \gamma^p \sigma^{p,i}) \cdot \sqrt{\frac{T}{q}} \cdot \sqrt{T} \cdot BL \\
=& c^R(-l \cdot \Phi^{-1}(1-p) \cdot \sqrt{\Delta t}) \cdot \gamma \cdot (\sigma^{m,i} + \gamma^p \sigma^{p,i}) \cdot \frac{T}{\sqrt{q}} \cdot BL
\end{aligned}
$$

Brownian Transfer Price of a Liquidity Facility

We are given a liquidity facility of maturity T$[\Delta t]$ and an amount F [€]. Liquidity facilities can be exercised daily, i.e. T times. Product-specific Brownian exposure per unit notional is $\sigma^{p,F}$ and systematic exposure $\sigma^{m,F}$.

The Brownian transfer price yields:

$$
\begin{aligned}
TP^{B,F} =& TP^B(\sigma^{p,F}, \sigma^{m,F}, T, T) \cdot F \\
=& c^R(-l \cdot \Phi^{-1}(1-p) \cdot \sqrt{\Delta t}) \cdot \gamma \cdot (\sigma^{m,F} + \gamma^p \sigma^{p,F}) \cdot \sqrt{T} \cdot \sqrt{T} \cdot F \\
=& c^R(-l \cdot \Phi^{-1}(1-p) \cdot \sqrt{\Delta t}) \cdot \gamma \cdot (\sigma^{m,F} + \gamma^p \sigma^{p,F}) \cdot T \cdot F
\end{aligned}
$$

The transfer price for the daily Liquidity facility is higher than for the quarterly backup line, other things being equal due to more exposure dates.

5.2.3 Transfer Price for the Jump Component

The jump component of product i is:

$$s^i \Delta J_{t_k}$$

It measures the unexpected outflows due to a loss of confidence. We determine the transfer price $TP^J(s^i, n_2^i, T^i)$ for one unit product volume.

Unlike Brownian risk, jump risk can only be backed with collateral, as unsecured funding is unavailable in a loss of confidence.[38] The transfer model of section 5.1.2 suggests that the reserve to back a loss of confidence is not a central reserve operated by Money Market, but a decentral one that consists of all liquid assets that are not owned by Money Market. The liquid assets held by Money Market are primarily used as reserve. By contrast, the decentral assets are not bought because they are liquid, but for business purposes as hedging and trading. The fact that they are liquid is used in the rare event of a loss of confidence.

The transfer price for jump risk derives from the expected cost that collateral holders bear if they have to liquidate their assets. The derivation of the transfer price takes the following steps:

1. Determination of required collateral $C(s^A)$ to back aggregate jump exposure s^A
2. Determination of cost implied by required collateral $C(s^A)$
3. Jump Transfer Prices for Product i
4. Transfer Prices for Arbitrary Maturities and Exercise Frequencies
5. Product Examples
6. Comparison with the Brownian Transfer Price

1. Determination of required collateral $C(s^A)$ to back aggregate jump exposure s^A

The aggregate jump component from section 4.2.3 is:

$$s^A \Delta J_{t_k}$$

The parameter s^A measures the aggregate jump risk sensitivity across all products. The jump is modelled by the Compound Poisson Process ΔJ_{t_k}. We assume that if customers lose confidence, customers of all products lose confidence. That is why there is only one J_{t_k}. The Compound Poisson Process is defined as follows:[39]

$$\Delta J_{t_k} = \sum_{j=1}^{N(\Delta t)} Y_j \tag{5.19}$$

It consists of a counting model $N(\Delta t)$ and a jump size model Y_j. One jump represents one loss of confidence.

---

38 See section 4.3.2.

39 See definition (4.3) on page 50 for details.

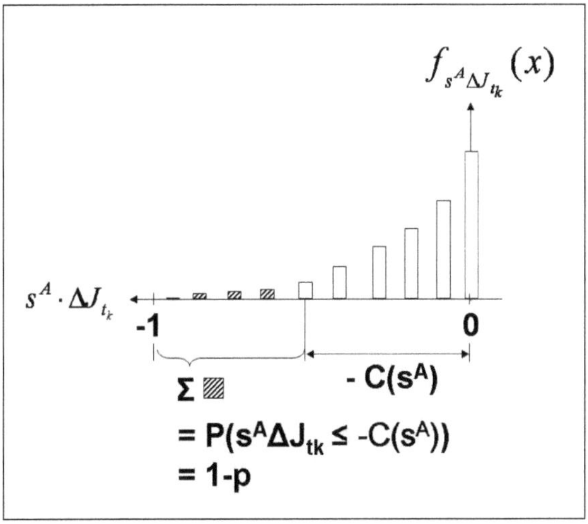

Fig. 5.12 Model of Required Collateral

We introduce the following notation:

$$\Delta J_{t_k} : \text{Covers a time period of } 1 \cdot \Delta t$$
$$\Delta J_n : \text{Covers a time period of } n \cdot \Delta t$$

The first step consists of determining the jump risk quantile, i.e. the quantile of the Compound Poisson Process. Figure 5.12 motivates our setup. It plots an exemplary density function of $s^A \Delta J_{t_k}$. The process can only take negative values (outgoing cash flows) since we only model 'losses' but not 'gains' of confidence. We assume that the bank wants to back jump risk up to a confidence level p.

The determination of the required collateral $C(s^A)$ resorts to determine the (1-p)-quantile of the Compound Poisson Process ΔJ_{t_k}:

$$P(s^A \cdot \Delta J_t \leq -C(s^A)) = 1 - p$$
$$F(\Delta J_{t_k} \leq -\frac{C(s^A)}{s^A}) = 1 - p$$
$$C(s^A) = -s^A \cdot F^{-1}_{\Delta J_{t_k}}(1 - p) \tag{5.20}$$

Being:

$$F^{-1}_{\Delta J_{t_k}}(1 - p) : \text{(1-p)-Quantile of } \Delta J_{t_k}$$

The determination of $F^{-1}_{\Delta J_{t_k}}(1-p)$ encounters two difficulties:

1. Rare Event
   A loss of confidence is a rare event: on average one might have one loss of confidence every 1.000 days. Consequently, the daily probability of a jump is very low and heavily skewed to the left ('No jumps'). Therefore, we cannot derive the quantile on the daily distribution ΔJ_{t_k}.[40]
2. Numerical Determination of Quantile
   The Brownian transfer price is based on the quantile of the standard normal distribution whose quantiles are tabulated and computationally available. By contrast, quantiles of Compound Poisson Processes are not readily available and have to be numerically determined.

We start with the difficulty implied by rareness.

Rareness refers to the counting model. Instead of using the daily distribution as in the Brownian case, we need a longer time horizon. We propose to use the horizon for which one loss of confidence is expected. We choose this horizon because we believe that it reflects the methodology that banks apply to determine the loss of confidence quantile. Banks measure jump risk by stress tests for different scenarios (e.g. bank-specific/ industry loss of confidence).[41] One scenario models one loss of confidence. Our horizon choice of one expected loss of confidence is inferred from banks stress testing. Certainly, the horizon of one expected loss of confidence varies across banks.[42]

The time horizon of one expected jump is set via the counting parameter lambda.

The number of jumps $N(\Delta t)$ for a period of $1 \cdot \Delta t$ is distributed as follows:[43]

$$P(N(\Delta t) = n) = \frac{e^{-\lambda \cdot \Delta t} \cdot (\lambda \cdot \Delta t)^n}{n!} \tag{5.21}$$

As our model time scale is normalized to Δt, we use the following abbreviation for T periods of Δt:

$$N(T \cdot \Delta t) = N(T)$$

The expected number of jumps per Δt is:

$$E[N(\Delta t)] = \lambda \cdot \Delta t$$
$$\lambda = \frac{E[N(\Delta t)]}{\Delta t}$$

[40] This contrasts with the Brownian transfer price that is indeed derived on the daily distribution. Note the difference between Brownian and jump component: a Brownian shock occurs in Δt almost sure as $P[\Delta W_{t_k} \neq 0] = 1$. In contrast, it is virtually 'almost certain' that **no jump** occurs in Δt as $P[\Delta J_{t_k} \neq 0] = 1 - P[N(\Delta t) = 0] = 0.001$. Hence, with a high probability, we have daily Brownian deviations. In comparison, daily jump movements are very improbable.

[41] See [Deutsche Bank Group, 2007, p.95f.] and [Commerzbank AG, 2008, 125] as examples.

[42] If one admits that our jump component reflects reputational risk, the horizon varies as reputational risk varies across banks. See [Pohl and Zaby, 2008].

[43] See [McNeil et al., 2005, p.484].

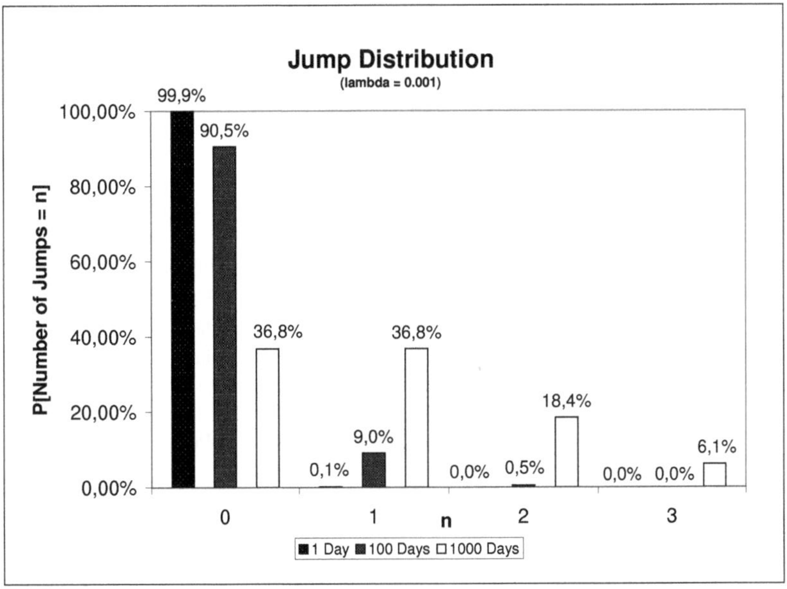

Fig. 5.13 Jump Distribution for Different Time Horizons

Hence, lambda can be interpreted as the expected number of jumps per Δt and λ^{-1} as the time, for which lambda jumps are expected. As we propose the horizon of one expected jump, the quantile calculation is not based on the distribution of Δt, but on $\lambda^{-1}\Delta t$.

For our numerical example, we need to specify the time horizon λ^{-1}.

We assume $\lambda^{-1} = 1000$.

Thus:

$$\begin{aligned}\lambda &= \frac{1}{1000} \\ &= 0.001\end{aligned}$$

From there, our quantile is based on the 1000-day distribution ΔJ_{1000}. Figure 5.13 plots the counting distributions for lambda=0.001 for 1 day, 100 days and 1000 days. It shows the probability $P(N(j \cdot \Delta t) = n)$ of n = 0, 1, ... jumps after j= 1 day, 100 days and 1000 days.[44] The daily probability of a jump is very small (0.1%). However, the probabilities of jumps increase with the time horizon: in 100 days a jump occurs with a probability of 9%. In 1000 days the probability of a jump is 36.8%. The probability for two jumps in 1000 days is already 18.4%. On average, one expects one jump in 1000 days.

Figure 5.13 makes clear that it is not reasonable to derive the quantile on the daily distribution.

[44] See (5.21).

The setup of figure 5.12 still holds, but the quantile is not based on ΔJ_{t_k}, but on $\Delta J_{\lambda^{-1}}$.[45]

Converting (5.20) from $1\Delta t$ to a horizon of $\lambda^{-1}\Delta t$, the required collateral to back s^A units of jump risk during $\lambda^{-1}[\Delta t]$ at a confidence level p is:

$$C_{\lambda^{-1}}(s^A) = -s^A \cdot F^{-1}_{\Delta J_{\lambda^{-1}}}(1-p) \tag{5.22}$$

Being:

$F^{-1}_{\Delta J_{\lambda^{-1}}}(1-p)$:(1-p)-Quantile of Compound Poisson Process for $\lambda^{-1} \cdot \Delta t$

(5.22) states that s^A units of jump risk have to be backed with collateral of $(-s^A \cdot F^{-1}_{\Delta J_{\lambda^{-1}}}(1-p))$ for a given confidence level p. (5.22) suggests that the required collateral is linear in the exposure s^A. After having overcome the difficulty implied by rareness, we discuss how the quantile can be numerically determined.

In order to determine the quantile, we have to specify the jump size model. As proposed in section 4.2.3, we use a binomial jump size model that distinguishes two types of crises: bank-specific and industry-wide crises. Our specified Compound Poisson Process is given by (5.23):

$$s^i \cdot \Delta J_{\lambda^{-1}} = s^i \cdot \sum_{j=1}^{N(T)} Y_j \tag{5.23}$$

$$Y_j = \begin{cases} a, P[Y_j = a] = p^{bs} \\ b, P[Y_j = b] = 1 - p^{bs} \end{cases} \tag{5.24}$$

Being:

ΔJ_{t_k} : Compound Poisson Process with horizon $\lambda^{-1}\ [\Delta t]$

a : Percentage of Volume Withdrawal in bank-specific crisis

b : Percentage of Volume Withdrawal in industry crisis

p : Given a Crisis, probability of being a bank-specific crisis

$1-p$: Given a Crisis, probability of being an industry crisis

$N(T)$: Counting Model

s^i : Product-specific Adjustment Factor

To determine the quantile of the confidence model, it is important to analyze the interaction of counting and jump size model.

The severities a and b measure the average percentage of product volumes that are withdrawn in a bank or industry-wide crisis. s^i allows for product-specific adjustments. They scale the averages up or down.[46] Hence, $s^i \cdot a$ and $s^i \cdot b$ are the percentages of product i that are withdrawn in a bank-specific and industry-wide crisis, respectively.

---

[45] It is based on ΔJ_{1000} for our numerical example.

[46] For example, the parameter s^i allows to distinguish wholesale and retail depositors.

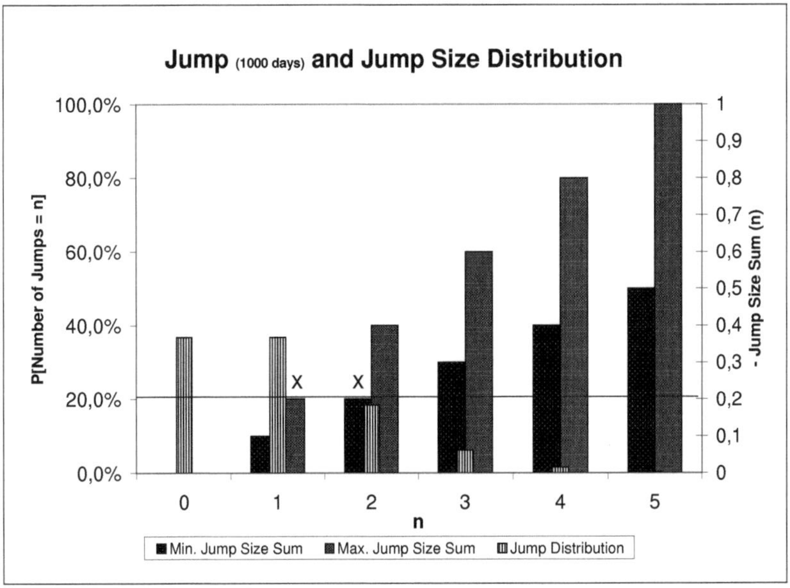

Fig. 5.14 Numerical Example, Jump and Jump Size Distributions

For our numerical example, we specify the jump size model as:

$$Y_j = \begin{cases} -0.1 & ,P[Y_j = -0.1] = 0.5 \\ -0.2 & ,P[Y_j = -0.2] = 0.5 \end{cases}$$

A numerical example of the Compound Poisson Process ΔJ_{1000} is given in figure 5.14. The parametrisation is as follows: a=10%, b=20%, $\lambda = 0.001$ and $\Delta t = 1000$. Figure 5.14 plots the jump probabilities for 1000 days as well as maximum and minimum jump sizes. In our setup, an industry-specific crisis is the more severe crisis. Thus, the jump size minima result for every crisis being a bank-specific crisis, and jump size maxima for every crisis being an industry crisis. However, the quantile is based on the jump sum and not on the number of jumps. Figure 5.14 shows that a given sum results from several combinations of jumps. The sum 0.2 (marked with 'x' in figure 5.14) results from one (0.2) jump or from two (0.1) jumps. Therefore, it is convenient to group jump combinations with the same sum. This leads to figure 5.15. The upper part orders jump combinations that sum up to the same number. The lower part consists of three sections: the number of jumps n, the probability of j 0.1-jumps and a table that counts the number of 0.1-jumps.[47] The probability to have j 0,1-jumps among n jumps follows the binomial distribution Bin(j,n,p).

[47] The number of 0.2-jumps is (n - number of 0.1-jumps).

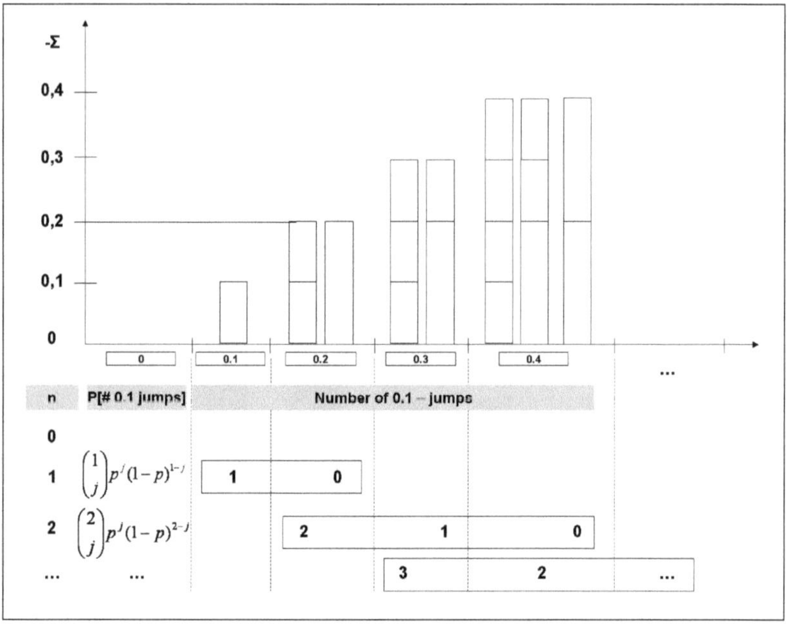

Fig. 5.15 Numerical Example, Groups with Same Cumulated Jump Sizes

The Compound Poisson Process has the following density:

$$P(J_t = s) = \sum_{k=0}^{\infty} p_N(n) \cdot P(\sum_{j=1}^{n} Y_j = s) \tag{5.25}$$

Being:

$$p_N(n) = \frac{e^{-(\lambda t)}(\lambda t)^n}{n!}$$

(5.25) suggests that the probability of J_{t_k} being equal to s is obtained by iterating across all possible number of jumps ($k = 0, ..., \infty$) and identifying those combinations that sum up to s ($\sum_{j=1}^{n} Y_j = s$), multiplying both probabilities and summing up the products.

For our example with jump sizes a= -0.1 and b= -0.2, a particular sum s results from a well-defined number of jumps. As suggested by figure 5.14, the jump sum for a given number of jumps n is in $[-0.1, -0.2] \cdot n$. To end up with s, we only have to consider $\{\lceil s/0.2 \rceil, ..., \lceil s/0.1 \rceil\}$ jumps.[48]

[48] $\lceil x \rceil$ is rounding x up to the next integer.

Hence:

$$P(J_t = s) = \sum_{n=\lceil s/0.2\rceil}^{\lceil s/0.1\rceil} p_N(n) \cdot P(\sum_{j=1}^{n} Y_j = s)$$

Given a number of jumps n, the number of 0.1-jumps j can be between 0,...,n. In fact, the jump sum is binomially distributed:

$$P(J_t = s) = \sum_{n=\lceil s/0.2\rceil}^{\lceil s/0.1\rceil} p_N(n) \cdot \sum_{j=0}^{n} \binom{n}{j} p^j (1-p)^{n-j}$$

However, only the combination (j,k-j) with $-0.1 \cdot j - 0.2 \cdot (k-j) = s$ is relevant for the density s. As a result, the binomial sum has to be restricted to these combinations. Thus:

$$P(J_t = s) = \sum_{n=\lceil s/0.2\rceil}^{\lceil s/0.1\rceil} p_N(n) \cdot \sum_{\substack{j=0 \\ -0.1\cdot j-0.2\cdot(n-j)=s}}^{n} \binom{n}{j} p^j (1-p)^{n-j}$$

Note that:

$$\begin{aligned} -0.1 \cdot j - 0.2 \cdot (n-j) &= s \\ j &= 0.1 \cdot s + 2 \cdot n \end{aligned}$$

Consequently, there is only one possible j for a given sum s and number of jumps n. This results in the fact that the binomial sum contains only one summand and j can be replaced by $0.1 \cdot s + 2 \cdot n$. This yields the density function for our confidence model:

$$P(J_t = s) = \sum_{n=\lceil s/0.2\rceil}^{\lceil s/0.1\rceil} p_N(n) \cdot \binom{n}{0.1 \cdot s + 2 \cdot n} p^{0.1\cdot s+2\cdot n} (1-p)^{n-0.1\cdot s} \tag{5.26}$$

The resulting density is plotted in figure 5.16. The jump sizes of '-0.1' and '-0.2' are equally weighted (p=0.5). The density is a weighted sum of jump and jump size probabilities. The probability of a sum of '-0.2' is higher than that of '-0.1' because '-0.2' can be reached by two jump events (1x(-0.2),1x(-0.2)) whereas -0.1 can only be reached by one jump event (1x(-0.1)).

The manual determination of the compound poisson density can be shortened by the Panjer algorithm.[49] This algorithm is a recursive approximation of the density. If the number of admissible jumps is finite (as in our example), the Panjer algorithm provides the exact density.

---

[49] See [McNeil et al., 2005, p.480].

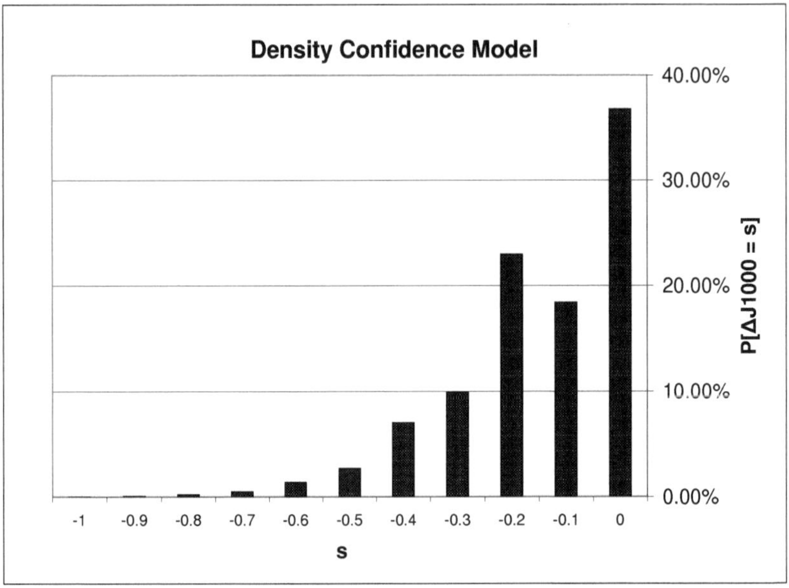

Fig. 5.16 Density of Confidence Model

The algorithm for the Compound Poisson Process and positive sums states:

$$
\begin{aligned}
P(s=0) &= p_0 \\
P(s=S) &= \sum_{i=1}^{S} \frac{\lambda \cdot i}{S} g_i \cdot s_{S-i} \\
\text{Being:}& \\
\text{Jump Size Density:}& \\
g_i &: P(Y=i)
\end{aligned}
\tag{5.27}
$$

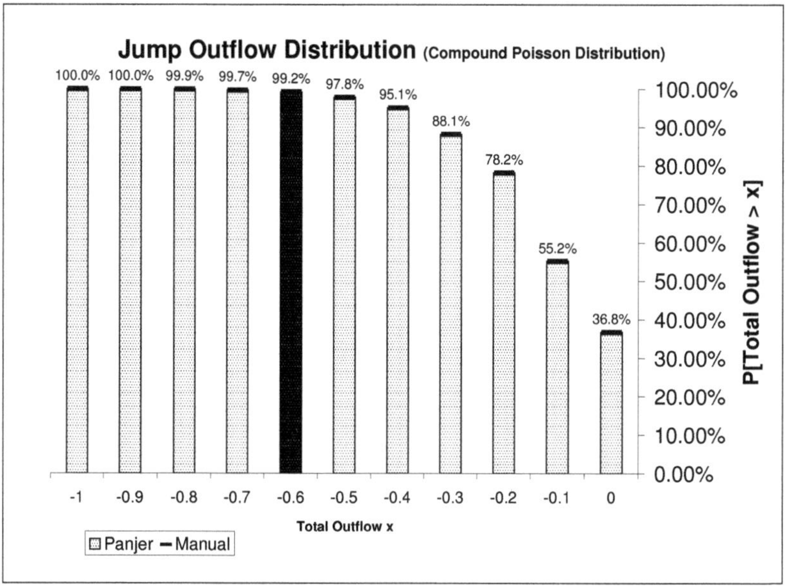

Fig. 5.17 Distribution Function of Jump Outflow

Applied to our example with negative sums we obtain:

$$
\begin{aligned}
P(s=0) &= e^{-\lambda^{-1}} \\
P(s=-0.1) &= \frac{\lambda^{-1}\cdot(-0.1)}{-0.1}P(Y_j=-0.1)\cdot s_0 \\
P(s=-0.2) &= \frac{\lambda^{-1}\cdot(-0.1)}{-0.2}P(Y_j=-0.1)\cdot s_{-0.1} \\
&\quad + \frac{\lambda^{-1}\cdot(-0.2)}{-0.2}P(Y_j=-0.2)\cdot s_0 \\
P(s=-0.3) &= \frac{\lambda^{-1}\cdot(-0.1)}{-0.3}P(Y_j=-0.1)\cdot s_{-0.2} \\
&\quad + \frac{\lambda^{-1}\cdot(-0.2)}{-0.3}P(Y_j=-0.2)\cdot s_{-0.1} \\
&\quad + \frac{\lambda^{-1}\cdot(-0.3)}{-0.3}\underbrace{P(Y_j=-0.3)}_{=0}\cdot s_0 \\
&\dots
\end{aligned}
$$

Figure 5.17 plots the distribution function of the jump outflow determined manually and by the Panjer recursion. As stated, they are identical in our setup.

The distribution function shows that within 1000 days, the outflow does not exceed 60% of the volume of liquidity options at 99% confidence (it is the 99.2%-quantile). Hence:

$$\begin{aligned} C_{1000}(1) &= -F_{\Delta J^{-1}_{1000}}(1\%) \\ &= 0.60 \end{aligned}$$

Note that the horizon of 1000 days was chosen so that there is one expected loss of confidence. The risk measure is not the expected outflow but the 99%-quantile outflow. The outflow of 60% results from several industry and/or bank-specific confidence crises. Thus, the model also covers sequences of confidence losses.

The quantile depends on the severity of confidence losses. Note the following relation:

$$\begin{aligned} P(m \cdot s^A \cdot \Delta J_t \leq -m \cdot C(s^A)) &= 1-p \\ P(m \cdot s^A \cdot \sum_{j=1}^{N(\Delta t)} Y_j \leq -m \cdot C(s^A)) &= 1-p \\ P(s^A \cdot \sum_{j=1}^{N(\Delta t)} m \cdot Y_j \leq -m \cdot C(s^A)) &= 1-p \\ P(s^A \cdot \sum_{j=1}^{N(\Delta t)} Y_j^m \leq -m \cdot C(s^A)) &= 1-p \\ P(s^A \cdot \Delta J_t^m \leq -m \cdot C(s^A)) &= 1-p \end{aligned}$$

Due to this, the quantile is linear in the jump size. Scaling the jump size with a constant factor m scales the quantile by m.

For our numerical example we assumed that only 10% and 20% of the volume of liquidity options are withdrawn in a bank-specific and industry-wide loss of confidence. This might be too optimistic. Increasing the severity also increases the quantile, as can be seen in figure (5.18). Doubling the jump size doubles the quantile. The 99%-quantile is now 1.2. Certainly, the 100% quantile should be 1.0 as it covers the complete liquidity option. More than the notional cannot be withdrawn. This model error results from the use of a Lévy-process instead of a Geometric Lévy process.

In (5.22) we have derived the required collateral:

$$C_{\lambda^{-1}}(s^A) = -s^A \cdot F^{-1}_{\Delta J_{\lambda^{-1}}}(1-p)$$

Furthermore, we described how to determine $F^{-1}_{\Delta J_{\lambda^{-1}}}(1-p)$. The next step is the definition of a cost function that measures the cost related to the required collateral.

2. Determination of cost implied by required collateral $C(s^A)$

Transfer prices are based on the cost to buffer risk. For jump risk, the cost is related to the collateral that is primarily held as part of the business strategy. More precisely, it would even be held if there was no jump risk at all.

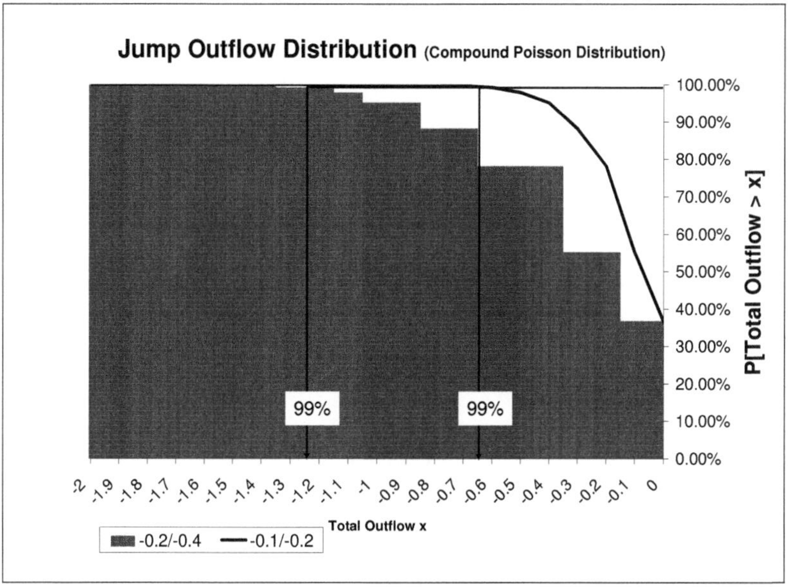

Fig. 5.18 Impact of Jump Size Doubling on Compound Poisson Quantile

Extra cost occurs if the collateral is liquidated in case of a loss of confidence: the liquidation might unwind hedging and trading positions and generate open risk positions in other risk classes. The positions cannot be closed before new liquidity (cash inflows, external funding) is available to repurchase the collateral. Collateral owners use the liquidation model from section 4.4 to estimate the market-induced cost that results from unexpected liquidation. Furthermore, they should consider the position-induced cost that occurs between the unwinding and re-establishing of positions. Both cost components have to be translated into a cost function $c^J(.)$. We do not specify the cost function here. We assume that the cost function is linear in the collateral amount.[50] The transfer price for one unit jump risk $TP^J(1)$ is as follows:

$$\begin{aligned} TP^J_{\lambda^{-1}}(1) &= c^J(C(1)) \\ &= c^J(-F^{-1}_{\Delta J_{\lambda^{-1}}}(1-p)) \end{aligned}$$

[50] This assumption is critical, providing that a large fraction of collateral is part of leveraged positions with non-linear P&L-functions.

Due to the linearity of the cost function, a jump risk exposure of s^A has the following transfer price for a time horizon $\lambda^{-1}[\Delta t]$:

$$\begin{aligned} TP^J_{\lambda^{-1}}(s^A) &= TP^J_{\lambda^{-1}}(1)\cdot s^A \\ &= c^J(-F^{-1}_{\Delta J_{\lambda^{-1}}}(1-p))\cdot s^A \end{aligned}$$

3. Jump Transfer Prices for Product i

We determined transfer prices for the aggregate jump risk. Nevertheless, we are interested in transfer prices for product jump risk s^i. In contrast to product-specific Brownian risk, jump risk does not diversify across products. Jump risk is modelled with one single systematic factor. Product-specific sensitivity is introduced by the factor s^i.

Due to the lack of diversification effects, product collateral and transfer prices sum up to their aggregates:

$$C(s^A) = C(\sum_{i=1}^{d} s^i) = \sum_{i=1}^{d} C(s^i)$$

$$TP^J_{\lambda^{-1}}(s^A) = TP^J_{\lambda^{-1}}(\sum_{i=1}^{d} s^i) = \sum_{i=1}^{d} TP^J_{\lambda^{-1}}(s^i)$$

There is one diversification effect that we have not discussed so far: the one between Brownian and jump risk.[51]

Brownian and jump components are assumed to be independent.[52] Hence, summing up central Money Market reserve and decentral collateral overestimates the risk. As these reserves are the basis for transfer prices, products are 'over'-charged.

The consideration of diversification effects between both stochastic sources is only reasonable if there is one common reserve. Diversification means that if one stochastic source materializes, the other does not necessarily do the same thing. Diversification can be considered as a sort of netting effect. If both stochastic sources are backed with the **same reserve**, only the netted effect has to be covered by it.

However, our organizational setup assumes two **separated reserves**. As a consequence, the decentral reserve for jump risk cannot be used to compensate Brownian risk and the Brownian reserve cannot be used to compensate jump risk. The reason is that Money Market cannot access the collateral pool since it does not have ownership. In a loss of confidence, an inter-department crisis committee is established and activates a contingency plan. Collateral owners renounce ownership and the crisis committee (not Money Market!) liquidates collateral. In contrast, the collateral pool cannot be used for Brownian deviations because Money Market does not have access to the collateral. However, if large Brownian deviations and jump risk occur at the same time (as if they were perfectly correlated), both can be compensated by their specific risk buffers.

---

[51] So far, we analysed diversification effects **within** each stochastic source (Brownian and jump risk).

[52] See section 4.2.2.

Due to the separated reserves, we do not incorporate diversification effects between Brownian and jump component.

The transfer price for jump risk on the product level results as:

$$\begin{aligned} TP^J_{\lambda^{-1}}(s^i) &= c^J(C(s^i)) \\ &= c^J(C(1)) \cdot s^i \\ &= c^J(-F^{-1}_{\Delta J_{\lambda^{-1}}}(1-p)) \cdot s^i \end{aligned} \tag{5.28}$$

(5.28) is the transfer price for a jump risk exposure of s^i at a confidence level p for the time horizon λ^{-1}

4. Transfer Prices for Arbitrary Maturities and Exercise Frequencies

For Brownian risk, we derived the quantile on the daily distribution and scaled it to longer maturities. The jump risk quantile is derived on a long-term distribution (λ^{-1}) and has to be scaled to shorter maturities.

The scaling rule for Brownian risk distinguishes maturity T and number of exercise dates n_2. The distinction was based on the argument that time without exercise dates (process times) scales the standard deviation by square root. The number of exercise dates just describes a sequence of (independent) options that enter in a linear manner.

Recall the Brownian rule (5.15) on page 106:

$$TP^B(...,T,n_2) = \sqrt{T} \cdot \sqrt{n_2} \cdot TP^B(...,\Delta t) \tag{5.29}$$

The transfer price (5.28) is based on the distribution with time horizon λ^{-1} ($T = \lambda^{-1}$). A jump can occur at every point in time ($n_2 = \lambda^{-1}$).

Applying the Brownian rule (5.29), we get the following for jump transfer prices:

$$\begin{aligned} TP^J(...,\Delta t) &= \frac{TP^J(...,T,n_2)}{\sqrt{T} \cdot \sqrt{n_2}} \\ &= \frac{TP^J(...,\lambda^{-1},\lambda^{-1})}{\sqrt{\lambda^{-1}} \cdot \sqrt{\lambda^{-1}}} \\ &= \lambda \cdot TP^J(...,\lambda^{-1},\lambda^{-1}) \end{aligned} \tag{5.30}$$

Hence, the transfer price for a daily exposure is found by re-scaling with λ. Based on the daily transfer price, the transfer price for a product with maturity T and n_2 exercise dates is:

$$TP^J(...,T,n_2) = \sqrt{T} \cdot \sqrt{n_2} \cdot TP^J(...,\Delta t) \tag{5.31}$$

Combining (5.31) and (5.30) we can directly infer from the $TP_{\lambda^{-1}}(...,\lambda^{-1},\lambda^{-1})$ to $TP(...,T,n_2)$ by:

$$TP^J(...,T,n_2) = \sqrt{T} \cdot \sqrt{n_2} \cdot \lambda \cdot TP^J(...,\lambda^{-1},\lambda^{-1}) \tag{5.32}$$

Finally, the jump transfer price per unit product volume, for an exposure of s^i, for a maturity T and n_2 exposure dates is obtained as:

$$\begin{aligned} TP^J(p,s^i,T,n_2) &= TP^J(p,s^i,\lambda^{-1},\lambda^{-1}) \cdot \lambda \cdot \sqrt{n_2} \cdot \sqrt{T} \\ &= c^J(-F^{-1}_{\Delta J_{\lambda^{-1}}}(1-p)) \cdot s^i \cdot \lambda \cdot \sqrt{n_2} \cdot \sqrt{T} \end{aligned} \tag{5.33}$$

Recall that (5.33) is normalized to one unit product volume.

5. Product Examples

Jump Risk Transfer Price of a Roll-over Liquidity Backup Line

We are given a liquidity backup line of maturity T $[\Delta t]$ and an amount BL [€]. The backup line can be drawn at every quarter, i.e. $\frac{T}{q}$ times. The length of a quarter is q Δt. Backup lines have a product-specific jump risk exposure per unit notional of s^{BL}. Based on (5.33), the jump risk transfer price is:

$$\begin{aligned} TP^J(s^{BL}) &= c^J(-F^{-1}_{\Delta J_{\lambda^{-1}}}(1-p)) \cdot s^{BL} \cdot \lambda \cdot \sqrt{n_2}\sqrt{T} \cdot BL \\ &= c^J(-F^{-1}_{\Delta J_{\lambda^{-1}}}(1-p)) \cdot s^{BL} \cdot \lambda \cdot \frac{T}{\sqrt{q}} \cdot BL \end{aligned}$$

Jump Risk Transfer Price of Demand Deposits

We are given a demand deposit of expected maturity E[T] $[\Delta t]$ and amount DD [€]. Demand deposits can be exercized daily, i.e. E[T] times. Product-specific jump risk per unit notional is s^{DD}.

The jump risk transfer price yields:

$$\begin{aligned} TP^J(s^{DD}) &= c^J(-F^{-1}_{\Delta J_{\lambda^{-1}}}(1-p)) \cdot s^{DD} \cdot \lambda \cdot \sqrt{n_2} \cdot \sqrt{E[T]} \cdot DD \\ &= c^J(-F^{-1}_{\Delta J_{\lambda^{-1}}}(1-p)) \cdot s^{DD} \cdot \lambda \cdot \sqrt{E[T]} \cdot \sqrt{E[T]} \cdot DD \\ &= c^J(-F^{-1}_{\Delta J_{\lambda^{-1}}}(1-p)) \cdot s^{DD} \cdot \lambda \cdot E[T] \cdot DD \end{aligned}$$

6. Comparison with the Brownian Transfer Price

Recall the transfer price (5.18) for one unit Brownian risk from page 106:

$$TP^B(\sigma^{p,i},\sigma^{m,i},T^i,n_2^i) = \underbrace{c^R(-l \cdot \Phi^{-1}(1-p) \cdot \sqrt{\Delta t})}_{(1)} \cdot \underbrace{\gamma \cdot (\sigma^{m,i} + \gamma^p \sigma^{p,i})}_{(2)} \cdot \underbrace{\sqrt{n_2^i} \cdot \sqrt{T^i}}_{(4)} \tag{5.34}$$

Recall the jump risk transfer price (5.33):

$$TP^J(p,s^i,T^i,n_2^i) = \underbrace{c^J(-F^{-1}_{\Delta J_{\lambda^{-1}}}(1-p))}_{(1)} \cdot \underbrace{s^i}_{(2)} \cdot \underbrace{\lambda}_{(3)} \cdot \underbrace{\sqrt{n_2^i} \cdot \sqrt{T^i}}_{(4)} \tag{5.35}$$

Both transfer prices are based on reserve cost. However, the Brownian transfer price is based on a reserve owned by Money Market (central reserve) whereas the jump transfer price is based on a decentral reserve that is only accessible in a loss of confidence.

The transfer prices have similar building blocks:

- (1) Quantile
  Both transfer prices are based on the (1-p)-quantile. For Brownian deviations, short-term funding is still available. Therefore, an additional parameter l is introduced. l represents the fraction of the quantile (funding capacity) that has to be backed with a reserve. For jump risk, external funding is not available. As a result, 100% of the quantile have to be backed with collateral.
- (2) Exposure
  We model Brownian exposure by a systematic factor and unsystematic noise. The Brownian exposure is measured in Brownian standard deviations. Due to diversification effects, the exposures have to be adjusted by γ and γ^p, respectively. The jump exposure is measured by s^i. s^i adjusts the jump size model for product particularities. Confidence is modelled with one single systematic factor. Thus, diversification is not an issue.
- (3) Horizon Scaling
  The Brownian quantile is derived from the distribution for Δt. As jumps are rare events, we cannot derive the jump quantile on the Δt-distribution of the Compound Poisson Process. We propose to use the $\lambda^{-1} \cdot \Delta t$-distribution. The horizon $\lambda^{-1}\Delta t$ corresponds to the period for which one jump is expected. As transfer prices are normalized to Δt, we have to rescale the transfer price by λ.
- (4) Time Rule
  The time rules are the same for both transfer prices.

5.2.3.1 Reconciliation with the Literature

The literature agrees on the pricing methodology for products with deterministic cash flows. The only pricing model for products with stochastic cash flows that we are aware of was presented by Neu et al. (2007).[53] It is a pricing model for the undrawn fraction of loan commitments. In our pricing model, loan commitments have a transfer price for the deterministic and Brownian component.[54] In the following, we compare our approach to that of Neu et al. (2007).

[53] See [Neu et al., 2007].

[54] We model loan commitments with a drift component for expected and a Brownian component for unexpected liquidity-driven cash flows. Loan commitments do not have a jump component.

Their pricing formula is noted as:

$$TP(\Delta^s,\sigma_c,t_k) = (TP^D(\Delta^s) + TP^{\text{Cash Flow Risk}}(\Delta^s) + TP^{\text{Spread Risk}}(\sigma_c)) \cdot V$$

$$TP^D(\Delta^s) := \underbrace{(\sum_s p_s \cdot \Delta^s)}_{E[CF]} \cdot c(0,t_k)$$

$$TP^{\text{Cash Flow Risk}}(\Delta^s) := \left(\sum_s p_s \cdot \Delta^s\right) \cdot c^R$$

$$TP^{\text{Spread Risk}}(\sigma_c) := \sigma_c \cdot c(0,t_k)$$

Being:

TP : Transfer Price for Undrawn Proportion of Loan Commitments

TP^D : Transfer Price for expected Cash Flow

$TP^{\text{Cash Flow Risk}}$:Transfer Price for Cash Flow Risk

$TP^{\text{Spread Risk}}$: Transfer Price (Premium) for Spread Risk

Δ^s : Drawdown Rate for scenario s

p_s : Probability of Scenario s

$c(0,t_k)$: Funding Spread for Maturity t_k

c^R : Reserve cost

σ_c : Volatility of Funding Spread

V : Undrawn Volume

The transfer price consists of a transfer price for expected cash flows, cash flow risk and spread risk. It does not cover the liquidity cost till the maturity of the commitment, but only to a key date t_k.[55]

The expected cash flow is the sum of scenario-drawdowns Δ^s weighted with the scenario probability p_s. The model is static, as only one drawdown per scenario and not a sequence of drawdowns is assumed.

The transfer price of expected cash flows, TP^D, is the corresponding maturity's funding spread. The transfer price for cash flow risk refers to the reserve cost. The calculating basis is, again, the expected cash flow. This argument is surprising, as the expected cash flow is not a risk. A risk is rather an unexpected cash out-flow beyond the expected cash flow (a type of quantile). The transfer price for spread risk can be interpreted as risk premium on spread changes. The funding spread is assumed to have a normal distribution. Neu et al. (2007) use one standard deviation above the current funding spread as quantile. This corresponds to a 81%-confidence level.

[55] They mention $t_k = 1$ (year) in their article, but other periods are possible.

According to (5.4) (transfer price for drift) and (5.18) (transfer price for Brownian component), our transfer price for loan commitments is written as:

$$\begin{aligned} TP(\mu_{t_0}^i,\ldots,\mu_{t_T}^i,\sigma^{m,BL},\sigma^{p,BL},T,T) =& (TP^D(\mu_{t_0}^i,\ldots,\mu_{t_T}^i) \\ &+ TP^{\text{Cash Flow Risk}}(\sigma^{p,F},\sigma^{m,F},T) \\ &+ TP^{\text{Spread Risk}}(\sigma_f)) \cdot V \\ TP^D :=& \sum_{j=0}^{T} c(0,t_j)\Delta t \cdot \mu_{t_j} \cdot (t_j - t_0) \\ TP^{\text{Cash Flow Risk}} :=& \underbrace{c^R(-l \cdot \Phi^{-1}(1-p) \cdot \sqrt{\Delta t})}_{\text{Cost } c^R(l,p)} \cdot \underbrace{\gamma \cdot (\sigma^{m,F} + \gamma^p \sigma^{p,F})}_{\text{Exposure } \Delta} \cdot T \\ TP^{\text{Spread Risk}} :=& 0 \end{aligned}$$

Our transfer price is not calculated for a period but for the lifetime of the product.[56]

As in Neu et al. (2007), the transfer price for deterministic cash flows is based on expected cash flows and the credit spread. This confirms that a consensus exists in the literature concerning the transfer prices for deterministic cash flows. However, our transfer price allows for a sequence of expected drawings $\mu_{t_0}^i,\ldots,\mu_{t_T}^i$ and not only for a single drawing.

As in Neu et al. (2007), our transfer price for cash flow risk can be split up into two components: (1) cost function and (2) exposure. In contrast to them, our exposure is based on a cash flow quantile whereas they use expected cash flows. Without additional arguments, this is not intuitive, as stated before. Furthermore, our pricing model distinguishes secured (reserve) and unsecured funding. Neu et al. (2007) do not allow for this degree of freedom. They implicitly assume that the risk fraction has to be backed at 100% with a reserve (this refers to l=100% in our model). Finally, we address product and aggregate level by specifying dependence structures between products. Our model distinguishes systematic and unsystematic liquidity risk and incorporates diversification effects. Neu et al. (2007) do not discuss the aggregate level, which is why their model can be interpreted as a stand-alone pricing model. This means that the loan commitment is priced as if it were the bank's only loan commitment.

Neu et al. (2007) price spread risk on expected cash flows. We do not price it since the spread management is in Origination and it is their decision how much spread risk they are willing to bear.[57]

We summarize that our pricing model for loan commitments uses the same methodology for the deterministic transfer price and a refined approach for the stochastic part. It does not price spread risk, as this is managed by Origination.

---

[56] However, it is possible to establish quarterly or annual transfer prices.

[57] It is likely that Neu et al. (2007) want to price the spread risk of unexpected cash flows. We do not price spread risk on unexpected cash flows either.

5.2.3.2 Pricing Examples

The complete transfer price of product i is the sum of the normalized deterministic, Brownian and jump transfer prices multiplied by product volume $X^i_{t_0}$:

$$\begin{aligned} TP^i(\mu^i_{t_0},\dots,\mu^i_{t_T},\sigma^{i,p}_{t_k},\sigma^{i,m},s^i,T^i,n^i_2) =&(TP^D(\mu^i_{t_0},\dots,\mu^i_{t_T}) \\ &+TP^B(\sigma^{i,p},\sigma^{i,m},T^i,n^i_2) \\ &+TP^J(s^i,T^i,n^i_2))\cdot X^i_{t_0} \end{aligned}$$

Replacing TP^D, TP^B and TP^J by their components, we obtain:

$$\begin{aligned} TP^i(\mu^i_{t_0},\dots,\mu^i_{t_T},\sigma^{i,p},\sigma^{i,m},s^i,n^i_2,T^i) =& \\ &(\sum_{j=0}^{T}\{(r(0,t_j)-r_s(0,t_j))\Delta t\cdot\mu_{t_j}\cdot(t_j-t_0)\} \\ &+c^R(-l\cdot\Phi^{-1}(1-p)\cdot\sqrt{\Delta t})\cdot\gamma\cdot(\sigma^{m,i}+\gamma^p\sigma^{p,i})\cdot\sqrt{n^i_2}\cdot\sqrt{T^i} \\ &+c^J(-F^{-1}_{\Delta J_{\lambda-1}}(1-p))\cdot s^i\cdot\lambda\cdot\sqrt{n^i_2}\cdot\sqrt{T})\cdot X^i_{t_0} \end{aligned} \tag{5.36}$$

For illustration purposes, we calculate the liquidity transfer price of the product 'Saving Deposits'. We choose saving deposits as they have all cash flow components: deterministic, Brownian and jump component.

First, the product-independent parameters have to be set (see (5.37)). We assume that the funding spread curve is flat at 40 BP per year. As our model is set up on a daily time scale, we convert the BP per year to BP per day. It is expected that 50% of saving deposits are withdrawn after six months. The remaining half is withdrawn in one year. For all other days, no payments are expected. It is assumed that only 60% of the required funding capacity to back Brownian shocks has to be ensured by a reserve. The Brownian shocks should be ensured at 99% confidence. Diversification between systematic and unsystematic liquidity factors requires an adjustment factor of 0.9. Diversification effects among products lead to an adjustment factor of 0.4. The cost is given per unit standard deviation and per unit s^i. We assume that the backing of 1 Brownian standard deviation implies a cost of 20 BP per year and that of jump risk 5 BP per year.

$$
\begin{aligned}
r(0,t_k) - r_s(0,t_k) &= 40 \text{ BP p.a.} \\
\mu_{t_k} &= \begin{cases} 0.5, & k \in \{180, 360\} \\ 0, & \text{else} \end{cases} \\
l &= 0.6 \\
\Phi(1-99\%) &= -2.3263 \\
\gamma &= 0.9 \\
\gamma^p &= 0.4 \\
c^R(1) &= 20[\frac{BP}{\text{Std p.a.}}] \\
c^J(1) &= 5[\frac{BP}{1.000 \text{ days}}] \\
F^{-1}_{\Delta J_{\lambda-1}}(1-99\%) &= -0.6
\end{aligned} \tag{5.37}
$$

The parameters that describe the products are:

$$
\begin{aligned}
\sigma^{i,m} &= 10\%[\text{p.a.}] \\
\sigma^{i,p} &= 30\%[\text{p.a.}] \\
s_{t_k} &= 1 \\
E[T] &= 360 \\
n_2 &= 360
\end{aligned}
$$

We assume that saving deposits have 10% systematic and 30% product-specific annual standard deviations. We expect that saving deposits can use the general jump sensitivity. No adjustment is necessary, which is reflected by the neutral adjustment of 1.0. The expected maturity is 360 days, which was reflected by the last expected payment. Saving deposits can be withdrawn daily. Therefore, n_2 is set to 360.

Inserting the values in (5.36) yields:

$$\begin{aligned}
TP^i_{t_k}(\mu^i_{t_k},\sigma^{i,p}_{t_k},\sigma^{i,m}_{t_k},s^i_{t_k},n^i_2,T^i) =& \frac{40}{360}[\frac{\text{BP p.a.}}{\text{days}}]\cdot 1\cdot 0.5\cdot 180[\text{days}]\\
&+\frac{40}{360}[\frac{\text{BP p.a.}}{\text{days}}]\cdot 1\cdot 0.5\cdot 360[\text{days}]\\
&+\frac{c^R(-0.6\cdot\Phi^{-1}(1\%)\cdot 1)\cdot 0.9\cdot(10\%+0.4\cdot 30\%)}{360}\cdot\sqrt{360^2}\\
&+c^J(0.6)\cdot 1\cdot 0.001\cdot\sqrt{360}\cdot\sqrt{360}\\
=&30[\text{BP}]\\
&+\frac{20[\frac{\text{BP p.a.}}{\text{Std p.a.}}]\cdot 1.4\cdot 0.9\cdot(10\%+0.4\cdot 30\%)[\text{p.a.}]}{360}\cdot 360[\text{days}]\\
&+5[\text{BP p. 1000 days}]\cdot 0.6[p.1000d]\cdot 0.001\cdot 360[\text{days}]\\
=&(30+5.53+1.08)[\text{BP}]\\
=&36.61[\text{BP}]
\end{aligned}$$

For the given parametrisation, the liquidity transfer price per unit 'Saving Deposits' is 36.61 BP.

5.3 Summary

Transfer model and pricing are at the heart of our bank liquidity management. Figure 5.19 summarizes the chapter. The management process starts at the sales departments, which sell products to customers. Products consist of nominal and interest rate cash flows. Fixed-rate interest rate cash flows are swapped to the interest rate department. As a result, the liquidity portfolio consists of floaters. The transfer price is the maturity-specific swap rate. The remaining notional cash flows consist of deterministic and stochastic cash flows. The latter are split up into a liquidity-driven Brownian, and a confidence-driven jump component. All three components are transferred to different departments at transfer prices. Transfer prices are derived as follows:

1. Deterministic Transfer Price
   The deterministic component is transferred to Origination. In order to determine the transfer price for deterministic cash flows, the funding cost is split up into swap rate and funding spread. The swap rate is transferred to the interest rate department while the remaining funding spread is transferred to Origination.
2. Brownian Transfer Price
   The Brownian component is transferred to Money Market. The component consists of a product and a systematic factor. The transfer price is based on the decentral reserve that Money Market holds to back aggregate Brownian deviations up to a confidence level p. In a first step, the confidence level is translated into a required aggregate funding capacity. However, only a secured fraction of the aggregate funding capacity has to be held as reserve. In a second step, the aggregate funding capacity is allocated to products.

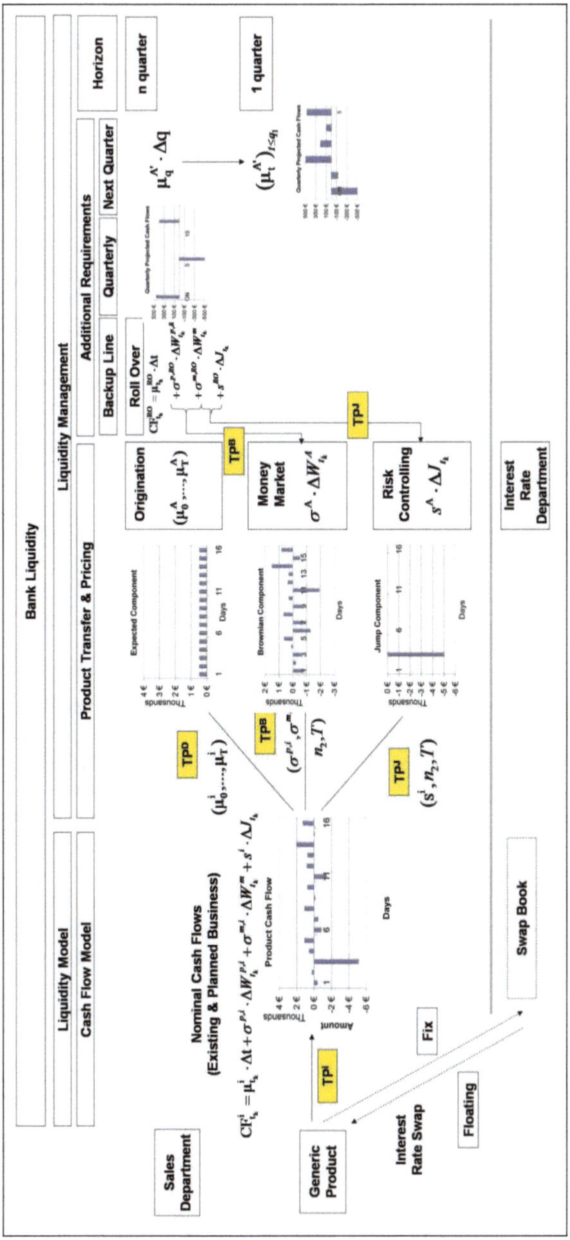

Fig. 5.19 Liquidity Management Process

The allocation mechanism incorporates diversification effects between unsystematic and systematic factors as well as between products. In a third step, transfer prices have to account for different maturities and exposure frequencies. It turns out that the transfer price is linear in the number of exposure dates and with square root for the time between two exposure dates.

3. Jump Transfer Price
   The jump component is transferred to Risk Controlling. It is not transferred to Money Market because Money Market uses external funding to manage Brownian cash flows. However, in a loss of confidence, external funding is unavailable. The jump component is backed with liquid assets that have been bought for reasons other than liquidity management. This type of reserve is called 'decentral' reserve and is only accessible in a loss of confidence and only by an inter-department crisis committee. The transfer price is based on expected liquidation costs. Diversification effects between Money Market and Risk Controlling are not taken into account, as the reserves are not used interchangeably.

Transfer prices are normalized to one unit notional. The final transfer price is obtained as the sum of normalized transfer prices times notional.

After the transfer, departments aggregate their components as seen in figure 5.19. The transfer prices compensate for cost without active management. The objective of Origination and Money Market is to realize lower cost by their active spread and reserve management. The difference between transfer prices and actual cost is the department performance. Hence, the performance of Origination and Money Market is measured relative to their ability to reduce the cost by active management.

The separation of components is the first step towards a separation of spread and cash flow risk. However, further requirements are necessary. Origination chooses a rolling-strategy to run spread positions. The rolling strategy is not only based on an uncertain spread, but also on uncertain roll-over volumes. Therefore, Origination transfers the Brownian roll-over risk to Money Market and the jump roll-over risk to Risk Controlling via two liquidity backup lines. Furthermore, Origination operates on quarterly instead of daily cash flows. As a result, cash flows are projected at quarter beginnings (quarterly projected cash flows). As Origination operates on instruments that have maturities beyond a quarter, it cannot manage the deterministic cash flows of the next quarter. The next quarter is transferred to Money Market. We propose to set the model horizon of Money Market to one quarter due to complexity reasons. Hence, Money Market manages the deterministic and Brownian cash flows of the next quarter.

If products are unrestricted by maturity or amount, Origination can operate on unconditional expected cash flows and on an unlimited time horizon. However, if products are restricted, Origination should operate on conditional expected cash flows. We opt for unconditional ones since conditional expected cash flows are random. We want Origination to operate on deterministic cash flows. In order to attenuate this model bias, the horizon of Origination has to be limited.

The separation and transfer of cash flow components leads to the risk profile as given in table 5.1: The Money Market department manages short-term liquidity, which comprises Brownian deviations and expected cash flows of the next quarter. Money Market

Table 5.1 Risk Profile after Liquidity Transfer

Risk Type	Money Market	Origination	Risk Controlling
Liquidity-driven Cash Flow Risk	x		
Short-term Funding Capacity Risk	x		
Overnight Rate	x		
Long-term Funding Capacity Risk	x		x
Funding Spread Risk		x	
Liquidation Risk			x
Confidence-driven Cash Flow Risk			x

uses Money Market instruments on the interbank and central bank market. The drivers for short-term liquidity management are stochastic liquidity-driven cash flows (Brownian component).

The Origination department operates on deterministic cash flows. The stochastic driver is the funding spread. The stochastic of the funding capacity resulting from roll-over risk is transferred to Money Market and Risk Controlling. Origination uses different instruments from the Money Market's: it issues securities. The separation of spread and cash flow risk is important as both risks are backed with different risk buffers: spread risk is a P&L-risk and backed with economic capital. Cash flow risk is a liquidity risk and backed with counterbalancing capacity.

The jump component is transferred to Risk Controlling. Jump risk is backed with collateral whose holders bear a liquidation risk. Liquidation risks are costs incurred in case of fire-sale liquidation.

The separation of components allows for local optimization: Money Market optimizes the reserve for (Brownian) cash flow risk. Origination optimizes the funding profile given a spread risk. The local optimization programmes are discussed in the next section.

Chapter 6
Liquidity Optimization

This chapter discusses the optimization of long-term and short-term liquidity. The first section restricts the setup in order to allow for explicit solutions. The second section analyses the optimization within Origination. The third presents the optimization within Money Market while the final section briefly describes the tasks of Risk Controlling.

6.1 Setup

This section analyzes the optimization of liquidity within the departments. The optimization programmes are analytically solved. In particular, we do not use 'black box' solver programmes. However, complexity sets narrow limits for explicit solutions. Therefore, we have to use a simplified setup with respect to the cash flow assumption and the model horizon. The simplification is justified, as the general proceeding is still apparent. Practical implementation has to be extended with respect to the cash flow process and horizon. The optimization follows the same procedure but has to be done numerically using optimization software.

Figure 6.1 describes our setup. It is divided into three sections:

1. Liquidity Model
2. Liquidity Management
3. Liquidity Optimization

1. Liquidity Model

The proposed cash flow is plotted in the cash flow maturity ladder in figure 6.1 on the left. We restrict the cash flow with the following assumptions:

Assumption 6.1. The bank has contracted loans that are paid out during the first quarter and repaid in the third quarter.

We take assets as given so that Origination has to optimize funding. Short-term assets are chosen to keep the model horizon short. It is important to have three time points. The first time point is needed to pay out loans, the second to roll-over funds. The third is required as a maturity date for long-term funds. Therefore, time points could also be 0, 1 year, 2 years. Loans are chosen as they form banks' core assets.

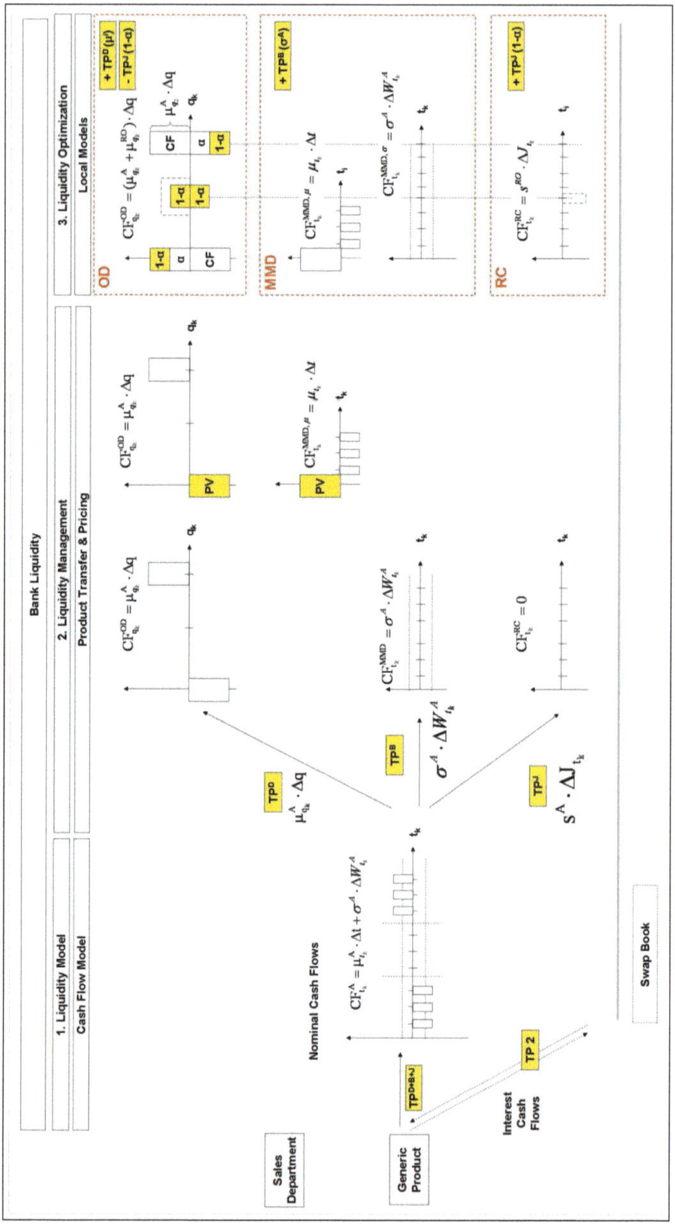

Fig. 6.1 Setup for Local Optimization

Assumption 6.2. Within a quarter, deterministic cash flows occur at a constant rate.

Intra-quarterly deterministic cash flows are optimized by Money Market. The constant rate is required because the optimization of the Money Market is solved for constant μ only.

Assumption 6.3. The cash flow volatility (prepayment) σ^{Loans} is constant.

The argument is the same as for the constant drift: the Money Market optimization is solved for constant σ only.

Assumptions 6.1-6.3 are summarized by:[1]

$$CF_{t_k}^{loan} = \mu_{t_k}^{loan} \cdot \Delta t + \sigma^{loan} \cdot \Delta W_{t_k}^{loan}$$

The loan cash flows are modelled with a deterministic and a Brownian component. It does not contain a jump component, as debtors cannot lose confidence. As we assume loans to be the only product, the aggregate cash flow is identical to the loan cash flow:

$$\begin{aligned} CF_{t_k}^{A} &= \mu_{t_k}^{A} \cdot \Delta t + \sigma^{A} \cdot \Delta W_{t_k}^{A} \\ &= CF_{t_k}^{loan} \end{aligned}$$

The deterministic components in figure 6.1 are displayed as boxes, the Brownian component as a dotted line. All loans are summarized in the aggregate cash flow.

2. Liquidity Management

The internal transfer mechanism separates the cash flow components: the deterministic cash flows are transferred to Origination at $TP^D(\mu_{q_k}^A)$. The cash flows are projected to quarter beginnings. The Brownian component is transferred to Money Market at $TP^B(\sigma^A)$. Origination sells its first quarter to Money Market at the present value.[2] This is seen in figure 6.1 in the section '2. Liquidity Management' in the PV-position graphs.

3. Liquidity Optimization

Once the cash flow components are allocated in the departments, they will be optimized. The departments have received transfer prices. The deterministic transfer price covers matched-maturity funding. The Brownian transfer price refers to a static liquidity reserve. The jump transfer price is derived from a static collateral reserve.

To realize the transactions that underlie the transfer prices, no active management is needed. Thus, transfer prices are the performance benchmark. The department performance is the difference between transfer price and actual cost. If the department replicates the activities underlying the transfer prices, the performance is zero. In the following, we outline the optimization programme for each department starting with Origination.

---

[1] As loans are the only product, there is no distinction between systematic and unsystematic risk.

[2] See section 5.1.2 for details.

Origination faces the following cash flows:

$$CF_{q_k}^{OD} = (\mu_{q_0}, \mu_{q_1}, \mu_{q_2}) \cdot \Delta q$$
$$= (-\mu_{q_2}, 0, \mu_{q_2}) \cdot \Delta q$$

Loans are paid out during the first $(-\mu_{q_2})$ and expected to be repaid during the third quarter μ_{q_2}. For q_1 no payments are expected. For easier notation, we set $CF := \mu_{q_2}$. CF is the asset cash flow that needs to be funded. The task of Origination is to determine an optimal funding mix of short-term $(1-\alpha)$ and long-term (α) funding. In our 2-quarter model, there is only one funding decision at q_0: $(1-\alpha)$.[3] The funding covers the outflow at q_0. α of the funding is repaid at q_2. $(1-\alpha)$ has to be rolled over at q_1. Origination funds by issuing securities. Funding decisions are taken on a quarterly basis.

To ensure the roll-over volume, Origination has to buy a backup line from Money Market against Brownian roll-over risk, and from Risk Controlling against jump roll-over risk at the volume of $(1-\alpha)CF$. The backup line costs the Brownian and jump transfer prices for q_1.

Assumption 6.4. The Brownian exposure of the roll-over is zero ($\sigma_{q_i}^{RO} = 0$).

The backup line ensures volume, but not the funding spread. We assume that securities can always be rolled over at a certain spread provided that investors have confidence. If investors lose confidence, they do not roll over, no matter how much the spread.

Origination maximizes the expected terminal value $E[TV^{OD}]$. The break-even for the performance is the jump transfer price:

$$\max_{1-\alpha} E[TV^{OD}] - TP^J(s_{q_1}^{RO}) \cdot (1-\alpha)CF$$

Money Market maximizes the return by choosing an optimal dynamic reserve policy. It optimizes the Brownian deviations together with the deterministic cash flows of the first quarter. Money Market uses loans and deposits in the inter-bank market to carry out its reserve policy. For its management, Money Market receives the Brownian transfer price. Reserve decisions are taken on a daily basis.

$$TP^B(\sigma^A) + \max_{d_{t_k}} E[TV^{MMD}]$$

The Brownian transfer price depends on σ^A. Seen from the Money Market perspective, σ^A is exogenuous. In particular, it does not depend on the reserve decision. Therefore, $TP(\sigma^A)$ is outside the optimization programme.

In contrast to Origination and Money Market, Risk Controlling is not an actively managing department. It is rather an actively monitoring department. Risk Controlling monitors jump risk exposure and available collaterals.[4]

---

[3] As we only have one funding decision (t_0) we omit the time index.

[4] See section 6.4 for more details.

Global versus Local Optimization

Liquidity can be optimized department-wise if underlying factors and decision variables are disjoint:

$$\max_{d_t,(1-\alpha)} E[TV^{MMD+OD}] \stackrel{(1)}{=} \max_{d_t,1-\alpha} E[TV^{MMD}] + E[TV^{OD}] \tag{6.1}$$

$$\stackrel{(2)}{=} \max_{d_t} E[TV^{MMD}] + \max_{1-\alpha} E[TV^{OD}] \tag{6.2}$$

The split is based on the following arguments:

1. Process Independence (See (6.1))
   Origination operates on deterministic cash flows. Money Market operates on Brownian cash flows and deterministic cash flows of the first quarter. Deterministic and Brownian cash flows are independent by construction. As the first quarter is transferred before the model starts, the transfer does not introduce dependencies. As Origination cannot influence the deterministic cash flow profile of the next quarter (as its instruments have at least one quarter maturity), it cannot manipulate the performance of the Money Market. As the Money Market cannot influence deterministic cash flows beyond a quarter, it cannot manipulate the performance of Origination. The independence process justifies splitting the expectations.
2. Disjoint Decision Variables (See (6.2))
   The decision variables (instruments) of the Money Market are interbank deposits and loans. By comparison, the decision variables of Origination are security issues. Hence, the departments use different decision variables. This justifies splitting the optimization programme.

The roll-over decision implies a jump exposure and establishes a link between Origination and Risk Controlling.

After having motivated local optimization, we specify and solve the optimization programmes for each department.

6.2 Origination Department

6.2.1 The Model

6.2.1.1 Setup

Figure 6.2 displays the roll-over decision of the bank as stated in section 6.1. The bank has to fund loans at the amount CF that matures in q_2. CF is the volume of q_2-loans:

$$\begin{aligned} CF &= E[CF_{q_2}] \\ &= \mu_{q_2} \cdot \Delta q \end{aligned}$$

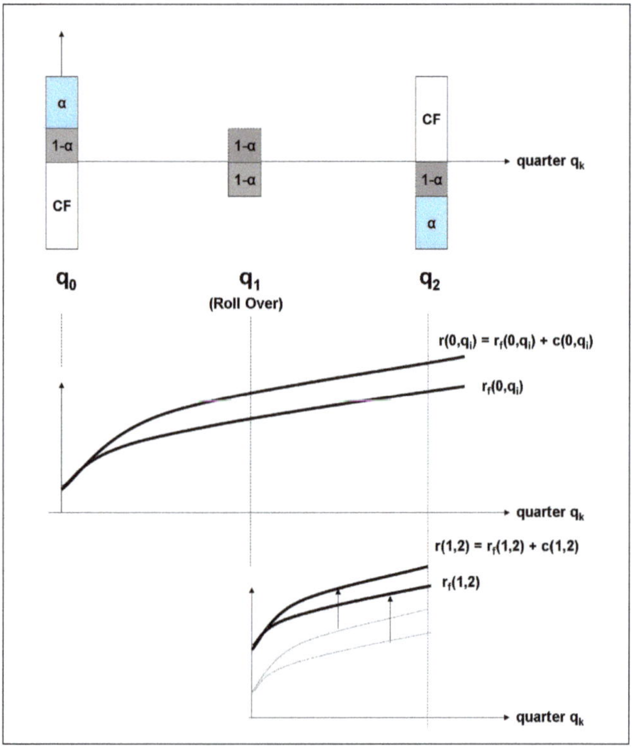

Fig. 6.2 Model Setup

The loans can be funded by a matched-funded strategy (1 x 2 periods), a rolling funding strategy (2 x 1 period) or a linear combination of both. The fraction of 2-period funding is α, the one of 1-period funding is $(1-\alpha)$. The gross funding cost at t_0 for a maturity t are r(0,t). The gross funding cost can be split up into the risk-free rate and the funding spread:

$$r(0,q_k) = r_f(0,q_k) + c(0,q_k)$$

The variables $r(0,q_k)$, $r_f(0,q_k)$ and $c(0,q_k)$ are spot variables. Origination operates on deterministic cash flows. They have been bought from the sales department and the transfer price is the funding spread $c(0,t_i)$.[5] The vectors $(r(0,q_k))_{k\in\{1,2\}}$, $(r_f(0,q_k))_{k\in\{1,2\}}$ and $(c(0,q_k))_{k\in\{1,2\}}$ are the corresponding term structures. The spot term structures imply the following arbitrage-free forward rates for the period [1,2]:

[5] See section 5.2 for details.

$$f_r(0,1,2) = \frac{(1+r(0,2))^2}{(1+r(0,1))} - 1$$

$$f_{r_f}(0,1,2) = \frac{(1+r_f(0,2))^2}{(1+r_f(0,1))} - 1$$

Being:

$f_r(0,1,2)$: Gross Forward Rate for [1,2]

$f_{r_f}(0,1,2)$: Risk-free Forward Rate for [1,2]

We define the implied forward spread $f_c(0,q_1,q_2)$ for [1,2]:

$$f_c(0,1,2) := f_r(0,1,2) - f_{r_f}(0,1,2)$$

As fixed-rates are swapped against variable rates, we assume the risk-free rate position to be closed on a forward rate basis. Origination manages the funding spread cost by choosing the proportion of matched (α) and mismatch-funding ($1-\alpha$).

More formally, Origination maximizes the terminal value of the liquidity portfolio. The terminal value is formulated as follows:[6]

$$TV := CF(1+r(0,2))^2 \tag{6.3}$$

$$- (1-\alpha)\cdot CF(1+r(0,1))(1+f_{r_f}(0,1,2)+c(1,2)) \tag{6.4}$$

$$- \alpha \cdot CF(1+r(0,2))^2 \tag{6.5}$$

$$- (1-\alpha)\cdot CF \cdot TP(1+r(0,2))^2 \tag{6.6}$$

being:

$1-\alpha$: Fraction of roll-over funding

$TP := TP^J(s^{RO})$

(6.3) is the terminal value of assets. (6.4) is the terminal value of the rolling funding. The interest rate for the future period [1,2] is already fixed at today's forward rates and the spread position is open. (6.5) is the terminal value of the matched funding. (6.6) is the transfer price paid to RC for the liquidity backup line at roll-over dates.

The rearrangement of terms yields:

$$\begin{aligned} TV =& (1-\alpha)CF(1+r(0,2))^2\cdot(1-TP) \\ &-(1-\alpha)CF(1+r(0,1))(1+f_{r_f}(0,1,2)+c(1,2)) \end{aligned} \tag{6.7}$$

Obviously, the transfer prices lower the terminal value. The only uncertain quantity in (6.7) is the future funding spread $c(1,2)$. The expected terminal value is:

$$\begin{aligned} E^{OD}[TV] :=& (1-\alpha)CF(1+r(0,2))^2\cdot(1-TP) \\ &-(1-\alpha)CF(1+r(0,1))(1+f_{r_f}(0,1,2)+E^{OD}[c(1,2)]) \end{aligned} \tag{6.8}$$

[6] The distinction risk-free rate/funding spread is only of interest for the (future) roll-over fraction. To shorten notation, all spot rates are expressed as gross rates. The deterministic transfer price (funding spread) is contained in r(0,2).

The expectation is the subjective expectation of Origination. In the following, we omit the superscript 'OD'.

6.2.2 Optimization without Funding Risk

In a first step, we demonstrate that the negligence of funding risk leads to 100% or 0% short-term funding.

We are looking for the roll-over volume $(1-\alpha^*)$ that maximizes expected terminal value:

$$\max_{1-\alpha} E[TV] \Leftrightarrow \frac{\partial E[TV]}{\partial(1-\alpha)} \stackrel{!}{=} 0 \tag{6.9}$$

The derivation of 6.8 w.r.t. $(1-\alpha)$ yields:

$$\begin{aligned}\frac{\partial E[TV]}{\partial(1-\alpha)} &= CF(1+r(0,2))^2(1-TP)\\ &\quad -CF(1+r(0,1))(1+f_{r_f}(0,1,2)+E[c(1,2)])\\ &\stackrel{!}{=} 0\end{aligned}$$

The rearrangement of terms yields:

$$\begin{gathered}\frac{(1+r(0,2))^2}{(1+r(0,1))}(1-TP) = (1+f_{r_f}(0,1,2)+E[c(1,2)])\\ \Leftrightarrow\\ (1+f_r(0,1,2))(1-TP) = (1+f_{r_f}(0,1,2)+E[c(1,2)])\\ \Leftrightarrow\\ (f_r(0,1,2)-f_{r_f}(0,1,2))-(1+f_r(0,1,2))TP = E[c(1,2)]\\ \Leftrightarrow\\ f_c(0,1,2)-(1+f_r(0,1,2))TP = E[c(1,2)]\end{gathered}$$

Hence, the optimal roll-over decision is:

$$1-\alpha^* = \begin{cases} 1, & f_c(0,1,2)-(1+f_r(0,1,2))TP \geq E[c(1,2)] \\ 0, & \text{else} \end{cases}$$

Our first observation is that only corner solutions are optimal. This is due to the linearity of the terminal value in $(1-\alpha)$. Our second observation is that rolling funding is preferable if Origination expects the funding spread to be far below the forward spread. Without transfer pricing, the break-even for a rolling strategy is exactly the forward spread. With transfer pricing, the transfer price (= volume insurance) has to be earned as well. Hence, the break-even is lower.

Note that the backup line is only bought for the roll-over volume. Consequently, the transfer price is linear in the roll-over volume. It affects the switching point, but it does not affect the optimal volume which is always either 1 or 0.

6.2.3 Optimization with Funding Capacity Risk

Origination pays a transfer price to Risk Controlling to lock in funding capacity. However, Risk Controlling only ensures the volume, but not the funding spread so the funding spread risk has not been incorporated yet. We model roll-over risk by introducing a stochastic long-term funding capacity β that triggers a penalty spread:[7]

$$FC_1^{\mathrm{lt}} := \beta$$

Up to β, Origination can issue securities at the standard spread. For amounts beyond β, Origination has to draw the liquidity backup line. Risk Controlling provides the funds, but at a penalty cost s. The penalty cost can be thought of as additional costs that are caused by the liquidation of collateral (decentral reserve).

Recall the terminal value **without** funding restrictions given by (6.7):

$$\begin{aligned} TV = &(1-\alpha)CF(1+r(0,2))^2 \cdot (1-TP) \\ &-(1-\alpha)CF(1+r(0,1))(1+f_{r_f}(0,1,2)+c(1,2)) \end{aligned}$$

The terminal value **with** funding limit β at t_1 is written as follows:

$$\begin{aligned} TV = &CF(1+r(0,2))^2 - \alpha CF \cdot (1+r(0,2))^2 \\ &-CF \cdot (1-\alpha)(1+r(0,2))^2 \cdot TP \\ &-CF \cdot \min((1-\alpha)(1+r(0,1)),\beta) \cdot (1+f_{r_f}(0,1,2)+c(1,2)) \\ &-CF \max((1-\alpha)(1+r(0,1))-\beta,0)(1+f_{r_f}(0,1,2)+c(1,2)+s) \end{aligned} \tag{6.10}$$

The roll-over up to β costs the usual funding rate $f_{rf}(0,1,2)+c(1,2)$. Rolling beyond β implies the additional penalty spread s. (6.10) is simplified as:

[7] We use beta instead of FC_1^{lt} to simplify notation.

$$
\begin{aligned}
TV = & CF \cdot (1-\alpha)CF(1+r(0,2))^2(1-TP) \\
& - CF \cdot (1+f_{rf}(0,1,2)+c(1,2)) \qquad (6.11)\\
& \cdot (\min((1-\alpha)(1+r(0,1)),\beta) + \max((1-\alpha)(1+r(0,1))-\beta,0)) \\
& - CF \cdot \max((1-\alpha)(1+r(0,1))-\beta,0) \cdot s \\
& = \ldots \\
& - CF \cdot (1+f_{r_f}(0,1,2)+c(1,2)) \qquad (6.12)\\
& \cdot (\beta + \min((1-\alpha)(1+r(0,1))-\beta,0) + \max((1-\alpha)(1+r(0,1))-\beta,0)) \\
& - \ldots \\
& = \ldots \\
& - CF \cdot (1+f_{rf}(0,1,2)+c(1,2))(\beta + (1-\alpha)(1+r(0,1))-\beta) \\
& \ldots \\
& = (1-\alpha)CF \cdot ((1+r(0,2))^2(1-TP) - (1+r(0,1)) \cdot (1+f_{r_f}(0,1,2)+c(1,2)) \\
& - \max((1-\alpha)(1+r(0,1))-\beta,0) \cdot s \qquad (6.13)
\end{aligned}
$$

Note that the decision regarding the roll-over volume $(1-\alpha)$ is taken at q_0, whereas the funding capacity is based at q_1. As a consequence, one of the variables has to be compounded/discounted. In (6.13), $(1-\alpha)$ is compounded. However, it turns out that calculations simplify if β is discounted instead.[8] Therefore, we introduce $\widetilde{\beta} := \beta \cdot (1+r(0,1))^{-1}$. With the discounted beta, (6.13) becomes:

$$
\begin{aligned}
TV = & CF(1-\alpha)((1+r(0,2))^2(1-TP) - (1+r(0,1)) \cdot (1+f_{r_f}(0,1,2)+c(1,2))) \\
& - CF(1+r(0,1)) \max((1-\alpha) - \underbrace{\frac{\beta}{1+r(0,1)}}_{=:\widetilde{\beta}},0) \cdot s \\
& = CF(1-\alpha)((1+r(0,2))^2(1-TP) - (1+r(0,1)) \cdot (1+f_{r_f}(0,1,2)+c(1,2) \\
& - CF(1+r(0,1)) \max((1-\alpha)-\widetilde{\beta},0) \cdot s
\end{aligned}
$$

$\widetilde{\beta}$ can be interpreted as the funding capacity that refers to the initial balance sheet. It describes the notional proportion that is 'fundable' in q_1. By contrast, β refers to the compounded t_1-balance sheet, i.e. to notional plus interest. Whereas β is defined in $[0, 1+r(0,1)]$, $\widetilde{\beta}$ is defined in [0,1]. In the following, our arguments are based on $\widetilde{\beta}$ and its density $f(\widetilde{\beta})$.

Assumption 6.5. We assume that spread dynamics and funding capacity are independent.

The expected terminal value is formulated below as:

$$
\begin{aligned}
E[TV] = & CF(1-\alpha)((1+r(0,2))^2(1-TP) - (1+r(0,1)) \cdot (1+f_{r_f}(0,1,2)+E[c(1,2)]) \\
& - CF(1+r(0,1)) \cdot E[\max((1-\alpha)-\widetilde{\beta},0)] \cdot s
\end{aligned}
$$

[8] This ensures that integrals operate on a beta that is defined on the interval [0,1].

Using lemma C.1 on page 201, the derivation of E[TV] w.r.t. $(1-\alpha)$ yields:

$$\begin{aligned}\frac{\partial E[TV]}{\partial(1-\alpha)} =& CF\cdot((1+r(0,2))^2(1-TP)-(1+r(0,1))\cdot(1+f_{r_f}(0,1,2)E[r(1,2)]))\\ &-CF\cdot(1+r(0,1))\cdot P[\widetilde{\beta}\leq(1-\alpha^*)]\cdot s\\ &\stackrel{!}{=}0\end{aligned}$$

Hence:

$$\begin{aligned}\Leftrightarrow (1+r(0,1))\cdot P[\widetilde{\beta}\leq(1-\alpha^*)]\cdot s =& (1+r(0,2))^2(1-TP)\\ &-(1+r_f(0,1)+c(0,1))\cdot(1+f_{r_f}(0,1,2)+E[c(1,2)])\\ \Leftrightarrow P[\widetilde{\beta}\leq(1-\alpha^*)]\cdot s =& \frac{(1+r(0,2))^2}{(1+r(0,1))}(1-TP)-1-f_{r_f}(0,1,2)-E[c(1,2)]\\ =& (1+f_r(0,1,2))(1-TP)-1-f_{r_f}(0,1,2)\\ &-E[c(1,2)]\\ =& f_r(0,1,2)-f_{r_f}(0,1,2)\\ &-E[c(1,2)]-(1+f_r(0,1,2))TP\\ =& f_c(0,1,2)-E[c(1,2)]-(1+f_r(0,1,2))TP\end{aligned}$$

The optimal roll-over fraction $(1-\alpha^*)$ satisfies (6.14):

$$\underbrace{P[\widetilde{\beta}\leq(1-\alpha^*)]\cdot s}_{\text{Expected marginal roll-over cost}} = \underbrace{f_c(0,1,2)-E[c(1,2)]-(1+f_r(0,1,2))TP}_{\text{Expected marginal roll-over gain}} \tag{6.14}$$

being:

$f_c(0,1,2)$: Forward Spread in 0 for [1,2]

$E[c(1,2)]$: Subjective Expectation about funding spread in t_1

$(1+f_r(0,1,2))TP$: Compounded Transfer Price

Hence, the optimal roll-over fraction (1-α^*) balances the expected marginal illiquidity cost (left) with the expected marginal roll-over gain (right). Without transfer pricing, the expected marginal roll-over gain is simply the difference between the implied forward spread and the funding spread expectation of Origination. Incorporating transfer prices lowers the expected gain.

Based on the general result (6.14), we analyse how particular choices of funding stochastics and penalty costs affect the optimal roll-over volume. The analysis focuses on model properties. Whether the model is a stand-alone model or part of an overall bank liquidity model does not change its properties. However, the analysis as a stand-alone model shortens notation as we can omit the transfer price term. As a result, transfer prices are set to zero in the following sections.

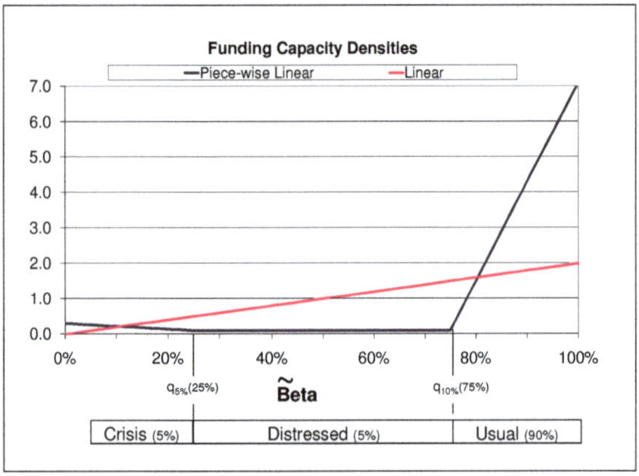

Fig. 6.3 Densities for Funding Capacities

6.2.3.1 Impact of Funding Stochastic

To analyze the impact of the funding stochastics, we choose a linear density and a piecewise linear density. Our motivation for the linear density is based on the following arguments:

1. Investment Bank Density
   A linear density represents the smooth density of a bank with sensitive wholesale funding.
2. Simplicity
   The linear density simplifies calculations.

The piecewise funding density incorporates the following additional features:

1. Retail Bank Density
   Retail Banks distinguish three fundamental scenarios: standard funding, distressed funding, and funding crisis. The probability distribution should account for these scenarios.
2. 'Distressed Funding' and 'Funding Crisis' have a low probability.
   Consequently, the bulk of probability mass is placed on standard funding.

The densities are plotted in figure 6.3. The piecewise density is calibrated so that the 5%- and 10%-quantiles are the boundaries for the funding scenarios: scenarios with less than 25% funding capacity are called 'funding crisis', covering a probability of 5%. Distressed funding encompasses all scenarios with more than 25%, but less than 75% funding capacity. The probability of distressed scenarios is 5%. Standard funding are scenarios with a funding capacity of more than 75%. Standard funding occurs with a probability of 90%.

Formally, the densities are given by (6.15) (linear) and (6.16) (piecewise linear):

$$f(\widetilde{\beta}) = \begin{cases} 2 \cdot \widetilde{\beta}, & \widetilde{\beta} \in [0,1] \\ 0, & \text{else} \end{cases} \tag{6.15}$$

$$g(\widetilde{\beta}) = \begin{cases} 0.3 - 0.8 \cdot \widetilde{\beta} & ,0 \leq \widetilde{\beta} \leq 25\% \\ 0.1 & ,25\% \leq \widetilde{\beta} \leq 75\% \\ -20.9 + 28 \cdot \widetilde{\beta} & ,75\% \leq \widetilde{\beta} \leq 1 \\ 0 & ,\text{else} \end{cases} \tag{6.16}$$

The corresponding distribution functions are given by (6.17) and (6.18):

$$P_f(\widetilde{\beta} \leq x) = F(X \leq x) = \begin{cases} 0, & x < 0 \\ x^2 \cdot x, & 0 \leq 1 \\ 1, & 1 < x \end{cases} \tag{6.17}$$

$$P_g(\widetilde{\beta} \leq x) = F(X \leq x) = \begin{cases} 0 & ,x < 0 \\ 0.3 \cdot x - 0.4 \cdot x^2 & ,0 \leq x \leq 25\% \\ 0.025 + 0.1 \cdot x & ,25\% \leq x \leq 75\% \\ 7.9 - 20.9 \cdot x + 14 \cdot x^2 & ,75\% \leq x \leq 1 \\ 1 & ,1 < x \end{cases} \tag{6.18}$$

Being:

x : Roll-over Volume $1 - \alpha$

The expected marginal costs are the distribution function times the penalty spread:

$$E_i[C(x)] = s \cdot P_i(\widetilde{\beta} \leq x), i \in \{f, g\} \tag{6.19}$$

Figure (6.4) plots the expected marginal cost functions for a penalty spread of 0.5% (50 BP). As our roll-over model does not imply fixed costs, all cost functions begin at their origin. As penalty costs have to be paid if 100% is rolled over, the second common point of the cost functions is (1,s). The size of the penalty spread determines the slope of the cost functions.

Between the two common points, the cost functions are shaped by the distribution function: the cost function with linear density is smooth whereas the cost function with piecewise linear density clearly reflects the switch from distressed to standard funding.

Given the expected marginal gain of 50 BP, the resulting optimal volumes are 31.63% for linear and 75% for piecewise density, respectively. Because the linear density assigns more probability to low funding scenarios, the optimal roll-over volume is lower than for piecewise density. The cost functions start almost in a linear fashion and become more convex with increasing funding. As the expected marginal gains are fairly small, the optimal volumes are determined in the linear region. The smaller the probability of adverse funding scenarios, the longer the linear region of the cost function. Within the linear region, the slope of the cost functions is very low: a small change in the expectation

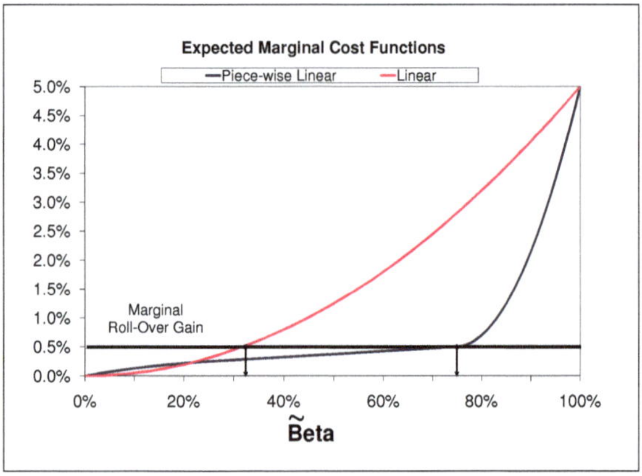

Fig. 6.4 Expected Marginal Cost Functions

of the funding spread has great impact on the optimal roll-over volume. As expectation is subjective, the optimal roll-over volume is also somewhat subjective.

We conclude that the choice of funding stochastic has a high impact on the shape of the expected marginal cost functions: shifting probabilities to good funding scenarios leads to substantial higher optimal roll-over volumes.

However, we believe that the number of reasonable funding stochastics is rather limited, as there is a consensus that little probability has to be placed on funding crises and large probabilities on usual funding circumstances. However, assuming funding stochastics where crises and distressed funding are rare leads to cost functions with a large linear region. Within the linear region the cost function only increases moderately. This implies that small changes in spread expectations translate into large changes in optimal volumes. Therefore, the model has a high arbitrary component.

After having discussed the sensitivity of the optimal roll-over volume with regard to the funding stochastics, we analyse the sensitivity with regard to the penalty definition.

6.2.3.2 Impact of Spread Definition

Until now, the penalty cost was constant. Within this section, we analyze the impact of volume dependent penalty spreads. The volume-dependent spread is called progressive spread in contrast to the constant spread.

For easier notation, we define:

$$x(\alpha) := (1 - \alpha)$$

We assume that the penalty cost increases with the volume shortage. As particular cost function we choose:

$$
\begin{aligned}
s(x(\alpha),\widetilde{\beta}) &:= k \cdot c1 \cdot \max(x(\alpha)-\widetilde{\beta}) \\
&\text{being:} \\
&c1 := (1+r(0,1))) \\
&k := \text{ Scaling Factor}
\end{aligned}
$$

The quantity $\max(x(\alpha)-\widetilde{\beta})$ measures the volume shortage in t_0-dollars. The c1-factor converts the amount to t_1-dollars. This way, the cost in t_1 exactly corresponds to the volume shortage in t_1. The scaling factor k regulates the tightness of the volume-cost relation: a scaling factor of one means that a 1% volume shortage leads to 1% (100 BP) increase in penalty costs. However, such a strong link lets penalty costs grow too quickly (a 10% volume shortage already implies 1.000 BP). A scaling factor of 0.1 or 0.05 (5 BP for every 1% volume shortage) is more realistic.

Recall the terminal value with **constant** illiquidity cost:

$$
\begin{aligned}
TV = {} & (1-\alpha)((1+r(0,2))^2 - c1 \cdot (1+f_{rf}(0,1,2)+c(1,2)) \\
& - c1 \cdot \max(x(\alpha)-\widetilde{\beta},0) \cdot s
\end{aligned}
$$

The terminal value with **progressive** illiquidity cost is written as:

$$
\begin{aligned}
TV = {} & (1-\alpha)((1+r(0,2))^2 - c1 \cdot (1+f_{rf}(0,1,2)+c(1,2)) \\
& - c1 \cdot \underbrace{\max(x(\alpha)-\widetilde{\beta})\, k \cdot c1 \cdot \underbrace{\max(x(\alpha)-\widetilde{\beta},0)}_{\text{t0-quantity}}}_{\text{Penalty Cost: t1-quantity}} \\
= {} & (1-\alpha)((1+r(0,2))^2 - c1 \cdot (1+f_{rf}(0,1,2)+c(1,2)) \\
& - k \cdot c1^2 \cdot \max(x(\alpha)-\widetilde{\beta},0))^2
\end{aligned}
\tag{6.20}
$$

The expected terminal value is:

$$
\begin{aligned}
E[TV] = {} & (1-\alpha)((1+r(0,2))^2 - c1 \cdot (1+f_{rf}(0,1,2)+E[c(1,2)]) \\
& - k \cdot c1^2 \cdot E[\max(x(\alpha)-\widetilde{\beta},0)^2]
\end{aligned}
\tag{6.21}
$$

Note that a progressive penalty spread function is a natural way of introducing the variance of $\widetilde{\beta}$ into the analysis, as it holds:

$$\begin{aligned}
Var(\max(x(\alpha)-\widetilde{\beta},0)) &= E[\max(x(\alpha)-\widetilde{\beta},0)^2]-E[\max(x(\alpha)-\widetilde{\beta},0)]^2\\
\Leftrightarrow E[\max(x(\alpha)-\widetilde{\beta},0)^2] &= Var(\max(x(\alpha)-\widetilde{\beta},0))+E[\max(x(\alpha)-\widetilde{\beta},0)]^2\\
E[TV] &= (1-\alpha)((1+r(0,2))^2-c\cdot(1+f_{rf}(0,1,2)+E[c(1,2)])\\
&\quad -k\cdot(1+r(0,1))^2\cdot(Var(\max(x(\alpha)-\widetilde{\beta},0))\\
&\quad +E[\max(x(\alpha)-\widetilde{\beta},0)]^2)
\end{aligned}$$

Hence, progressive penalty spreads imply balancing expected roll-over gain to the cost-weighted variance of funding shortage.

Using lemma (C.2) on page 203, the derivation of (6.21) w.r.t. α yields:

$$\begin{aligned}
\frac{\partial E[TV]}{\partial \alpha} &= -(c2-c1\cdot c12)\\
&\quad -k\cdot c1^2\cdot(-2)(x(\alpha)-E[\widetilde{\beta}|\widetilde{\beta}\leq x(\alpha)])P(\widetilde{\beta}\leq x(\alpha))\\
&= -(c2-c1\cdot c12)\\
&\quad +2\cdot k\cdot c1^2\cdot((1-\alpha)-E[\widetilde{\beta}|\widetilde{\beta}\leq(1-\alpha)])P(\widetilde{\beta}\leq(1-\alpha))
\end{aligned}$$

We obtain the same optimality condition with the exception that the constant s is substituted:[9]

$$P[\widetilde{\beta}\leq(1-\alpha^*)]\cdot\underbrace{k\cdot 2\cdot c1[(1-\alpha^*)-E[\widetilde{\beta}|\widetilde{\beta}\leq(1-\alpha^*)]}_{\text{Previous s}}=f_s(0,1,2)-E[s(1,2)] \tag{6.22}$$

The former constant penalty spread is substituted with an expression that reflects how much the required funding $(1-\alpha^*)$ exceeds the available funding $\widetilde{\beta}$. The expression $E[\widetilde{\beta}|\widetilde{\beta}\leq(1-\alpha^*)]$ is the expected funding capacity shortfall, i.e. the expected funding capacity given a funding shortage.

As $E[\widetilde{\beta}|\widetilde{\beta}\leq(1-\alpha)]\leq(1-\alpha)$, the expected marginal costs are always positive.

In order to study the sensitivity of the optimal roll-over volume to the type of spread function, we choose the piecewise density as particular funding stochastic.

Compared to the cost function with constant spreads, those with volume-dependent spreads incorporate the expected funding capacity shortfall.

[9] Note that we are situated within the local model where transfer prices are outside the optimization programme. Therefore, we omitted the transfer prices.

Based on the density (6.16), the expected funding capacity shortfall of the piecewise linear density is noted as follows:

$$E[\widetilde{\beta}|\widetilde{\beta} \le x] = \begin{cases} 0 & ,x < 0 \\ x^2 \cdot [0.15 - \frac{0.8}{3}x] & ,0 \le x \le 25\% \\ 0.05 \cdot x^2 + 0.00208 & ,25\% \le x \le 75\% \\ x^2 \cdot [-10.45 + \frac{28}{3}x] + 1.970833 & ,75\% \le x \le 1 \end{cases} \tag{6.23}$$

The expected marginal cost with constant spreads is:

$$E_g[C^c(x)] = s \cdot \begin{cases} 0 & ,x < 0 \\ 0.3 \cdot \widetilde{\beta} - 0.4 \cdot \widetilde{\beta}^2 & ,0 \le x \le 25\% \\ 0.025 + 0.1 \cdot \widetilde{\beta} & ,25\% \le x \le 75\% \\ 7.9 - 20.9 \cdot \widetilde{\beta} + 14 \cdot \widetilde{\beta}^2 & ,75\% \le x \le 1 \\ 1 & ,1 < \widetilde{\beta} \end{cases}$$

Based on (6.18) and (6.23), the expected marginal cost function with volume dependent spread is formulated as:

$$E_g[C^p(x)] = 2k \cdot c1 \cdot \begin{cases} 0 & ,x < 0 \\ (0.3 \cdot x - 0.4 \cdot x^2) \\ \cdot (x - x^2 \cdot (0.15 - \frac{0.8}{3}x)) & ,0 \le x \le 25\% \\ (0.025 + 0.1 \cdot x) \\ \cdot (x - (0.05x^2 + 0.00208)) & ,25\% \le x \le 75\% \\ (7.9 - 20.9 \cdot x + 14 \cdot x^2) \\ \cdot (x - (-10.45x^2 + \frac{28}{3}x^3 + 1.970833)) & ,75\% \le x \le 1 \\ (1 - \underbrace{0.8542}_{= E[\widetilde{\beta}]}) & ,1 < x \end{cases}$$

Figure 6.5 plots the expected marginal cost functions with constant and volume dependent penalty cost for a given 1-period risk-free rate of 5% and a scaling factor of 0.05. With respect to figure 6.5, we make the following observations:

- Cost functions differ for high volumes.
  The different definitions of penalty cost lead to a substantial divergence of cost functions for high roll-over volumes ($\geq 90\%$). The shape for lower roll-over volumes is primarily determined by funding stochastics. The reason is obvious: as the progressive spreads are volume-linked, the particularity of the spread definition is more pronounced

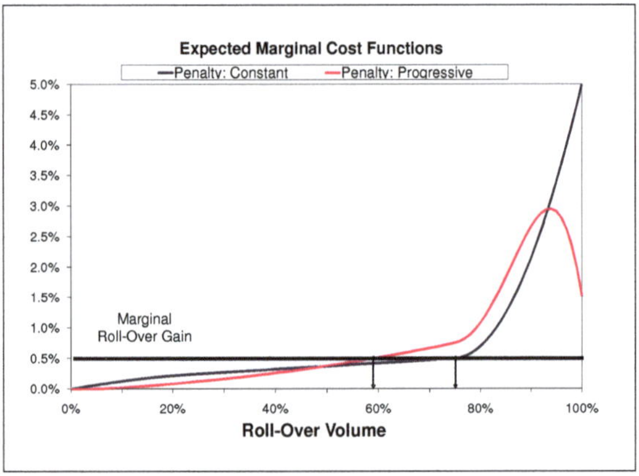

Fig. 6.5 Cost Functios for Constant and Progressive Spreads

for high volumes. The hump indicates that the expected funding-capacity shortfall increases faster than the roll-over volume. This results from the skewness of the density: for high volumes, the volume and its probability quickly increase. As both factors are the main inputs, the expected funding-capacity shortfall increases faster than the shortfall volume.

- The impact of the spread definition on the roll-over volume is of second order.
  The roll-over volume is determined in the linear region where the shape of cost functions is similar for constant and progressive penalty spreads alike. Although the spread definition also implies minor changes in the linear region, they are of second order compared to the changes in the non-linear region. The same impact can easily be effected by adjusting the constant spread level or the scaling factor k for progressive spreads. In particular, the spread definition does not change the fact that the optimal roll-over volumes are determined in the linear region.

The optimal volumes are of 58,78% for progressive and 75% for constant penalty cost. If the constant penalty cost were slightly higher, the order of optimal volumes would be inversed. The model instability results from the extreme stochastic of the funding capacity that places 90% probability on the last quartile.

The fact that the choice of the density function affects the optimal results more than the choice of the penalty function can be seen in figure 6.6. Figure 6.6 suggests that the expected marginal cost function can be split up into a linear and non-linear part. The former lies between 0% and approximately 80%. The distribution function determines the length of the linear part whereas the spread definition determines the shape of the non-linear part. As the roll-over volume is determined in the linear part, the choice of the distribution function affects the optimal volume more than the choice of the spread function. Figure 6.6 shows that the cost functions of the same distribution are closer than the cost functions of the same spread.

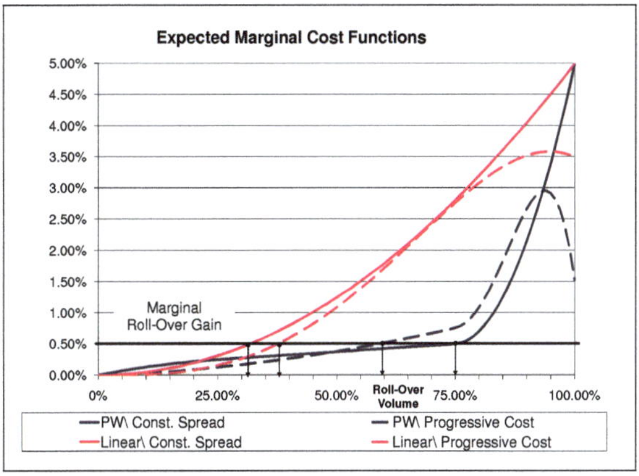

Fig. 6.6 Comparison of Expected Marginal Cost Functions

Table 6.1. summarizes the optimal volumes for different distribution and spread functions. This underlines the importance of the density choice: the distances between the

Table 6.1 Optimal Roll-Over Volumes

Spread Density	Linear	Piece-wise	Distance
Constant	32%	75%	33%
Progressive	37%	59%	22%
Distance	5%	16%	—

optimal volumes of different densities are 22% and 33% whereas the difference between the optimal volumes of different spread definitions are 5% and 16%.

6.2.4 Comparison with the Literature

Figure 6.7 situates the roll-over model within the bank liquidity model. The variables and optimization programme of Origination are greyed. Origination operates on the expected cash flow $\mu^A_{q_k}$. We introduced β as stochastic long-term funding capacity. The second stochastic driver is the funding spread $c(1,2)$ that is uncertain in q_0. The long-term interest rate position was closed: future rates are replaced by forward rates. Origination maximizes the expected terminal return from the portfolio of expected cash flows. Figure 6.8 summarizes the model by Dempster and Ireland (1988).[10]. Their model is driven by interest rates. Our model, however, is driven by the key liquidity variables funding capacity and funding spread. Their model is not a liquidity model because their funding capacity is deterministic. It is rather an interest rate management model. With the existence of interest rate swaps, interest rates do not determine a funding profile. A target

[10] We introduced the model in section 1.2.2.1.

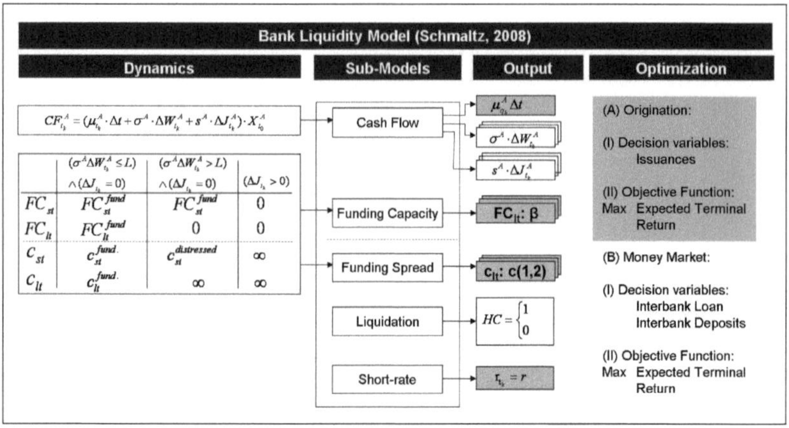

Fig. 6.7 Funding Optimization within the Bank Liquidity Model

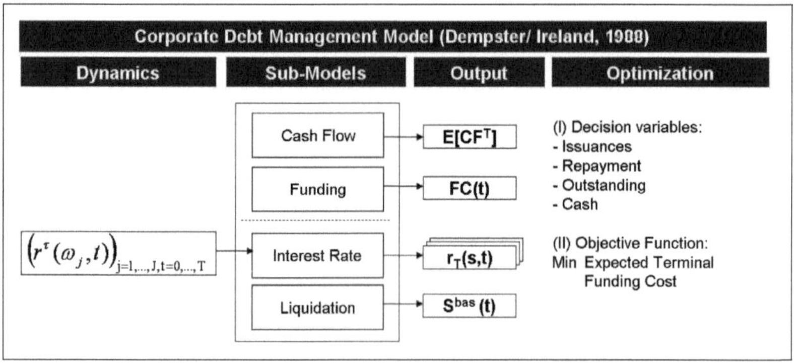

Fig. 6.8 Corporate Debt Model by Dempster/ Ireland (1988)

interest-rate position can be established given any funding profile. They account for market liquidity by considering a deterministic bid-ask spread. The optimization programme of Origination does not require a liquidation model because Origination does not bear cash flow risk. Thus, there is no need to unexpectedly liquidate assets.

Like us, they optimize an expected terminal value. However, they minimize the terminal cost. We maximize the terminal return.

6.2.5 Conclusion

Origination runs a Maturity Mismatch Strategy. It optimizes the funding-maturity profile by trading-off benefits and risks of short-term versus long-term funding. The benefits of short-term funding are low current funding spreads while the risks of short-term funding are future elevated spreads and insufficient roll-over volume.

Origination maximizes the expected terminal value of the portfolio of expected cash flows. We demonstrated that the negligence of roll-over risk leads to extreme funding profiles, 100% short-term or 100% long-term. We introduced roll-over risk that translates a funding constraint into a penalty spread. We illustrated that to consider roll-over risk leads to optimal funding profiles where short and long-term funding coexist.

Further, we analysed the sensitivity of the optimal volume with respect to the funding stochastics and penalty spread definition. We found that the optimal volume is much more sensitive to the funding stochastics than to the definition of the penalty spread. Thus, particular attention must be paid to the estimation of the distribution function of the funding capacity.[11]

Finally, we compared our roll-over optimization with the debt-management model presented by Dempster and Ireland (1988). Our optimization programme is similar with respect to the objective function. However, their model is driven by interest rates whereas our Origination model is driven by two key liquidity variables, namely funding capacity and funding spread.

6.3 Money Market Department

6.3.1 The Model

6.3.1.1 Setup

According to section 6.1, Money Market manages the following cash flow on a daily basis:

$$CF_{t_k}^{MMD} = \underbrace{\mu \cdot \Delta t}_{\substack{\text{Deterministic Cash Flow} \\ \text{Next Quarter}}} + \underbrace{\sigma^A \cdot \Delta W_{t_k}^A}_{\text{Brownian Component}} \tag{6.24}$$

$$CF_{t_0} : \text{ given}$$

[11] The estimation of the functing capacity has been discussed in section 4.3.3.

We approximate (6.24) by the following binomial cash flow model:[12]

$$CF_{t_0} := \mu_0 \cdot \Delta t$$

$$CF_{t_k} := \begin{cases} CF^+, & P[CF_{t_k} = CF^+] = p^{CF} = \frac{1}{2} \\ -CF^-, & P[CF_{t_k} = CF^-] = (1 - p^{CF}) = \frac{1}{2} \end{cases}$$

Being:

$$CF^+ = f(\mu, \sigma) = \sigma\sqrt{\Delta t} + \mu \Delta t$$

$$CF^- = g(\mu, \sigma) = \sigma\sqrt{\Delta t} - \mu \Delta t$$

Money Market faces a net cash inflow of CF^+ with probability p^{CF} and a net cash outflow CF^- with probability $1 - p^{CF}$. The initial cash flow CF_{t_0} is given. Note that the sum $(CF^+ + CF^-)$ refers to the amount of Brownian cash flow risk:

$$(CF^+ + CF^-) = 2\sigma\sqrt{\Delta t} \tag{6.25}$$

Apart from cash flows, funding is stochastic. The idea of a reserve given a stochastic funding capacity is formulated as follows:

$$FC_{t_{k+1}} = \max(R_{t_k}, FC_{t_k} + \xi_{t_{k+1}})$$

Being:

FC_{t_k} : Funding Capacity in t_k

R_{t_k} : Reserve in t_k

$\xi_{t_{k+1}}$: Funding Capacity Shock

The funding capacity is exposed to shocks $\xi_{t_{k+1}}$ which can reduce or extend funding capacity. A reserve is useful as the funding capacity can not fall below the reserve R_{t_k}. The reason is that a reserve is funded as well.[13] Assuming that used funding cannot be cancelled, the funding capacity is floored at the reserve level. Hence, the distribution of $FC_{t_{k+1}}$ depends on the reserve decision. For technical reasons, this is not allowed.[14] We avoid that drawback by translating the volume constraint into elevated funding cost.

[12] Appendix C.2.1 derives this result.

[13] A reserve is a combination of funding and investment where funding has a longer maturity than investment.

[14] See [Marohn, 1998, p.94].

Our funding distribution is motivated as follows:

k = 1,...,T:

$$r_{t_k}^{-} = r^{-} + c_{t_k} \tag{6.26}$$

$$= r^{-} + \begin{cases} c_{st}^{\text{distressed}}, & p^c \\ c_{st}^{\text{fund.}}, & 1 - p^c \end{cases} \tag{6.27}$$

$$= r^{-} + \begin{cases} c_{st}^{\text{distressed}}, & p^c \\ 0, & 1 - p^c \end{cases} \tag{6.28}$$

$$= \begin{cases} r^{--}, & p^c \\ r^{-}, & 1 - p^c \end{cases} \tag{6.29}$$

k=0:

$$r_0^{-} = r^{-} \tag{6.30}$$

(6.26) suggests that the gross funding costs $r_{t_k}^{-}$ are the sum of the risk-free funding rate r^{-} and the funding spread c_{t_k}. We assume the risk-free rate to be constant. The stochastic enters by the funding spread that translates funding capacity constraint into a price. The funding spread models different funding scenarios: (6.27) states that the funding spread is the fundamental short-term funding spread in normal market circumstances. In distressed circumstances, it is the distressed short-term spread. (6.28) assumes that the fundamental funding spread is zero.[15] In distressed funding, the elevated funding spread has to be paid reflecting the limited available volume of external funding.

To solve the Money Market optimization, only gross funding rates are relevant. Thus, (6.29) is the notation that we use: r^{-} refers to the fundamental funding cost in normal, r^{--} to the funding cost in distressed markets. With probability $1 - p^c$, funding conditions will be at the fundamental rate. With probability p^c, external funding is expensive. Hence, our capacity model has only two states: unlimited or reduced external funds. (6.30) states that the funding rate at t_0 is the fundamental rate r^{-}.

For investments, we assume a constant rate r^{+}.

The model is based on the key assumption (6.31):

$$0 < r^{+} < r^{-} << r^{--} \tag{6.31}$$

(6.31) states that it is costly to set up a reserve ($r^{+} < r^{-}$), but even more costly to have no reserve if funding is distressed ($r^{-} << r^{--}$). The difference between the fundamental funding and investment rate ($r^{-} - r^{+}$) is the bid-ask spread that accounts for market illiquidity. It reflects reserve cost.

Thus, Money Market has to trade off reserve cost ($r^{-} - r^{+}$) against elevated funding cost ($r^{--} - r^{-}$). In section 5.2.2, we suggested that a reserve stabilizes funding cost. Here, the reserve stabilizes funding cost at a level r^{-}. Without a reserve, the cost can go up to r^{--}.

[15] In fact, prior to the subprime crisis, the spreads for unsecured funding on the interbank market were very small.

Money Market determines the optimal reserve by solving (6.32) with constraints (6.33):

$$\max_{d_t} E[\sum_{t=0}^{T-1} (d_{t,1}^{+} + d_{t,2}^{+} \cdot 2) \cdot r^{+} + (d_{t,1}^{-} + d_{t,2}^{-} \cdot 2) \cdot r_t^{-}] \tag{6.32}$$

$$\text{s.t.}:$$

$$d_{t,1} + d_{t,2} = CF_t + d_{t-1,1} + d_{t-2,2} \tag{6.33}$$

Being:

$d_{t,m}$: Interbank Deal at t with maturity m

$d_{t,m}^{+}$: Interbank Deposit

$d_{t,m}^{-}$: Interbank Loan

$$d_{t,m} = d_{t,m}^{+} + d_{t,m}^{-} = \begin{cases} d_{t,m}^{+} + 0, & d_{t,m}^{+} \geq 0 \\ 0 + d_{t,m}^{-}, & d_{t,m}^{-} < 0 \end{cases} \tag{6.34}$$

(6.34) states that either loans or deposits are held for the same maturity, but not both at the same time.

We define:

$$\begin{aligned} [x]^{+} &= x^{+} := \max(x,0) \\ [x]^{-} &= x^{-} := \min(x,0) \end{aligned} \tag{6.35}$$

In contrast to the split notation, our x^{-} is negative. When applying (6.35) to the interbank deals, deposits are the positive, loans the negative part of $d_{t,m}$:

$$\text{Deposits}: d_{t,m}^{+} := \max(d_{t,m}, 0)$$
$$\text{Loans}: d_{t,m}^{-} := \min(d_{t,m}, 0)$$

Money Market maximizes the expected return by an optimal mix of interbank funding (-) and investments (+) $d_{t,m}^{+/-}$ whereas t refers to the time in which the funding/investment starts and m to the maturity. To take decisions in t, Money Market can use all information up to t:

$$d_{t,i} \sim \sigma(CF_s, r_s^{-} : s \leq t) \tag{6.36}$$

(6.36) states that decisions at t are taken knowing the cash flow and the prevailing funding conditions in t plus all cash flows and funding conditions of the past. However, decision taking does not use information beyond t.

The optimization has to honour the accounting constraint (6.33). (6.33) ensures that funds cannot 'leave the model'. The right hand side of (6.33) summarizes the sources, the left hand side the use of funds. (6.33) is an intertemporal constraint. To manage Bronwian cash flow deviations, Money Market receives the Brownian transfer prices.

The performance of Money Market is:

$$TP^B(\sigma^{MMD}) + \max_{d_t} E[\sum_{t=0}^{T-1} (d_{t,1}^+ + d_{t,2}^+ \cdot 2) \cdot r^+ + (d_{t,1}^- + d_{t,2}^- \cdot 2) \cdot r_t^-] \tag{6.37}$$

s.t. :

$$d_{t,1} + d_{t,2} = CF_t(\sigma^{MMD}, \mu^{MMD}) + d_{t-1,1} + d_{t-2,2} \tag{6.38}$$

(6.37) states that the performance of Money Market is measured relative to the received Brownian transfer prices. Hence, the transfer price is Money Market's break-even. The volume of Brownian cash flow risk determines the cash flow distribution in (6.38). Therefore, the optimal reserve policy depends on the amount of Brownian cash flow risk.

6.3.1.2 Choice of Model Horizon

As the model complexity grows exponentially in the number of time points, we choose the shortest model horizon (T=3) that still allows for a dynamic setup, i.e. that allows for t_0- and t_1-reserve decisions.

The explicit setup for T=3 is given by (6.39).

$$\begin{aligned}
\max_d E[&(d_{0,1}^+ + d_{0,2}^+ \cdot 2) \cdot r^+ + (d_{0,1}^- + d_{0,2}^- \cdot 2) \cdot r_0^- \\
&+ (d_{1,1}^+ + d_{1,2}^+ \cdot 2) \cdot r^+ + (d_{1,1}^- + d_{1,2}^- \cdot 2) \cdot r_1^- \\
&+ d_{2,1}^+ \cdot r^+ + d_{2,1}^- \cdot r_2^-]
\end{aligned} \tag{6.39}$$

s.t. :

$$\begin{aligned}
t = 0 &: d_{0,1} + d_{0,2} = CF_0 \\
t = 1 &: d_{1,1} + d_{1,2} = CF_1 + d_{0,1} \\
t = 2 &: d_{2,1} = CF_2 + d_{1,1} + d_{0,2}
\end{aligned}$$

The resulting model dynamic with its decision variables is summarized in figure 6.9. Node [i,j] refers to a cash flow scenario i (i = 1: inflow, i= 2: outflow) and funding scenario j (j = 1: normal funding, j= 2: funding crisis). Our variables of interest are 2-period reserve variables $d_{t,2}$. Replacing all 1-period variables and using (6.35), we obtain (6.40): Note that according to figure 6.9, 2-period decision variables are only at t_0 ($d_{0,2}$) and t_1 ($d_{1,2}[i,j]$).

$$\begin{aligned}
\max_{d_{02}, d_{1,2}} E[&([CF_0 - d_{02}]^+ + 2 \cdot [d_{02}]^+) r^+ \\
&+ ([CF_0 - d_{02}]^- + 2 \cdot [d_{02}]^-) r^- \\
&+ ([CF_1 + CF_0 - d_{02} - d_{12}]^+ + 2 \cdot [d_{12}]^+) r^+ \\
&+ ([CF_1 + CF_0 - d_{02} - d_{12}]^- + 2 \cdot [d_{12}]^-) r_1^- \\
&+ ([CF_0 + CF_1 + CF_2 - d_{12}]^+) r^+ \\
&+ ([CF_0 + CF_1 + CF_2 - d_{12}]^-) r_2^- \\
&]
\end{aligned} \tag{6.40}$$

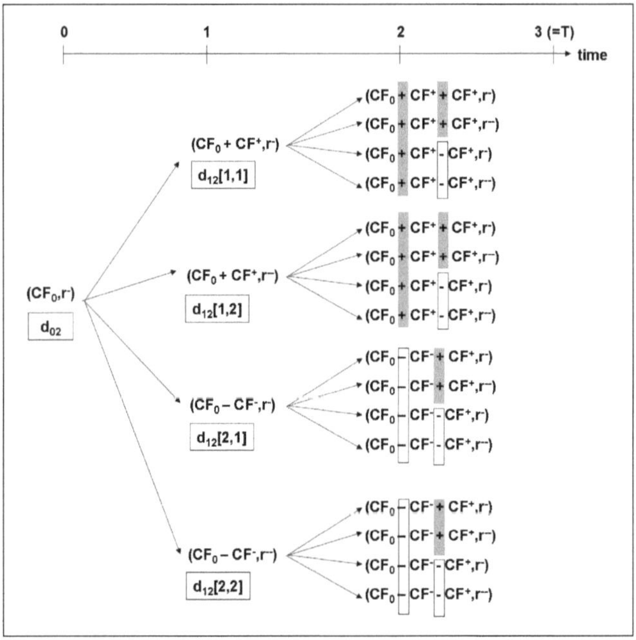

Fig. 6.9 Tree of Cumulated Cash Flows

The objective function can be decomposed into three terms:

1. t_0-terms that only depend on d_{02}

$$
\begin{aligned}
& E[\sum_{t=0}^{2}([CF_0 - d_{02}]^+ + 2\cdot[d_{02}]^+)r^+ \\
& + ([CF_0 - d_{02}]^- + 2\cdot[d_{02}]^-)r^- \\
& \dots \\
]
\end{aligned}
$$

2. t_1-terms that depend on both d_{02} and d_{12}

$$
\begin{aligned}
& E[\sum_{t=0}^{2}\dots \\
& + ([CF_1 + CF_0 - d_{02} - d_{12}]^+ + 2\cdot[d_{12}]^+)r^+ \\
& + ([CF_1 + CF_0 - d_{02} - d_{12}]^- + 2\cdot[d_{12}]^-)r_1^- \\
& \dots]
\end{aligned}
$$

3. t_2-terms that only depend on d_{12}

$$
\begin{aligned}
&E[\sum_{t=0}^{2}\\
&\dots\\
&+([CF_0+CF_1+CF_2-d_{12}]^+)r^+\\
&+([CF_0+CF_1+CF_2-d_{12}]^-)r_2^-\\
&]
\end{aligned}
$$

The t_1-terms constitute the linking element between the decision variables. Without the t_1-terms we could separately optimize in t_0 and t_2.

Replacing the expectation by its explicit presentation, the complete intertemporal objective function is given by (6.41):

$$
\begin{aligned}
\max_{d_{02},d_{12}[i,j]} & ([CF_0-d_{02}]^+ + 2\cdot[d_{02}]^+)r^+ \\
& ([CF_0-d_{02}]^- + 2\cdot[d_{02}]^-)r^- \\
& +p^{CF}(1-p^c)\cdot(\\
& ([CF_0+CF^+-d_{02}-d_{12}[1,1]]^+ + 2\cdot[d_{12}[1,1]]^+)r^+ \\
& +([CF_0+CF^+-d_{02}-d_{12}[1,1]]^- + 2\cdot[d_{12}[1,1]]^-)r^- \\
& +p^{CF}(1-p^c)\cdot((([CF_0+CF^+ +CF^+ -d_{12}[1,1]]^+)r^+ \\
& +([CF_0+CF^+ +CF^+ -d_{12}[1,1]]^-)r^-) \\
& +p^{CF}p^c\cdot((([CF_0+CF^+ +CF^+ -d_{12}[1,1]]^+)r^+ \\
& +([CF_0+CF^+ +CF^+ -d_{12}[1,1]]^-)r^{--}) \\
& +(1-p^{CF})(1-p^c)\cdot((([CF_0+CF^+ -CF^- -d_{12}[1,1]]^+)r^+ \\
& +([CF_0+CF^+ -CF^- -d_{12}[1,1]]^-)r^-) \\
& +(1-p^{CF})p^c\cdot((([CF_0+CF^+ -CF^- -d_{12}[1,1]]^+)r^+ \\
& +([CF_0+CF^+ -CF^- -d_{12}[1,1]]^-)r^{--}) \\
&)\text{ End of Node }[1,1] \\
& +p^{CF}p^c\cdot(([CF_0+CF^+-d_{02}-d_{12}[1,2]]^+ + 2\cdot[d_{12}[1,2]]^+)r^+ \\
& +([CF_0+CF^+-d_{02}-d_{12}[1,2]]^- + 2\cdot[d_{12}[1,2]]^-)r^{--} \\
& +p^{CF}(1-p^c)\cdot((([CF_0+CF^+ +CF^+ -d_{12}[1,2]]^+)r^+ \\
& +([CF_0+CF^+ +CF^+ -d_{12}[1,2]]^-)r^-) \\
& +p^{CF}p^c\cdot((([CF_0+CF^+ +CF^+ -d_{12}[1,2]]^+)r^+ \\
& +([CF_0+CF^+ +CF^+ -d_{12}[1,2]]^-)r^{--}) \\
& +(1-p^{CF})(1-p^c)\cdot((([CF_0+CF^+ -CF^- -d_{12}[1,2]]^+)r^+ \\
& +([CF_0+CF^+ -CF^- -d_{12}[1,2]]^-)r^-) \\
& +(1-p^{CF})p^c\cdot((([CF_0+CF^+ -CF^- -d_{12}[1,2]]^+)r^+ \\
& +([CF_0+CF^+ -CF^- -d_{12}[1,2]]^-)r^{--}) \\
&)\text{ End of Node }[1,2]
\end{aligned}
\tag{6.41}
$$

$$
\begin{aligned}
&+(1-p^{CF})(1-p^c)\cdot(([CF_0-CF^- -d_{02}-d_{12}[2,1]]^+ +2\cdot[d_{12}[2,1]]^+)r^+\\
&+([CF_0-CF^- -d_{02}-d_{12}[2,1]]^- +2\cdot[d_{12}[2,1]]^-)r^-\\
&+p^{CF}(1-p^c)\cdot(([CF_0-CF^- +CF^+ -d_{12}[2,1]]^+)r^+\\
&+([CF_0-CF^- +CF^+ -d_{12}[2,1]]^-)r^-)\\
&+p^{CF}p^c\cdot(([CF_0-CF^- +CF^+ -d_{12}[2,1]]^+)r^+\\
&+([CF_0-CF^- +CF^+ -d_{12}[2,1]]^-)r^{--})\\
&+(1-p^{CF})(1-p^c)\cdot(([CF_0-CF^- -CF^- -d_{12}[2,1]]^+)r^+\\
&+([CF_0-CF^- -CF^- -d_{12}[2,1]]^-)r^-)\\
&+(1-p^{CF})p^c\cdot(([CF_0-CF^- -CF^- -d_{12}[2,1]]^+)r^+\\
&+([CF_0-CF^- -CF^- -d_{12}[2,1]]^-)r^{--})\\
&\quad)\text{ End of Node [2,1]}\\
&\quad +(1-p^{CF})p^c\cdot(([CF_0-CF^- -d_{02}-d_{12}[2,1]]^+ +2\cdot[d_{12}[2,1]]^+)r^+\\
&+([CF_0-CF^- -d_{02}-d_{12}[2,1]]^- +2\cdot[d_{12}[2,1]]^-)r^{--}\\
&+p^{CF}(1-p^c)\cdot(([CF_0-CF^- +CF^+ -d_{12}[2,1]]^+)r^+\\
&+([CF_0-CF^- +CF^+ -d_{12}[2,1]]^-)r^-)\\
&+p^{CF}p^c\cdot(([CF_0-CF^- +CF^+ -d_{12}[2,1]]^+)r^+\\
&+([CF_0-CF^- +CF^+ -d_{12}[2,1]]^-)r^{--})\\
&+(1-p^{CF})(1-p^c)\cdot(([CF_0-CF^- -CF^- -d_{12}[2,1]]^+)r^+\\
&+([CF_0-CF^- -CF^- -d_{12}[2,1]]^-)r^-)\\
&+(1-p^{CF})p^c\cdot(([CF_0-CF^- -CF^- -d_{12}[2,1]]^+)r^+\\
&+([CF_0-CF^- -CF^- -d_{12}[2,1]]^-)r^{--})\\
&\quad)\text{ End of Node [2,2]}
\end{aligned}
$$

To solve (6.41), we proceed in three steps:

1. Optimality candidates
   The optimization programme is linear in the decision variables. Hence, the optimal investment/funding mix is either a corner solution or unbounded. Therefore, we determine the potential corners and show that the problem is always bounded in section 6.3.2 ('Optimality Candidates').
2. t_1-Decisions
   After having determined the candidates we determine optimal decisions for t_1 ($d_{1,2}[i,j]$) for given t_0-decisions in section 6.3.3 ('t1-Decisions').
3. t_0-decisions
   After having determined optimal t_1-decisions for all possible t_0-decisions, we determine the optimal t_0-decision in section 6.3.4 ('t0-Decisions').

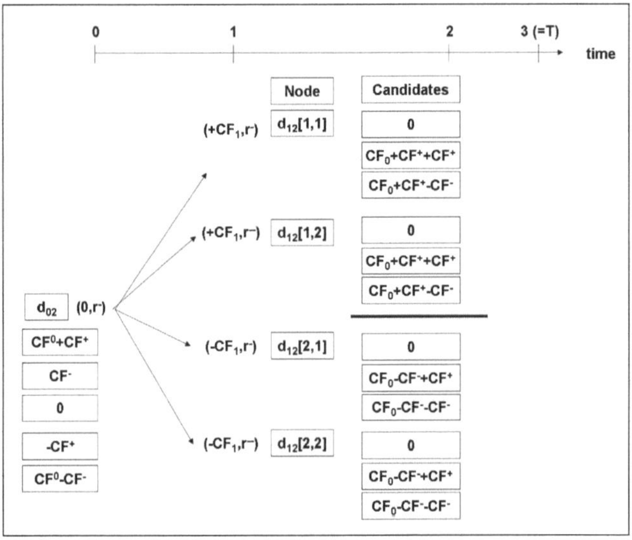

Fig. 6.10 Optimality Candidates

6.3.2 Optimality Candidates

The value function is only continuous piecewise as it contains max()- and min()-functions. In order to verify that the optimal decision is never $\pm\infty$, it is sufficient to check whether the optimum of unbounded intervals $[-\infty,k]$ or $[l,+\infty]$ is the lower/higher well-defined interval boundary.

Section C.2.2 checks this condition and identifies candidates.

We find that the optimization problem is well posed, i.e. that an optimal solution always exists. The optimal solution is a combination of the eligible d_{02}- and $d_{12}[i,j]$-values. Figure 6.10 summarizes the optimal candidates $d*_{1,2}[i,j]$ and $d*_{0,2}$. After having determined the optimal candidates, we have to determine the optimal decision vector $(d_{0,2},d_{1,2}[1,1],d_{1,2}[1,2],d_{1,2}[2,1],d_{1,2}[2,2])$.

As we are facing a 2-stage optimization problem, we proceed as follows:

1. Optimize across $d_{12}[i,j]$ for given d_{02}
   As we have five d_{02} candidates, we obtain 5 trees with a different root.
2. Optimize across d_{02} for optimal $d_{12}[i,j]$-combinations
   After having found the optimal $d_{12}[i,j]$-combination for each d_{02}, we optimize across the d_{02}

As we found 5 candidates for t_0 and 3 in each of the 4 t_1-nodes, there are $5 \cdot 3^4 = 405$ possible decision vectors (value functions). The following arguments are best understood using a numerical example. The cash flow dynamic is given in figure 6.11. The bank starts

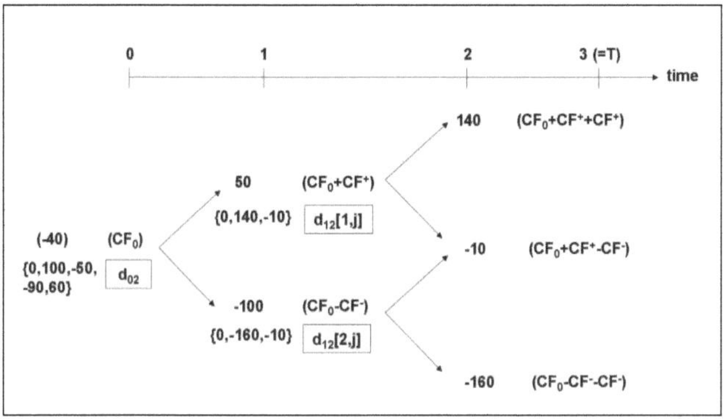

Fig. 6.11 Setup Numerical Example, $r^+ = 4\%$, $r^- = 5\%$, $r^{--} = 100\%$

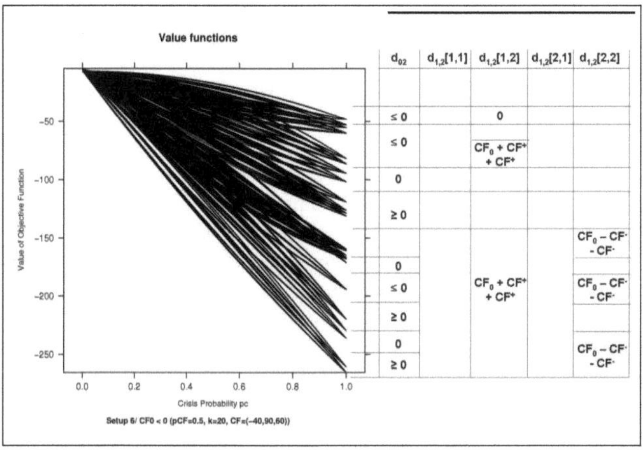

Fig. 6.12 All Possible Value Functions with Patterns

with a cash flow deficit of -40. In t_1, there might be a net inflow of 90 or a net outflow of 60, each with a probability of 0.5.

The bundle of possible value functions under this setup is given by figure 6.12. Based on figure 6.12, we make the following observations:

1. Value Functions are decreasing in crisis probability
2. Value functions are negative in that cash flow setup
   As the tree is skewed to deficits, no reserve policy achieves a positive return.
3. Value functions are either linear or parabolic
4. Value functions intersect
   There is no dominant policy across all crisis probabilities. However, many value functions intersect for small crisis probabilities.

In the evolution of value functions, patterns (bundles of value functions) can be distinguished for $p^c = 1$. In order to identify a pattern, we plot the common variables for each region on the right hand side.

Obviously, the worst policy are investments today ($d_{0,2} \geq 0$), investments in node [1,2] ($d_{1,2}[1,2] = +140$) and reserve setting in a funding crisis ($d_{1,2}[2,2] = -160$). The same is valid for future policy, but to choose ($d_{0,2} = 0$) today is the second worst policy. Whenever there is no entry, it means that there are several combinations of that variable at work and no pattern is observable.

We can state that no dominant pattern is distinguishable and we need a systematic approach to determine the optimal dynamic reserve policy.

6.3.3 Reserve Decisions in t1

The optimization programme is solved backwards. Hence, we first determine optimal future decisions for given t_0-decision. Secondly, we optimize across all t_0-decisions having derived optimal t_1-decisions.

We describe our approach for the [1,1]-node. All other nodes are solved in a similar manner.

In order to determine the optimal decision $d_{1,2}[1,1]$ in node [1,1], only expressions containing $d_{1,2}[1,1]$ are of interest. The value function consists of mixed $d_{0,2}/d_{1,2}[1,1]$-terms (e.g. $[CF_0 + CF^+ - d_{0,2} - d_{1,2}[1,1]]$...) and exclusive $d_{1,2}[1,1]$-terms (e.g. $[CF_0 + CF^+ + CF^+ - d_{1,2}[1,1]]$). Therefore, we obtain 15 equations (3 optimal $d_{1,2}[1,1]$-candidates x 5 optimal $d_{0,2}$-candidates) that are taken as given. Each expression of the value function is weighted with r^+, r^- or r^{--}. In a tabular form, the $d_{1,2}[1,1]$-value function is given by table 6.2. For table 6.2 the following color codes apply:

- $d_{02} = CF_0 + CF^+$
- $d_{02} = CF^-$
- $d_{02} = 0$
- $d_{02} = -CF^+$
- $d_{02} = CF_0 - CF^-$

The expressions in standard text are the same for all d_{02}. The first column lists the optimal candidates for t_1 $\{0, CF_0 + CF^+ + CF^+, CF_0 + CF^+ - CF^-\}$. The second column contains positive t_1-terms (that are invested). The third column contains negative t_1-terms that are funded at the standard rate r^-.[16] The fourth column contains t_2-amounts in form of expected funding cost $E[r_f]$.

The coloured fields represent 'mixed terms' that depend on both d_{02} and d_{12}-decision. Hence, the value function $f(d_{0,2} = 0, d_{1,2}[1,1] = 0)$ is given by (6.42).

[16] Note that node [1,1] is a non-crisis node. Node [1,2] contains the same expressions, but the negative expressions are funded at r^{--}.

Table 6.2 Intervalwise Derivations w.r.t. $d_{12}[1,i]$

[1] $d_{12}[1,1]$	[2] r^+	[3] r^-	[4] $E[r_f]$
0	$[CF_0+CF^+-CF^-]$ $p^{CF}\cdot(CF^++CF^-)$ $[CF_0+CF^+]$ $[CF_0+CF^++CF^+]$ (CF^++CF^-) $[CF_0+CF^+-CF^-]$		
$CF_0+CF^++CF^+$	$2\cdot[CF_0+CF^++CF^+]$	$-[CF_0+CF^++CF^+]$ $-(CF^++CF^-)$ $-(CF^+)$ $-[CF_0+CF^+-CF^-]$	$-(1-p^{CF})\cdot(CF^-+CF^+)$
$CF_0+CF^+-CF^-$	$2\cdot[CF_0+CF^+-CF^-]$ $p^{CF}\cdot(CF^++CF^-)$ (CF^-) (CF^++CF^-)	$-[CF_0-CF^-+CF^+]$ $-[CF_0-CF^--CF^-]$	

$$f(d_{0,2}=0,d_{1,2}[1,1]=CF_0+CF^+)= \qquad (6.42)$$
$$CF_0+CF^+-CF^-+p^{CF}\cdot(CF^++CF^-)$$
$$+[CF_0+CF^+]\cdot r^+$$

Of course, table 6.2 already contains an assumption about the cash flow profile: it assumes that $[CF_0+CF^+]$ is positive. It also assumes that $[CF_0+CF^+-CF^-]$ is positive.

In fact, the value function contains cash flow expressions that can be positive or negative depending on the cash flow configuration. These expressions are given in []. Expressions with determined signs are given in (). For example, (CF^++CF^-) is always positive. All possible cash flow setups are summarized in figure 6.3.3. On the left side, the scenarios are numbered. The lines indicate the possible locations of the 'zero'-line. Expressions above a line are positive, those below a line are negative. The scenarios are numbered from 9 (all expressions are positive) to 1 (all expressions are negative). In scenario 1 all expressions are below the zero line. Hence, this is a scenario in which even the highest value $CF_0+CF^++CF^+$ is still negative because the model starts with a high deficit and incoming cash flows CF^+ are too low to overcompensate it. Even after two incoming cash flows in t_1 and t_2, the balance is still negative.

It is important to consider all possible cash flow configurations to concatenate the model as a sequence of models. In this manner, the resulting balance of one model is the input balance of the next.

Note that there is a particularity for $[CF_0+CF^+-CF^-]$. This term can be both smaller or larger than CF_0 depending on the relative size of CF^+ and CF^-. Figure 6.3.3 displays a tree with $CF^+>CF^-$. In a tree with $CF^+<CF^-$, we obtain figure 6.14. All other terms are unchanged. Therefore, we have one setup for $CF_0+CF^+-CF^-<0$ and $CF_0>0$ (setup 6) and one setup for $CF_0+CF^+-CF^->0$ and $CF_0<0$ (setup 5). The

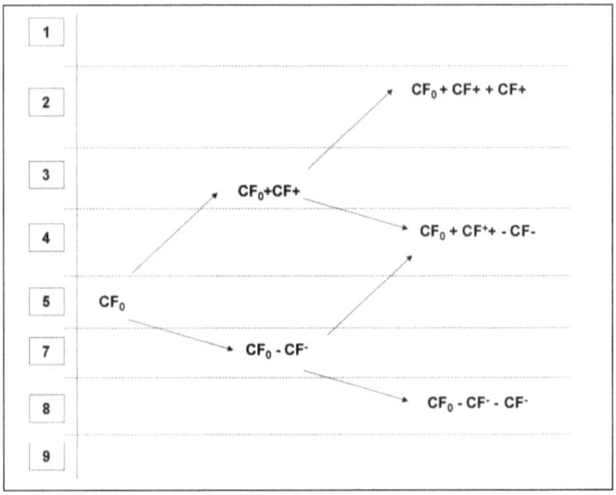

Fig. 6.13 Possible Cash Flow Setups (I)

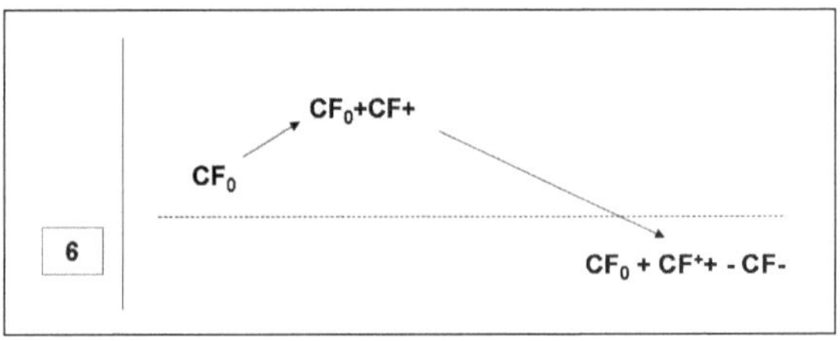

Fig. 6.14 Possible Cash Flow Setups (II)

configuration $CF_0 + CF^+ - CF^- < 0$ and $CF_0 < 0$ is covered by setup 4, the configuration $CF_0 + CF^+ - CF^- > 0$ and $CF_0 > 0$ is covered by setup 7.

Table 6.2 summarizes the $d_{12}[1,1]$-terms for setup 9. Apart from setup 9 (all terms are positive) we have to check setup 1 (all terms are negative).

For node [1,1], we also have to check the following setups as the corresponding terms have [] in table 6.3.3:

- Setup 8 (as $CF_0 - CF^- - CF^-$ occurs) (for $d_{02} = CF_0 - CF^-$ only)
- Setup 6 (as $CF_0 + CF^+ - CF^-$ occurs)
- Setup 3 (as $CF_0 + CF^+$ occurs) (for $d_{02} = 0$ only)

To check the optimality, we have to calculate the deltas between:

$$f(d_{1,2}[1,1] = 0, d_{0,2} = X)$$
$$f(d_{1,2}[1,1] = CF_0 + CF^+ + CF^+, d_{0,2} = X)$$
$$f(d_{1,2}[1,1] = CF_0 + CF^+ - CF^-), d_{0,2} = X)$$
X : Given common t0-decision

More precisely, we perform the following steps for each cash flow setup:

1. Calculate $\Delta(f(d_{1,2}[1,1]=0, d_{0,2}=X), f(d_{1,2}[1,1]=CF_0+CF^{+}+CF^{+}, d_{0,2}=X))$ In case of a stable sign, one decision dominates the other. In case of an unstable sign, the value functions intersect. We determine the intersection point at the (critical) expected funding cost $E[r_f]$
2. In case of a stable sign, we calculate whether the dominating decision also dominates $f(d_{1,2}[1,1]=CF_0+CF^{+}-CF^{-})$ by calculating the delta $\Delta(f(d_{1,2}[1,1]=0, d_{0,2}=X), f(d_{1,2}[1,1]=CF_0+CF^{+}-CF^{-}, d_{0,2}=X))$
3. In case of an unstable sign in (1), we check the dominance between $[CF_0+CF^{+}+CF^{+}]$ and $[CF_0+CF^{+}-CF^{-}]$.
   As the objective function is linear in $E[r_f]$, it can only intersect once and it is sufficient to check the relation with the remaining variable.

This procedure is the same for all other nodes [1,2], [2,1] and [2,2].

After some calculations, we obtain optimal (reserve) decisions for each cash flow setup. The decisions are summarized in figure 6.15. Figure 6.15 begins on the left hand side with the tree structure. For each node, the optimal $d_{1,2}[i,j]$-decision (horizontal logic) for each cash flow setup (vertical logic) is determined. The decisions are marked with different colours that are indicated in the legend at the bottom. Each decision is only valid for a certain $E[r_f]$-interval on the $[r^{-}, r^{--}]$-bar. In fact, each bar is plotted for the whole $E[r_f]$-interval from r^{-} to r^{--}.[17] Whenever a bar changes color (decision), the value functions intersect. The intersection points are given by (6.43).

$$
\begin{aligned}
a :=& \frac{r^{-} - p^{CF} r^{+}}{1 - pCF} \\
b :=& \frac{2r^{-} - (1 + p^{CF}) r^{+}}{1 - pCF} \\
c :=& \frac{\frac{CF^{-}}{CF^{+} - CF^{-}} \cdot (r^{-} - r^{+}) + r^{-} - p^{CF} r^{+}}{1 - pCF} \\
d :=& 2r^{-} - r^{+} \\
e :=& \frac{\frac{CF^{-}}{CF_0 - CF^{-} - CF^{-}} \cdot (r^{+} - r^{-}) + r^{-} - p^{CF} r^{+}}{1 - pCF} \\
f :=& \frac{\frac{CF_0 + CF^{+} - CF^{-}}{CF^{+} + CF^{-}} \cdot (r^{+} - r^{-}) + r^{-} - p^{CF} r^{+}}{1 - pCF}
\end{aligned}
\tag{6.43}
$$

$$
g := r^{-} + \frac{CF_0 + CF^{+} + CF^{+}}{CF_0 + CF^{+} - CF^{-}} \cdot (r^{-} - r^{+}) \tag{6.44}
$$

[17] Recall the definition of $E[r_f] := p^c \cdot r^{--} + (1 - p^c) \cdot r^{-}$. For $p^c = 0$ we obtain $E[r_f] = r^{-}$. For $p^c = 1$, we obtain $E[r_f] = r^{--}$.

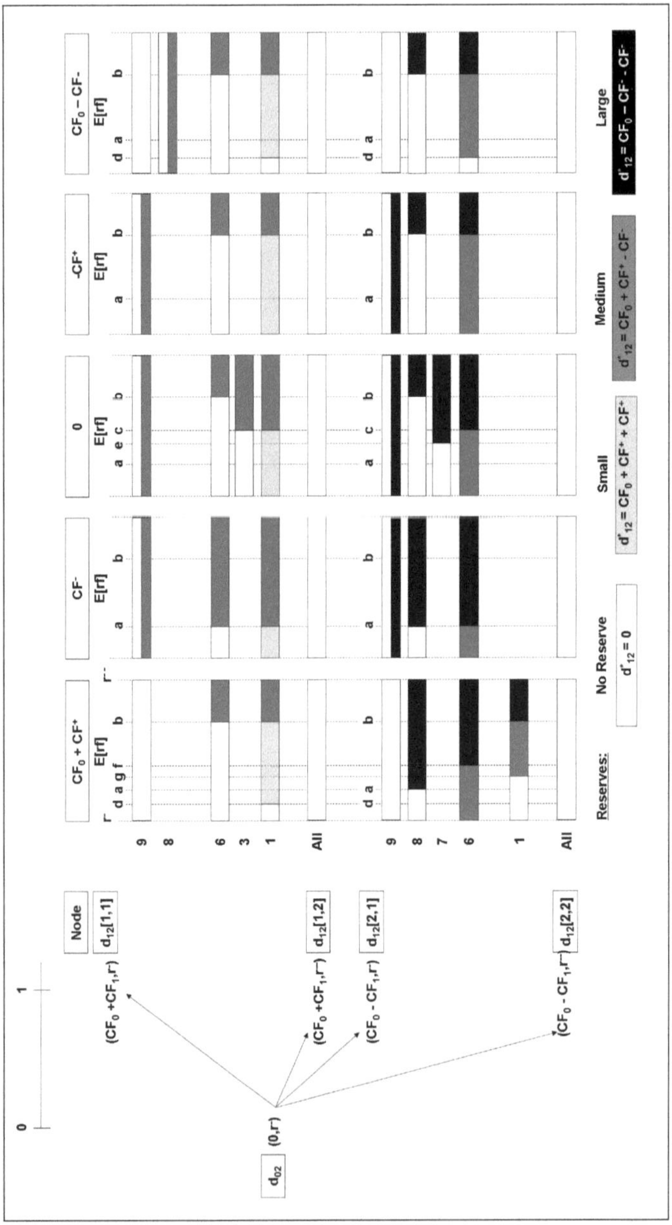

Fig. 6.15 Optimal Reserve Decisions in t1

The intersection points are setup-specific. The decreasing order of the intersection points can be shown for all cash flow configurations. Only the relative situation of d/a is conditional on p^{CF}:

$$p^{CF} > 0.5 \leftrightarrow d = 2r^{-} - r^{+} > \frac{r^{-} - p^{CF} r^{+}}{1 - p^{CF}} = a \tag{6.45}$$

We make the following observations:

1. In crisis nodes [i,2], the optimal decision is always $d_{1,2}[i,2] = 0$. This is in line with intuition, as setting up a reserve is never optimal in distressed markets.
2. For setup 9 (the balance is always positive), the optimum is undetermined. This is a somewhat pathological setup, as Money Market never needs external funding. Hence, distressed funding does not affect Money Market and reserve setting is unnecessary.
3. Reserve setting is more pronounced (reserves are set earlier (at lower critical $E[r_f]$) and with higher reserve amounts) in the net outflow node [2,1] than in the net inflow node [1,1]. This is in line with intuition, as Money Market is in a 'safer' position towards distressed funding in the inflow node than in the outflow node.
4. There is space for intermediary reserves. The reserve setting in the outflow node [2,1] in setup 6 always requires a reserve (except for $d_{0,2} = CF_0 - CF^{-}$). However, for small $E[r_f]$, a small reserve is preferable ($d_{1,2}[2,1] = CF_0 + CF^{+} - CF^{-}$) whereas for high $E[r_f]$, the higher reserve ($d_{1,2}[2,1] = CF_0 - CF^{-} - CF^{-}$) is optimal. Hence, it is not the case that the model jumps directly from '0'-reserve to the highest reserve without taking intermediary reserve states.

After having determined the optimal $d_{1,2}[i,j]$-decisions for given $d_{0,2}$, we have to find the optimal $d_{0,2}|d_{1,2}[i,j]$-vector.

6.3.4 Reserve Decisions in t0

We only solve setup 6 and 4 since these are most likely. Recall from figure 6.3.3 and figure 6.14 that setup 4 and 6 are defined as follows:

$$\text{Setup 6: } CF_0 \geq 0, CF_0 + CF^+ - CF^- \leq 0$$
$$\text{Setup 4: } CF_0 \leq 0, CF_0 + CF^+ - CF^- \leq 0$$

The optimal $d_{12}[i,j]$-decisions for setup 4 and 6 are summarized in figure 6.16. According to figure 6.16, we have to distinguish the following regions:

$$\begin{gathered}
\text{Region 1} \\
r^- \leq E[r_f] \leq 2r^- - r^+ (= d) \\
\text{Region 2} \\
2r^- - r^+ \leq E[r_f] \leq \frac{r^- - p^{CF} r^+}{1 - pCF} (= a) \\
\text{Region 3} \\
\frac{r^- - p^{CF} r^+}{1 - pCF} \leq E[r_f] \leq \frac{\frac{CF_0 + CF^+ - CF^-}{CF^+ + CF^-} \cdot (r^+ - r^-) + r^- - p^{CF} r^+}{1 - pCF} \\
(= f) \\
\text{Region 4} \\
\frac{\frac{CF_0 + CF^+ - CF^-}{CF^+ + CF^-} \cdot (r^+ - r^-) + r^- - p^{CF} r^+}{1 - pCF} \leq E[r_f] \leq \frac{\frac{CF^-}{CF^+ - CF^-} \cdot (r^- - r^+) + r^- - p^{CF} r^+}{1 - pCF} \\
(= c) \\
\text{Region 5} \\
\frac{\frac{CF^-}{CF^+ - CF^-} \cdot (r^- - r^+) + r^- - p^{CF} r^+}{1 - pCF} \leq E[r_f] \leq \frac{2r^- - (1 + p^{CF}) r^+}{1 - pCF} (= b) \\
\text{Region 6} \\
\frac{2r^- - (1 + p^{CF}) r^+}{1 - pCF} \leq E[r_f] \leq r^{--}
\end{gathered} \tag{6.46}$$

The region boundaries are intersection points between value functions of the same t_0-, but different t_1-decisions. Whenever value functions intersect, the optimal policy changes. Hence, we have to proceed region by region. Within each region, we have to check the relation between the value functions for all different $d_{0,2}$-values given the optimal t_1-decisions. This leads to optimal reserve decisions today. The t_1-decisions split up the $E[r_f]$-interval that runs from r^- to r^{--} into 6 regions. Their boundaries are given by (6.46).

As the value functions of f($d_{02} = 0$) contain a single CF_0-term, we have to distinguish the two regimes $CF_0 \geq 0$ and $CF_0 \leq 0$. [18] With the assumptions of $CF_0 + CF^+ - CF^- \leq 0$

[18] Note that we did not need this distinction for the derivation of t_1-decisions.

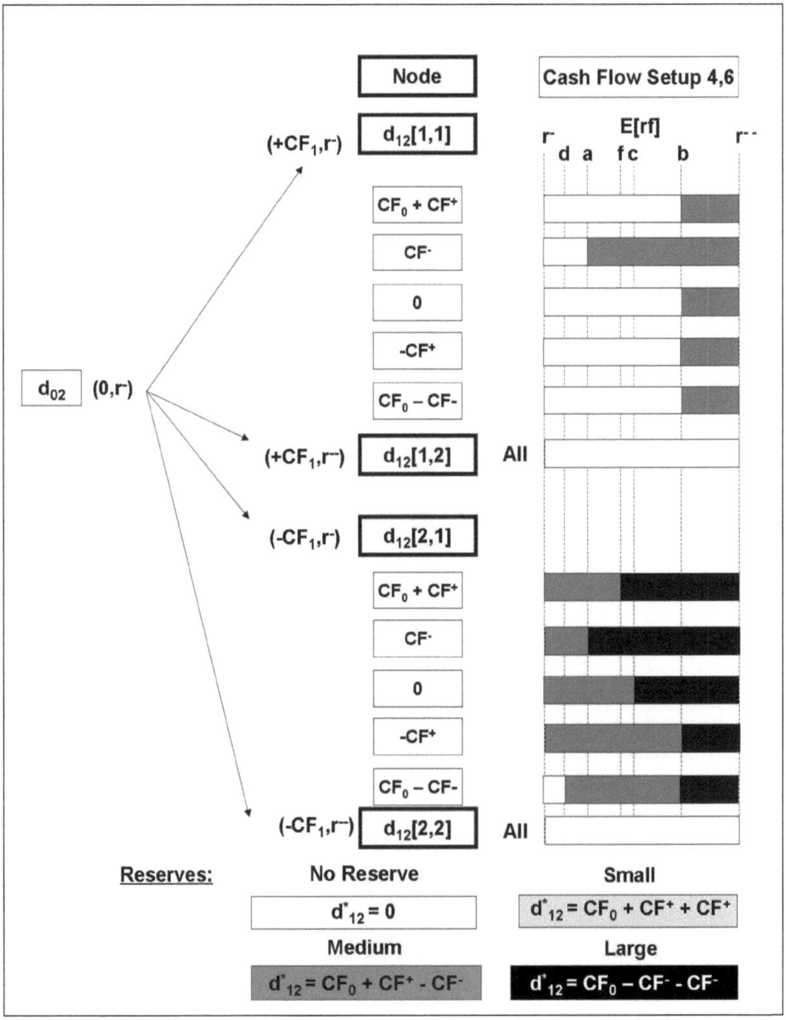

Fig. 6.16 Optimal Decision Rules, Setup 4 and 6

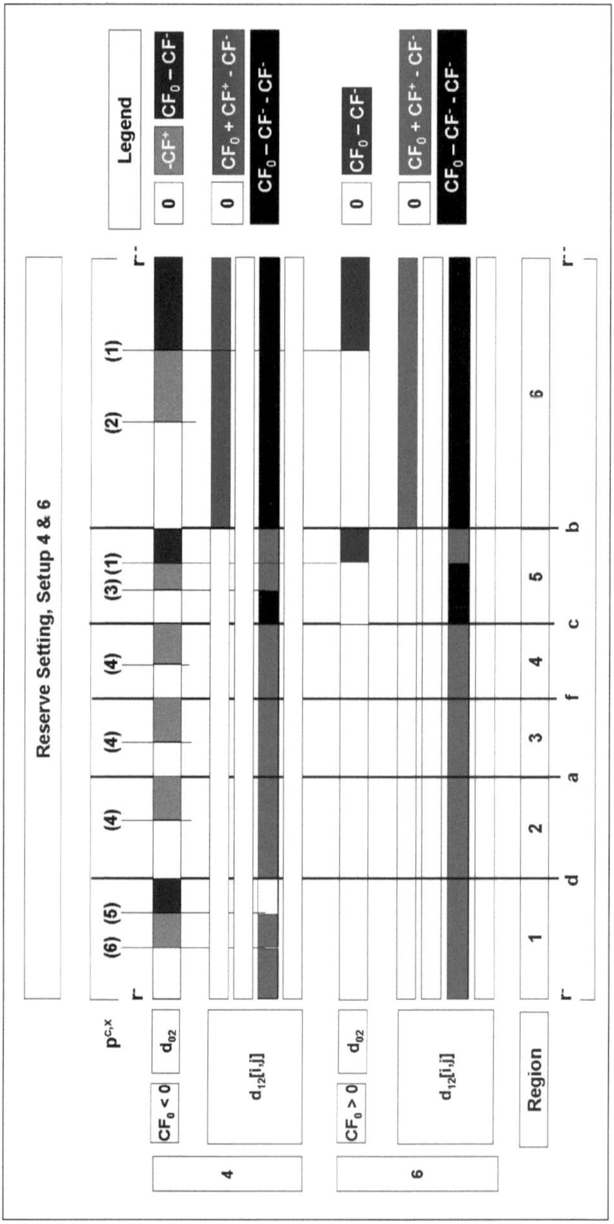

Fig. 6.17 Optimal Reserve Setting in Setup 4 and 6

and $CF_0 \geq 0$, we are in setup 6. With the assumption of $CF_0 \leq 0$, we are in setup 4. The upper block of figure 6.17 summarizes optimal decisions for setup 4, the bottom block setup 6.

The legend on the right hand side lists all optimal decisions that are used. Note that investments ($d_{t,2} > 0$) are never optimal. This is in line with intuition, as investments bear cost of carry.

For the decision vector, we use the following notation:

$$(d_{0,2} \mid d_{1,2}[1,1] \mid d_{1,2}[1,2] \mid d_{1,2}[2,1] \mid d_{1,2}[2,2])$$

The corresponding value function is determined as:

$$f(d_{0,2} \mid d_{1,2}[1,1] \mid d_{1,2}[1,2] \mid d_{1,2}[2,1] \mid d_{1,2}[2,2])$$

In the following, we explain the reserve setting region by region starting with region 6.

Region 6

Depending on critical crisis probabilities, the following reserve policies are optimal in region 6:

$$\begin{aligned}
(0|CF_0+CF^+-CF^-|0|CF_0-CF^- -CF^-|0)\\
(-CF^+|CF_0+CF^+-CF^-|0|CF_0-CF^- -CF^-|0)\\
(CF_0-CF^-|CF_0+CF^+-CF^-|0|CF_0-CF^- -CF^-|0)
\end{aligned}$$

The policies only differ in their $d_{0,2}$-decision. All three $d_{0,2}$-decisions $(0, -CF^+$ and $CF_0 - CF^+)$ might be optimal for $CF_0 < 0$. For $CF_0 \geq 0$, only 0 and $CF_0 - CF^+$ are optimal. The reason is that all three value functions intersect in the same point for $CF_0 \geq 0$ (in (1)), but in different points for $CF_0 < 0$ (in (2)). As the CF_0-term only occurs in the f(0)-function, the intersection point between $f(-CF^+)$ and $CF_0 - CF^-$ is the same for $CF_0 > 0$ and $CF_0 < 0$. However, for $CF_0 \leq 0$, the intersection points $f(0)/f(-CF^+)$ and $f(0)/f(CF_0 - CF^-)$ are left of the intersection point $f(-CF^+)/f(CF_0 - CF^-)$.

We obtain the following optimal t_0-decisions for region 6:

$$CF_0 \leq 0:$$

$$d^*_{02} = \begin{cases} 0, & p^c \leq p^{c1} \\ CF_0 - CF^-, & \text{else} \end{cases}$$

$$CF_0 \geq 0:$$

$$d^*_{02} = \begin{cases} 0, & p^c \leq p^{c2} \\ -CF^+, & p^{c2} \leq p^c \leq p^{c,1} \\ CF_0 - CF^-, & else \end{cases}$$

being:

$$p^{c,1} = 2 \cdot \frac{(r^- - r^+)}{(1 - p^{CF})(r^{--} - r^+)}$$

$$p^{c,2} = p^{c,1} + \frac{CF_0}{CF^+} \cdot \frac{(r^- - r^+)}{(1 - p^{CF})(r^{--} - r^+)}$$

As $CF_0/CF^+ < 0$, it holds:

$$p^{c,2} \leq p^{c,1}$$

However, it is possible that region 6 does not exist at all because it is completely beyond r^{--}. This is true if (6.47) holds:

$$p^{CF} \geq \frac{(r^{--} - r^-) - (r^- - r^+)}{r^{--} - r^+} \tag{6.47}$$

The condition has an intuitive interpretation: the nominator is the difference between the marginal benefits $(r^{--} - r^-)$ and the marginal cost $(r^- - r^+)$ of a reserve. The excess reserve benefits are normalized with the total cost.

Region 5

If region 6 is beyond r^{--}, the intersection point between $f(-CF^+,...)$ and $f(CF_0 - CF^-,...)$ is still at $p^{c,1}$ in region 5. Although both changed their t_1-decisions with respect to region 6, this change in t_1-decisions neither affect the delta nor the intersection point.[19] This holds for both setups $CF_0 \geq 0$ and $CF_0 \leq 0$, as there are single CF_0-terms in neither $f(-CF^+)$ nor in $f(CF_0 - CF^-)$. In comparison, for $d_{0,2} = 0$ the t_1-decisions did not change entering region 5, and the (same) value function f(0) of region 6 now intersects with the new value function of $f(-CF^+)$ of region 5, leading to a different intersection point $(p^{c,3})$.

[19] Note that the value functions $f(-CF^+)$ and $f(CF_0 - CF^-)$ in region 5 are not the ones from region 6.

$p^{c,3}$ is obtained by:

$$f(0) > f(-CF^+) \leftrightarrow p^c \leq \frac{-b \pm \sqrt{b^2 - 4ac}}{2a} \tag{6.48}$$

being:

$$\begin{aligned} a &:= -(1-p^{CF})^2(CF^+ + CF^-)(r^{--} - r^-) \\ b &:= -(1-p^{CF})CF^+ r^{--} \\ &\quad -(1-p^{CF})(CF^- r^+ + (CF^+ + CF^-)(2r^- + p^{CF} r^+ + (1-p^{CF})r^-)) \\ c &:= CF_0 * r^- - (CF_0 + CF^+) \cdot r^+ + CF^+ \cdot (2r^- - p^{CF} r^+) \end{aligned}$$

Hence, we obtain the following decision rules (similar with respect to region 6):

$$CF_0 \leq 0: \quad d_{02}^* = \begin{cases} 0, & p^c \leq p^{c1} \\ CF_0 - CF^-, & \text{else} \end{cases}$$

$$CF_0 \geq 0: \quad d_{02}^* = \begin{cases} 0, & p^c \leq p^{c3} \\ -CF^+, & p^{c3} \leq p^c \leq p^{c,1} \\ CF_0 - CF^-, & else \end{cases}$$

Region 5 is the last region where $d_{0,2}$ can be different from zero for $CF_0 \leq 0$. For all lower regions (4,...,1), reserve setting in t_0 is not optimal. Therefore, from now on all statements refer to setup $CF_0 \leq 0$.

Region 4

From region 4 onwards, we have a dominance of $f(-CF^+)$ over $f(CF_0 - CF^-)$ as long as t_1-decisions of $f(-CF^+)$ and $f(CF_0 - CF^-)$ do not change. As the next change is not before region 1, we do not have to test this relationship again before region 1.

The only change from region 5 to 4 concerns $d_{02} = 0$ where the $d_{12}[2,1]$-decision shifts from $[CF_0 - CF^- - CF^-]$ to $[CF_0 + CF^+ - CF^-]$.

For negative initial values there might be an intersection in region 4. The critical expected funding cost is:

$$f(0) > f(-CF^+) \leftrightarrow E[r_f] \leq \frac{\frac{(CF_0 + CF^+)(r^- - r^+)}{CF^+} + r^- - p^{CF} r^+}{1 - p^{CF}} \tag{6.49}$$

Please note that the f(0)-value function of region 4 is different from the value function of region 5. Only the $f(-CF^+)$-value function is still the same, as its t_1-decision vector is unchanged.

The decision rule for region 4 is:

$$CF_0 \le 0:$$

$$d_{02}^* = \begin{cases} 0, & p^{c,4} \\ -CF^+, & else \end{cases}$$

being :

$$p^{c,4} := \frac{\frac{\frac{(CF_0+CF^+)(r^- - r^+)}{CF^+} + r^- - p^{CF} r^+}{1-p^{CF}} - r^-}{r^{--} - r^-}$$

Region 3 & 2

The change from region 4 to 3 concerns neither f(0) nor $f(-CF^+)$. Hence, their region 3-value functions are still the same as in region 4. Consequently, intersection point $p^{c,4}$ and the decision rule of region 4 also apply for region 3.

The same argument applies for region 2 where the only change concerns $d_{02} = CF^-$. One can show that the dominance of f(0) still holds for the new $f(CF^-)$-function. Hence, the relation f(0)/ $f(-CF^+)$ is not affected by the region change.

Region 1

In region 1, $CF_0 - CF^-$ comes back into the game as its t_1-decision $d_{12}[2,1]$ changes from $CF_0 + CF^+ - CF^-$ to 0.

Thus only the relation between $f(CF_0 - CF^-)$, $f(-CF^+)$ and $f(CF_0 - CF^-)$ needs to be re-valued.

We obtain the following decision rule:

$$CF_0 \ge 0:$$

$$d_{02}^* = \begin{cases} 0, & p^c \le p^{c,6} \\ -CF^+, & p^{c,6} \le p^c \le p^{c,5} \\ CF_0 - CF^-, & else \end{cases}$$

being:

$$p^{c,6} = \frac{\frac{\frac{(CF_0+CF^+)(r^- - r^+)}{CF^+} + r^- - p^{CF} r^+}{1-p^{CF}} - r^-}{r^{--} - r^-}$$

$$p^{c,5} = \sqrt{\frac{2r^- - (1+p^{CF})r^+ 1 - p^{CF} - r^-}{r^{--} - r^-}}$$

One can show that $p^{c,6} \le p^{c,5}$.

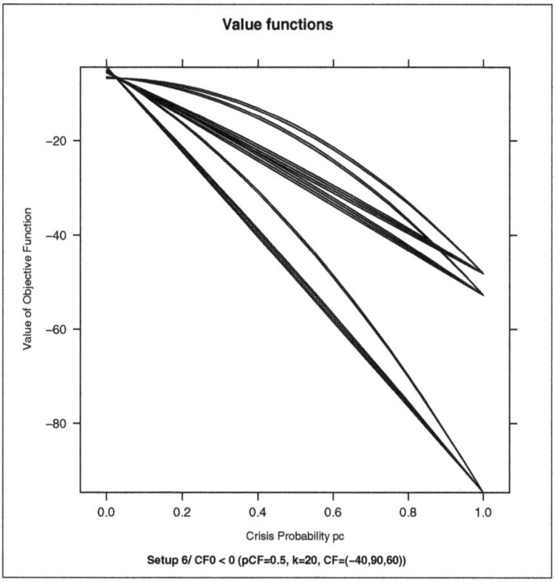

Fig. 6.18 Value Functions After Analytical Exclusion

6.3.5 Numerical Example

By the systematic analysis of value functions and their deltas, we could discard many value functions from figure 6.12. If we exclude all value functions with investment decisions ($d_{0,2} > 0$, $d_{1,2}[i, j] > 0$) as well as all reserve decisions in crisis nodes, we are left with the value functions in figure 6.18.[20] Based on these value functions, we are now verifying the determined policies and intersection points. We obtain the following regions and critical probabilities:

[20] We exclude investment decisions in general and reserve decisions in distressed nodes as we demonstrated that they are never optimal.

Region 6 : $[3.16\%, 100\%]$

$$d^{*,R6} = \begin{cases} (0|-10|0|-160|0), & 3.16\% \leq p^c \leq 3.24\% \\ (-90|-10|0|-160|0), & 3.24\% \leq p^c \leq 4.17\% \\ (-100|-10|0|-160|0), & \text{else} \end{cases}$$

Region 5 :$[1.89\%, 3.16\%]$

$$d^{*,R5} = \begin{cases} (0|0|0|-160|0), & p^c \leq 5.42\% \\ (-90|0|0|-10|0), & p^c \leq 3.24\% \\ (-100|0|0|-10|0), & \text{else} \end{cases}$$

Region 4,3,2 : $[1.05\%, 1.89\%]$

$$d^{*,R4/3/2} = \begin{cases} d(0|0|0|-10|0), & p^c \leq 2.22\% \\ d(-90|0|0|-10|0), & \text{else} \end{cases}$$

Region 1 : $[0\%, 1.05\%]$

$$d^{*,R1} = \begin{cases} d(0|0|0|-10|0), & p^c \leq 2.22\% \\ d(-90|0|0|-10|0), & 2.22\% \leq p^c \leq 17.8\% \\ d(-100|0|0|0|0), & \text{else} \end{cases}$$

As the regions are determined by t_1-decisions, the critical probabilities for t_0-decisions are not identical with region boundaries. In fact, they can be thought of as a new layer that superposes the t_1-regions. In this manner, every additional time step splits the decision set into more and more $(t_0, t_1, ..., t_n)$-intervals.

We verify our findings with graphs from each region. Figure 6.19 verifies the dominance of $(CF_0 - CF^-, ...)$ over $(-CF^+, ...)$ and $(0, ...)$ over all other policies in region 6. However, for small crisis probabilities, reserve setting is less profitable and value functions intersect.

Figure 6.20 displays the value functions in region 5. Please note that the region boundary was an intersection point where t_1-decisions change. Therefore, the value function $f(CF_0 - CF^-)$ of region 6 was the value function $f(CF_0 - CF^-|-10|0|-160|0)$. The value function $f(CF_0 - CF^-)$ of region 5 is $f(CF_0 - CF^-|0|0|-10|0)$. As the complete region 5 is below the critical probability $p^{c,3}$, the dominating policy is $(0|0|0|-160|0)$ as figure 6.20 suggests. Within region 4, 3 and 2, the dominance of $f(0|...)$ over $f(-CF^+|...)$ holds because these regions are below the critical crisis probability $p^{c,4} = 2.22\%$ as figure 6.21 suggests.

The dominance of $f(0|...)$ over f($CF_0 - CF^-|$... and f($-CF^+|$... continues in region 1, as the critical probabilities are beyond the interval. Please note that one can not demonstrate that critical probabilities are always beyond the corresponding intervals. The exact situation of probability and interval heavily depends on the cash flow probability.

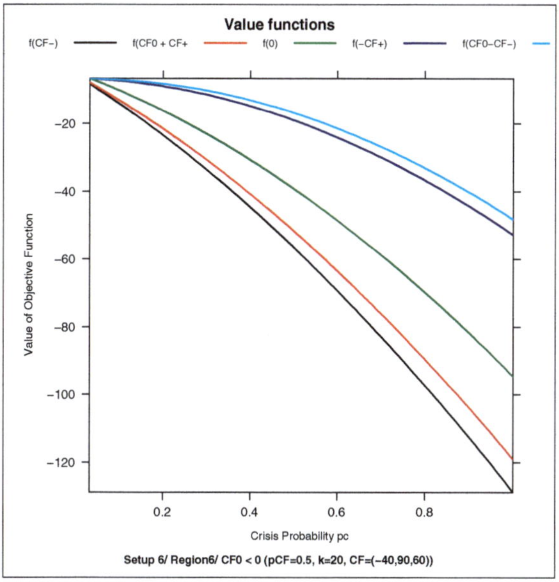

Fig. 6.19 Value Functions in Region 6

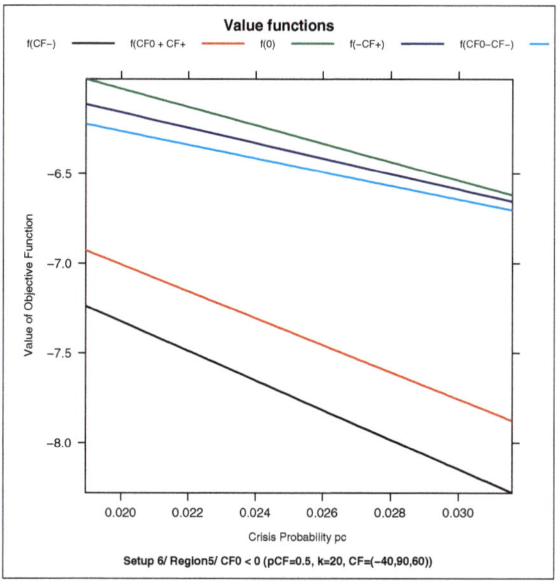

Fig. 6.20 Value Functions in Region 5

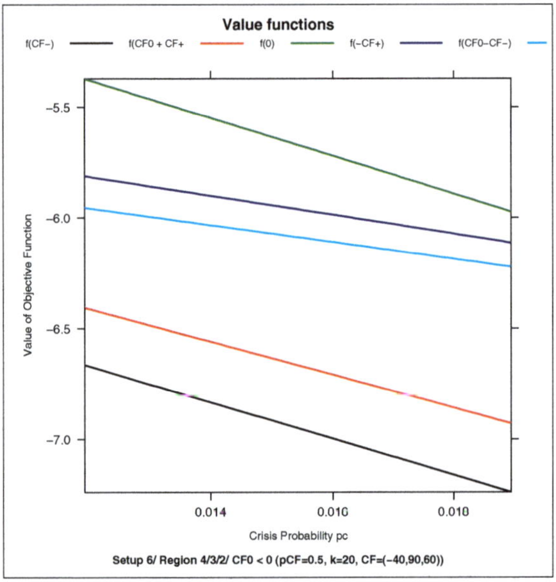

Fig. 6.21 Value Functions in Region 4,3,2

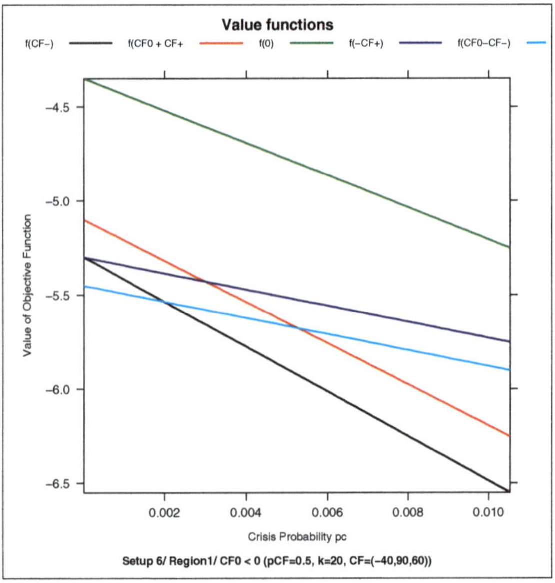

Fig. 6.22 Value Functions in Region 1

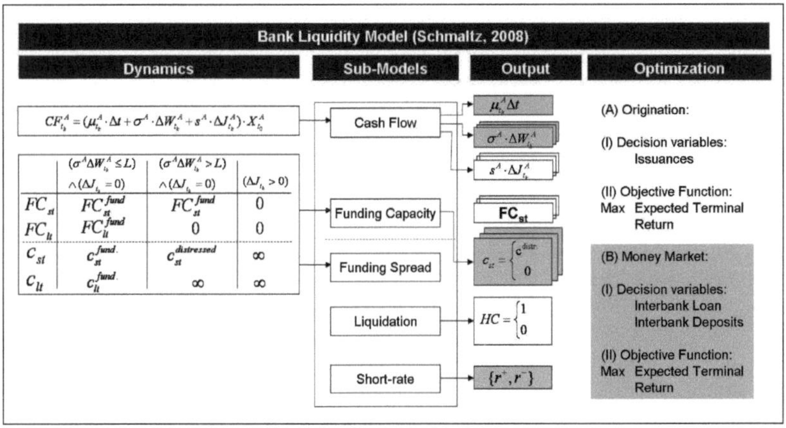

Fig. 6.23 Reserve Optimization within the Bank Liquidity Model

6.3.6 Comparison with the Literature

Figure 6.23 summarizes the reserve optimization in the Money Market department. Money Market optimizes Brownian deviations and deterministic cash flows of the next quarter facing a funding capacity risk. As reserve decisions affect the distribution of the funding capacity, we have to translate the capacity risk into a price risk. The gross funding cost is the sum of the constant risk-free funding rate plus funding spread. The price risk is that funding is unavailable at the fundamental, but at a distressed funding spread. Thus, the funding spread is stochastic in our model. Risk-free rates are constant. We also account for market illiquidity in form of a constant bid-ask spread that describes the reserve cost. Our objective function is the maximization of expected terminal return. For complexity reasons, we have to restrict the model horizon to 3 days. Figure 6.24 summarizes the cash management model of Schmid (2000).[21] The cash flow is of a similar structure as the one in our model. It consists of the budgeted cash flow plus a normally distributed forecast error. However, Schmid (2000) does not incorporate funding risk. His stochastic return drivers are interest rates and stock prices. In our setup, interest rates are constant. Only the bank-specific funding spread varies. Like us, Schmid's (2000) cash manager maximizes expected return. However, his basis is the present value of the return, not the terminal value.

[21] We introduced the model in section 1.2.2.1.

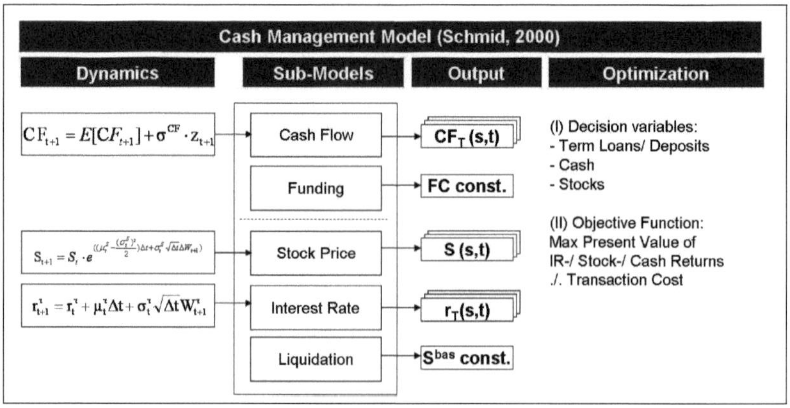

Fig. 6.24 Cash Management Model by Schmid (2000)

6.3.7 Conclusion

We analysed the reserve setting in a stochastic and dynamic framework where Money Market faces both cash flow and funding risk. As in other reserve models, Money Market has to balance marginal benefits (avoided distress costs) and marginal cost (cost of carry) from holding a reserve. Our reserve model is a 2-stage Stochastic Optimization that we solved backwards analytically. In a first step, we showed that optimal (bounded) solutions exist for all possible (cash flow) setups. This way, we obtained a bundle of candidates for optimal decisions that have to be analysed systematically. We start at t_1 and derive optimal t_1-decisions by freezing the t_0-decision and optimizing across the t_1-candidates. Whenever value functions intersect and a change in t_1-decisions is optimal, we obtained a region till the next intersection. In total, we obtained six t_1-regions. Having derived optimal t_1-decisions for all kinds of t_0-decisions, we step back to t_0 by determining the optimal joint decision $(d_{02}|d_{1,2}[i,j])$ for each region. We obtained critical crisis probabilities (intersecting probabilities) where $d_{0,2}$-decisions change. In general, t_0-intervals do not coincide with t_1-regions. The policy recommendations are in line with intuition, as investments are never optimal and reserves are never set up in crisis situations. The reserve amount increased with the crisis probability.

Using a numerical example, we verified the derived policy recommendations. We found that many intersection points lay outside the intervals. This indicated that there is a certain dominance of the t_0-decision for small crisis probabilities within the given configuration. Furthermore, one could see that the model is very sensitive to small crisis probabilities: five of six regions are below 4% crisis probability. If one assumes that the crisis probability is a parameter that is difficult to estimate, one might argue that the model incorporates a large estimation uncertainty.

Unfortunately, it is not ensured that the introduction of correlation effects or illiquid assets still allow for analytical solutions. As soon as policies with different t_1-decisions have to be compared, closed-form solutions are impossible.[22]

6.4 Risk Controlling

In contrast to Origination and Money Market, Risk Controlling does not have an optimization programme. Obviously, it is not reasonable to establish a performance measurement conditioned on a very rare event. Furthermore, Risk Controlling operates before jumps occur. If they occur, they are managed by another entity: the liquidity crisis committee.

There are three tasks that Risk Controlling is responsible for:

1. Determination of Optimal Jump Risk Quantile
   The transfer price is based on a confidence level up to which jump risk has to be backed with collateral. The confidence level should be an optimal one. Assuming that jumps beyond the quantile lead to illiquidity, the optimal level balances expected marginal illiquidity cost and marginal avoidance cost.
2. Balancing Jump Risk Exposure with Decentral Collateral
   Risk Controlling calibrates the cost function that translates the jump exposure into a transfer price:[23] if the jump exposure exceeds the available collateral, Risk Controlling makes jump risk taking less attractive by increasing the jump risk transfer price. As the transfer price is allocated to collateral holders, holding of collateral becomes more attractive. Via this mechanism, Risk Controlling balances jump risk exposure and decentral collateral.
3. Determination of Optimal Liquidation Policy
   Although decentral collateral is assumed to consist of liquid assets, the liquidity might vary across scenarios. In order to limit liquidation losses, optimal liquidation policies have to be derived.[24]

6.5 Summary

This section discussed liquidity optimization. We restricted the setup to allow for analytical solutions. In particular, we reduced the product spectrum to loans with constant drift and Brownian component for each quarter. Furthermore, we restricted the model horizon to three quarters and assumed that only a loss of confidence threatens roll-over.

Liquidity can be optimized locally if decision variables are distinct and underlying processes are independent. As this is the case, Origination optimizes the funding profile and Money Market optimizes reserve setting. The optimization is the basis of their perfor-

---

[22] The reason for this is that the crisis probability appears in terms of order two and higher.

[23] See section 5.2.3 for the jump risk cost function.

[24] For details on how to derive optimal liquidation strategies, please refer to [Mönch, 2005]. Within this context, he discusses the optimal order size that determines the liquidation horizon. Furthermore, he addresses practical aspects such as how to time order submissions and how to choose limits.

mance measurement. Risk Controlling optimizes as well. However, the optimization is not a basis for its performance measurement.

Given quarterly deterministic cash flows, Origination optimizes the funding maturity structure (Maturity Mismatch Strategy). It balances gain and risk of short (roll-over) and long-term funding. The gain from rolling over is a low funding cost. The risk are possible high funding cost and a volume risk. We showed that the negligence of risk leads to optimal roll-over volumes of either 100% or 0%. The crucial variable is 'expected future funding spread': if expectations are above the forward funding spread, Origination only funds in the long term. If they are below it, it only funds short-term. The volume insurance against jump risk (transfer price) affected the switching point, but not the optimal volume. Obviously, this setup cannot explain the coexistence of short and long-term funds. Therefore, we introduced roll-over risk. We model roll-over risk with a stochastic funding capacity. The stochastic introduces a non-linearity that leads to optimal maturity structures with both short and long-term funds. We model the capacity so that the volume is always ensured, but an additional penalty spread has to be paid for rolling beyond the capacity. This mechanism can be implemented by a liquidity backup line that ensures the volume but not the funding spread.[25] A subsequent sensitivity analysis revealed that the optimal volume is very sensitive to the stochastic of the funding capacity, but less sensitive to the definition of the penalty spread.

Money Market optimizes reserve holding during the next quarter, given deterministic and Brownian cash flows. We approximated cash flow and funding process by binomial models. To allow explicit solutions we limit the horizon to three days. Incoming and outgoing cash flows as well as the short-term funding spread are stochastic. If outgoing cash flows and elevated funding spreads coincide, Money Market faces distressed funding. Money Market can prevent this scenario by setting up a liquidity reserve. The optimal reserve balances current reserve cost (bid-ask spread) and the avoidance of expensive future funding. The decision variables of Money Market are interbank loans and deposits. The reserve optimization is linear in the reserve quantity. Thus, optimal reserves are boundary solutions. We verified that unlimited reserves are never optimal. In contrast, we found that candidates for optimal reserves are the cash flow balance.[26] As the number of possible reserve strategies is 405 (for T=3) we needed a systematic approach. The systematic comparison of value functions revealed whether a decision dominates or whether value functions intersect. In this manner, we obtain optimality regions across expected funding cost. We found that the higher the expected funding cost, the higher the optimal reserve in t_1. Furthermore, we found that investment is only optimal as part of a reserve strategy. After having determined optimal (t_1)-reserve decisions for each given (t_0)-decision, we determined the optimal (t_0,t_1)-combination. As for t_1, we found that there is no dominant (t_0,t_1)-vector, but depending on the probability of distressed funding, several strategies are optimal.

A numerical example revealed that the majority of value functions already intersect for very small crisis probabilities. For high crisis probabilities, the decision to set up a high reserve dominates. As the crisis probability is an unobservable quantity and intersections

[25] We introduced this internal backup line in section 5.1.2 to immunize Origination against any cash flow risk.

[26] Hence, clearing the account might be optimal.

concentrate on a small interval, the model is not robust. Furthermore, we do not find a high interaction between (t_0)- and (t_1)-decisions. This questions whether the model has to be dynamic. However, this result might partly be due to our short model horizon. Extensions (correlation pattern, longer horizon) are possible, but require numerical solving methods.

Risk Controlling determines the optimal confidence level up to which jump risk should be backed. Furthermore, it balances jump risk exposure and available collateral. For that purpose, it adjusts the cost function to make either jump risk or collateral holding more expensive. Finally, it elaborates an optimal scenario-dependent liquidation policy. In contrast to Origination and Money Market, the performance of Risk Controlling is not based on its optimizations.

Chapter 7
Conclusion

The motivation for this work was threefold: firstly, regulators encourage banks to develop internal models for liquidity management. Secondly, quantitative and complete liquidity models for banks are unavailable. Thirdly, corporate liquidity models disregard bank particularities.

The objective of the analysis was the development of an internal, quantitative and complete liquidity model for banks. We understand 'quantitative' as equation-based. For us, completeness covers several dimensions: firstly, the model has to cover product and aggregated level. Secondly, it has to incorporate short-term and long-term liquidity. Thirdly, it has to describe a variety of scenarios such as the expected and stress scenarios. Fourthly, it has to address modelling, managing, and optimizing bank liquidity. As bank particularity, we consider that some bank products are based on confidence.

The derivation of the liquidity model took the following steps: in chapter 2 we introduced the different liquidity concepts. Chapter 3 derived the key variables while chapter 4 discussed their requirements and modelling approaches. Chapter 5 presented a management approach that splits product cash flows and transfers the components to different departments. Finally, chapter 6 described how liquidity is optimally managed within the departments.

In the following, we present the results of each chapter and use figure 7.1 to stress how chapters and findings are related. Chapter 2 ensures a common definitional basis. We point out that liquidity refers to different concepts depending on the context: literature distinguishes asset, institutional and national liquidity. Asset liquidity measures the cost of asset liquidation, which is measured by haircuts. Asset liquidation is important for liquidity management, as it is the only way to generate liquidity if external funding is unavailable. Institutional liquidity refers to the ability of an institution to fulfill its payment obligations. Furthermore, national liquidity encompasses the means of payment of an economy. Liquidity concepts are not independent. Banks manage their institutional liquidity by using assets (asset liquidity) and central bank money (national liquidity). Chapter 3 is a preparatory step to model bank liquidity. Based on the liquidity strategies that banks run, it derives the key liquidity variables. We stated that banks run Maturity Mismatch and Liquidity Option strategies. A Maturity Mismatch strategy seeks to reduce funding costs. However, it implies a roll-over volume and funding spread risk. The key variables to model a Maturity Mismatch strategy are cash flows, long-term funding capacity, funding spread, and haircuts. Long-term interest rates are swapped to floating

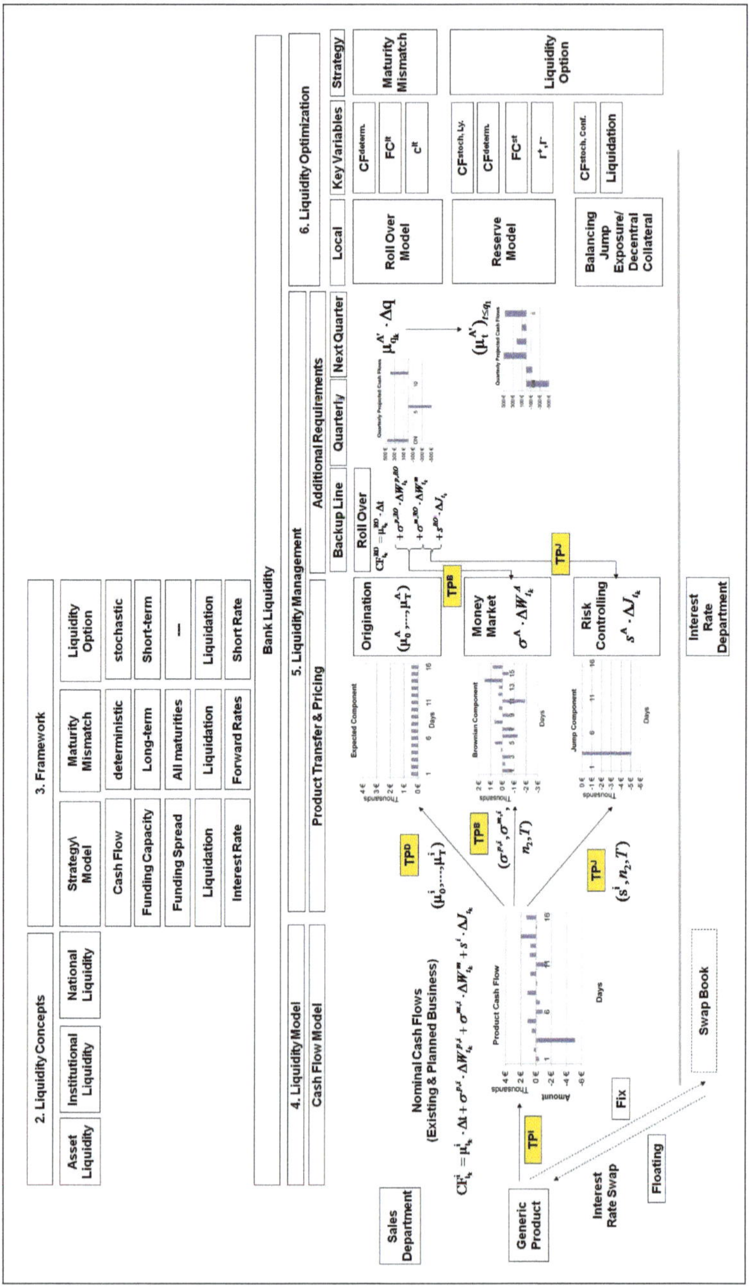

Fig. 7.1 Summary

rates and modelled by forward rates. The Liquidity Option strategy provides an attractive margin, but it implies cash flow risk. The key variables to model a liquidity option strategy are cash flows, short-term funding capacity, haircuts, and short-term interest rates. The key variables of Maturity Mismatch and Liquidity Option Strategy form the liquidity framework, which is not a model but rather a family of models. A liquidity model is obtained by specifying the dynamic of the key variables. The framework postulates that each complete liquidity model has to incorporate these key variables. A framework simplifies the comparison of liquidity models. Chapter 4, 5 and 6 span the bank liquidity model. Chapter 4 models the key variables and chapter 5 integrates them in banks' organisational setup. Chapter 6 discusses optimization.

Chapter 4 specifies a liquidity model that consists of sub-models for product cash flows, funding, liquidation and short-rate. Our focus lies on the cash flow model. We model product cash flows as a jump-diffusion process consisting of a drift, Brownian and jump component. The drift component represents contractual and planned cash flows. The Brownian component accounts for liquidity-driven unexpected cash flows. The jump component models confidence-driven unexpected cash flows, which is a bank particularity. Our process assumption covers all products. Product particularities are accounted for by product-specific parameters. We discussed the model horizon and argued that it is necessary to regularly update cash flow expectations. As our model is based on unconditional expectations, we cannot update expectations within the model. Thus, we have to stop the model, assess the new information and set up a new one with updated expectations. Therefore, the model horizon has to be limited. As liquidity management is performed on the aggregate level, we discussed the aggregation of product cash flows. Aggregation requires the specification of the dependency structure. We use a one factor-model for the Brownian component consisting of 'one' systematic factor and unsystematic (product-specific) risk. We assume independence between systematic and product-specific factors as well as between product-specific factors. The jump component is modelled by one systematic confidence factor.

The funding model specifies the dynamic of funding capacity and funding spread. With respect to the variables, we distinguish a long and a short-term version. With respect to the dynamic, we distinguish three scenarios: normal funding, distressed funding, and funding crisis. In a funding crisis, unsecured funding is unavailable. In distressed funding, long-term funding is unavailable. The funding dynamic is linked to the cash flow dynamic: a funding crisis is triggered by a jump. Funding is distressed if jumps are absent and high Brownian outgoing cash flows are present. We discussed methods to calibrate funding capacity, as it is an unobservable quantity.

The liquidation model determines haircuts for asset liquidation. The short-rate model describes the dynamic of the short-term risk-free rate. We assume very simple models for both variables, as they lie outside our focus.

Chapter 5 analyzes the separation and transfer of cash flow components to different departments. The framework suggested that the Maturity Mismatch Strategy is based on deterministic, and Liquidity Option Strategy on stochastic cash flows. Furthermore, the Maturity Mismatch strategy is based on the funding spread whereas the funding spread is of no interest for the Liquidity Option strategy.[1] The motivation of the cash flow separation is the isolation of strategies and their performances. The drift component is transferred to the Origination department. The Brownian component is transferred to the Money Market department; the jump component is transferred to Risk Controlling. Thus, Origination operates on deterministic cash flows and manages spread risk whereas Money Market manages liquidity-driven cash flow risk. Risk Controlling monitors the confidence-driven cash flow risk. Furthermore, the separation is also motivated by different instruments: Origination issues securities whereas Money Market uses short-term interbank loans and deposits. Money Market therefore manages Brownian risk with a reserve that is set up by interbank deals. Risk Controlling does not have an active instrument, but balances jump risk exposure with collateral that is owned by other departments (decentral reserve). We extended the basic transfer model with the help of additional requirements. The Maturity Mismatch Strategy implies a cash flow risk that Origination should not bear. Thus, it transfers the volume risk to Risk Controlling and Money Market with liquidity backup lines. The spread risk remains in Origination, as the backup line only ensures the volume, but not the spread. Moreover, Origination operates on a quarterly time scale due to the long-term horizon. Finally, Origination transfers the deterministic cash flows of the next quarter to Money Market, as it does not dispose of adequate instruments to manage inter-quarterly cash flows.

Components are transferred at transfer prices. The transfer price of the deterministic component is based on the funding spread. The transfer price for Brownian cash flow risk, however, is based on the cost that a Money Market reserve at a certain confidence level implies. The transfer price for jump risk is based on the expected liquidation cost of the decentral liquidity reserve.

Chapter 6 is dedicated to the liquidity optimization in each department. In order to allow for tractable optimization models, we restricted the setup with regard to product cash flows and model horizon. As underlying processes and instruments of Origination and Money Market are disjoint, liquidity can be optimized locally. Origination determines the optimal split between long and short-term funding, facing roll-over risk. We solved a model with a three-quarter horizon. Furthermore, we stressed that funding risk has to be taken into account to obtain an optimal co-existence of short and long-term funding. The sensitivity analysis revealed that the optimal volume is more sensitive to the specification of funding risk than to the specification of the penalty spread.

Money Market derives an optimal reserve policy facing Brownian cash flow and short-term funding capacity risk. We solved a dynamic reserve model for a three-day horizon. The reserve amount increased in the crisis probability. However, the probability region within which the reserve amount has to be adjusted is very small. This means that intermediary reserves have a very small slot and the two reserve decisions 'No reserve' and 'Maximal reserve' dominate.

Risk Controlling does not run an optimization as it does not have an active instrument. However, it adjusts the transfer price for jump risk to encourage or discourage jump risk taking or collateral holding. Furthermore, it determines the optimal confidence level for

[1] It becomes of interest if funding capacity constraints have to be translated into elevated funding spreads, as we did in the Money Market model.

jump risk and parameterizes the liquidation model. We are the first to present a quantitative liquidity model for banks that is complete as defined above. The model can be extended in several ways.

Within the section 'Liquidity Model', submodels can be refined. With respect to the cash flow model, a geometric jump-diffusion process is preferable, as it avoids negative product balances. In such a process, parameters refer to the current volume. In our process, they refer to the initial volume. Nonetheless, this is not crucial for the drift term. However, Brownian and jump exposures should refer to the current volume. The liquidation and interest rate models played a marginal role in our setup. We specified both, but assumed a simple structure. In particular, the liquidation model is needed to specify the cost function of the jump risk transfer price.

Due to the recent subprime turmoils, regulators stress the link between distressed funding and distressed asset liquidation. This link is important as funding and asset liquidation are the only ways to generate additional liquidity. Funding is done on primary, asset liquidation on secondary markets. Yet both are connected since the same investors operate on them. As we did not specify the liquidation model, we did not account for that particular link.[2] However, we incorporated the link between funding model and (perceived) asset quality as we linked the funding crisis to a loss of confidence.[3]

Within the section 'Liquidity Management', the cost functions need to be specified. We provided indications regarding the factors that underly the cost. However, the implementation of a transfer pricing system requires the specification of the cost function.

Within the section Liquidity Optimization, we discussed the general procedure. Implementable models follow that procedure, but need a longer model horizon. Additionally, the optimization should be based on a present value objective function. We maximized the terminal value. A present value-based optimization is preferable as the performance can be tracked at every time point. A terminal value-based optimization usually cannot track the performance prior to the model horizon. Given these extensions, solutions can only be determined numerically by using solver software. We did not formalize the tasks of Risk Controlling. Further work should be dedicated to the determination of the optimal jump risk quantile. Additionally, one should specify the rule how Risk Controlling adjusts the jump transfer price to rebalance jump exposure and decentral collateral. It might be possible to adapt inventory models that determine lower and upper boundaries for the collateral. If the jump exposure is within the boundaries, no action is needed. If the exposure hits the upper boundary, Risk Controlling should encourage further collateral holding and discourage further jump risk taking by increasing the jump risk transfer price. If the lower boundary is hit, the transfer price has to be lowered as well.

Our work did not address implementation, which requires time series of key liquidity variables. The quality and size of the time series that are needed to ensure a sound implementation depend on the banks' product portfolio. The required data might contrast the available data: time series of cash flows might be short or virtually unavailable. Funding capacity is an unobservable variable whose estimation requires additional actions that might not have been taken yet. Time series of funding spreads might not have been sys-

[2] [Preat and Herzberg, 2008] describe the link between asset and funding liquidity. [Brunnermeier and Pedersen,] provide a model that links market and funding liquidity.

[3] Note that the loss of confidence is defined on the cash flow process.

tematically tracked because the funding spread has not been considered a key liquidity variable. As the majority of key liquidity variables are internal, data is a more critical issue than for models that require market data. Therefore, implementation is highly bank-specific. However, we indirectly contribute to implementation since, by determining the key variables, we encourage banks to begin collecting the relevant information to ensure future implementation.

A logical step that follows implementation is the linking of stochastic sources to macroeconomic variables. In fact, our model has one systematic liquidity and one systematic confidence factor. It is desirable to identify economic variables that proxy these factors. Due to the rare event of a loss of confidence, it might be more difficult to identify proxies for the confidence factor. However, confidence could be proxied by reputational risk. At this point, there are first approaches to quantify that risk type. If stochastic drivers are linked to external variables, Brownian and jump transfer prices become more transparent as they are linked to observable variables.

Our model spans the spectrum of banks' liquidity management from identifying and modelling to managing and optimizing. It considers both short and long-term cash flows, shows the aggregation from product to aggregate liquidity, transfers and prices cash flow components, and addresses confidence. We hope that it serves as a departure point for future research and implementation projects.

Appendix A
Liquidity Model

A.1 Cash Flow Expectations

Conditional versus Unconditional Expectations

Unconditional expectations are expectations for a future time point t_{k+1} taken at t_0. Unconditional cash flow expectation writes as:

$$E[CF_{t_{k+1}}|F_{t_0}] = E[CF_{t_{k+1}}]$$
$$F_{t_0} = \{\Omega, \oslash\}$$

At t_0, the minimal information is available: 'something will happen'. This is formalized by the information set $F_{t_0} = \{\Omega, \oslash\}$.

Conditional expectations are expectations for the same future time point t_{k+1}, but taken at t_k. Conditional expectations are denoted:

$$E[CF_{t_{k+1}}|F_{t_k}]$$

Conditional expectations use the information set F_{t_k} instead of F_{t_0}. F_{t_k} contains all information that have been revealed between t_0 and t_k. Applied to our context, F_{t_k} contains all past cash flows. Seen from t_0, the conditional expectation is a random variable as it is not known which information will be revealed.

Conditional and unconditional expectations are identical if the process is independent on the revealed information. This means that the process is path-independent. Applied to our context this implies that past cash flows do not provide any information about future cash flows.

The following section discusses the implications of the expectation type for unrestricted and restricted products. We base our arguments on a product without jumps. However, the arguments also hold for products with jumps.

Unrestricted Products

In a first step, we discuss conditional and unconditional expectations for ideal (unrestricted) products. An unrestricted product can take balances between $(-\infty, +\infty)$ and does never expire.

With respect to inventories $X_{t_{k+1}}$, the conditional expectation $E[X_{t_{k+1}}|F_{t_k}]$ differs almost sure from unconditional expecation $E[X_{t_{k+1}}|F_{t_0}]$ as (A.1) suggests:

$$\begin{aligned} E[X_{t_{k+1}}|F_{t_0}] &= E[X_{t_k}] + \mu_{t_{k+1}}\Delta t \\ &\overset{a.s.}{\neq} X_{t_k} + \mu_{t_{k+1}}\Delta t \\ &= E[X_{t_{k+1}}|F_{t_k}] \end{aligned} \tag{A.1}$$

With respect to t_0, the inventory X_{t_k} is unknown. Thus, it has to be estimated by $E[X_{t_k}]$. With respect to t_k, the particular realization of X_{t_k} is known. As X_{t_k} differs almost sure from its expectation, conditional and unconditional expectations are different.

The fact that unconditional expectation requires an additional estimation of X_{t_k} is reflected by a higher variance:

$$\begin{aligned} Var[X_{t_{k+1}}|F_{t_0}] &= Var[X_{t_k} + \mu_{t_{k+1}}\Delta t + \sigma\Delta W_{t_{k+1}}|F_{t_0}] \\ &= Var(X_{t_k}|F_{t_0}) + \sigma^2 \cdot \Delta t \\ &> \sigma^2 \cdot \Delta t \\ &= Var[X_{t_{k+1}}|F_{t_k}] \end{aligned}$$

The variance of the t_{k+1}-inventory is higher seen from t_0 than seen from t_k. The intuition is that it is easier to forecast the level of the next time point knowing where the process currently is than to forecast the level from the starting point.

Obviously, taking into account information between t_0 and t_k reduces uncertainty about the inventory in t_{k+1}.

This is not true with respect to cash flows:

$$\begin{aligned} E[CF_{t_{k+1}}|F_{t_k}] &= (\mu^i_{t_{k+1}} \cdot \Delta t + \sigma^i_{t_{k+1}}\Delta W^i_{t_{k+1}}) \\ &= (\mu^i_{t_{k+1}}) \cdot \Delta t \\ E[CF_{t_{k+1}}|F_0] &= (\mu^i_{t_{k+1}} \cdot \Delta t + \sigma^i_{t_{k+1}}\Delta W^i_{t_{k+1}}) \\ &= (\mu^i_{t_{k+1}}) \cdot \Delta t \\ &= E[CF_{t_{k+1}}|F_{t_k}] \end{aligned}$$

The level is not relevant for the cash flow forecast: the cash flow for t_{k+1} as expected at t_0 is exactly the same as expected at t_{k+1}. Hence, knowing past cash flows does not improve the cash flow forecast for t_{k+1}. This is confirmed by the variance:

$$\begin{aligned} Var[CF_{t_{k+1}}|F_{t_k}] &= Var[\mu^i_{t_{k+1}} \cdot \Delta t + \sigma^i_{t_{k+1}} \Delta W^i_{t_{k+1}} |F_{t_k}] \\ &= (\sigma^i_{t_{k+1}})^2 \Delta t \\ Var[CF_{t_{k+1}}|F_0] &= Var(\mu^i_{t_{k+1}} \cdot \Delta t + \sigma^i_{t_{k+1}} \Delta W^i_{t_{k+1}}) \\ &= (\sigma^i_{t_{k+1}})^2 \cdot \Delta t \\ &= Var[CF_{t_{k+1}}|F_{t_k}] \end{aligned}$$

Uncertainty with respect to CF_{t_k+1} is not reduced knowing past cash flows. Knowing past cash flows does not provide any information about future cash flows. This property is termed path-independence.

We conclude that knowing past cash flows reduces the uncertainty about future inventories, but not about future cash flows. Using conditional expectations improves the forecast of inventories, but not that of cash flows.

Restricted Products

Real products are usually restricted in amount and/ or time (maturity). In the following, we analyze the implications for the statistical properties of cash flows. To illustrate our ideas, we take the example of a loan commitment with a lower bound of 0 and an upper bound of Z. Inventory and cash flow of the loan commitment restricted to [0,Z] are described by:

$$\begin{aligned} \underline{\overline{X}}_{t_{k+1}} &= \min(\max(\underline{\overline{X}}_{t_k} + CF_{t_{k+1}}, 0), Z) \\ &= \underline{\overline{X}}_{t_k} + \min(\max(CF_{t_{k+1}}, -\underline{\overline{X}}_{t_k}), Z - \underline{\overline{X}}_{t_k}) \\ &= \underline{\overline{X}}_{t_k} + \underline{\overline{CF}}_{t_{k+1}} \end{aligned}$$

Being:

$\underline{\overline{CF}}_{t_{k+1}}$:Restricted Cash Flow

$$\begin{aligned} \underline{\overline{CF}}_{t_{k+1}} &= \min(\max(CF_{t_{k+1}}, -\underline{\overline{X}}_{t_k}), Z - \underline{\overline{X}}_{t_k}) \\ &= \min(\max(CF_{t_{k+1}}, -\sum_{j=0}^{k} \underline{\overline{CF}}_{t_j}), Z - \sum_{j=0}^{k} \underline{\overline{CF}}_{t_j}) \end{aligned} \quad (A.2)$$

Hence, the restricted cash flow is the original cash flow restricted to $[-\underline{\overline{X}}_{t_k}, Z - \underline{\overline{X}}_{t_k}]$. Product restrictions translate into cash flow restrictions. (A.2) suggests that future cash flows depend on past cash flows. Product restrictions make cash flows path-dependent. This is in contrast to unrestricted products.

Now, it makes a difference for the cash flow forecast whether the current level is known (t_k-information) or has to be estimated (t_0-information). Obviously, using the information revelead between t_0 and t_k reduces the uncertainty about future cash flows:[1]

$$Var(\underline{\overline{CF}}_{t_{k+1}}|F_{t_k}) \leq Var(\underline{\overline{CF}}_{t_{k+1}}) \quad (A.3)$$

[1] The conditional variance defines [Shiryaev, 1996, p.214].

In contrast to unrestricted products, cash flow forecasts of restricted products should use conditional expectations and not unconditional expectations. The level-depending restrictions make past information F_{t_k} valuable to forecast cash flows. Consider the following example: knowing that the loan commitment is completely drawn in t_k, ($X_{t_k} = Z$) implies that the probability of additional cash outflows $CF_{t_{k+1}}$ is zero.

The more restricted a product, the more additional information reduces cash flow uncertainty all other things being equal. Consider the following example: loan commitments that are restricted to $[0,X_{t_k}]$ are more restrictive than loan commitments that are restricted to [0,Z]. The restriction $[0, X_{t_k}]$ means that the next balance has to be either lower than the current balance or equal. In other words: the commitment has to be repaid and cannot be drawn again. This property is called 'non-revolving' and ensures a monotonicity in the inventory evolution. Obviously, 'non-revolving' is more restrictive than a constant upper boundary Z.

Setting $Z = X_{t_k}$, (A.2) becomes:

$$\overline{\underline{CF}}_{t_{k+1}} = \min(\max(CF_{t_{k+1}}, -\underline{X}_{t_k}), 0)$$

To illustrate how the knowledge of the current level can reduce uncertainty, let us assume that the loan commitment has been repaid, i.e. $\underline{X}_{t_k} = 0$. For that particular case, we get:

$$\begin{aligned}\overline{\underline{CF}}_{t_{k+1}} &= \min(\max(CF_{t_{k+1}}, 0), 0)\\ &= 0\end{aligned}$$

Knowing that the non-revolving loan commitment has been repaid eliminates any uncertainty: $CF_{t_{k+1}}$ must be zero. From a t_0-perspective, the level is always uncertain. Consequently, a t_0-forecast can never discard cash flow uncertainty.[2]

We conclude that product restrictions make future cash flows depending on past cash flows. Knowing past cash flows reduces cash flow uncertainty. For non-revolving products, knowing the past might even lead to complete certainty. As a result, the use of conditional expected cash flows is preferable to the use of unconditional expected cash flows. The more products are restricted, the more valuable is the use of conditional expectations.

Suboptimality and Attenuation

Clearly, using unconditional expectations for real (restricted) products is suboptimal.

This section discusses how the suboptimality can be reduced.

As table A.1 suggests products have different degrees of restrictions: X_{t_k} denotes the product volume at t_k. Products 2-5 describe restricted products. Product 1 is an (ideal) unrestricted product. The products 2-4 are restricted in amount, product 5 is restricted in time (fixed maturity). Products can be restricted with respect to amount- and/ or time.

The importance of conditional expectations is decreasing in the degree of restrictions.

There are three ways to attenuate the suboptimality of using unconditional instead of conditional expectations:

[2] An exception is the rather 'pathological' case that the loan committment is already repaid in t_0.

Table A.1 Degrees of Product Restrictions

Number	Example	Amount	Maturity
1	Current Account incl. ∞-Overdraft	—	—
2	Saving Deposits	$0 \leq X_{t_k}$	—
3	Loan Committments	$0 \leq X_{t_{k+1}} \leq Z$	—
4	Amortizing Loans	$0 \leq X_{t_{k+1}} \leq X_{t_k}$	—
5	Like (1), fixed maturity	—	t_m

1. Limiting Model Horizon
   Clearly, the divergence between conditional and unconditional expectations increase in time as every time step reveals information which conditional expectations incorporate and unconditional expectations ignore. Limiting the model horizon limits the suboptimality.
2. Make 'Non-revolving' products revolving
   Non-revolving products can be made 'revolving' by modelling existing and future new business (incl. prolongations) as one product. Deviations of the new business net with deviations of the existing business. As a result, the expectation stabilizes and unconditional expectations exhibit a smaller model error.
3. Customer Modelling instead of product modelling
   Products are an artificial segmentation of customer needs: a customer that holds a savings and a current account can continue to withdraw on the current account if the savings account is on zero. Seen as one unit, the product 'savings and current account' is unrestricted. Hence, it might be preferable to use the customer as modelling unit instead of products. However, customer modelling can only be done for customers that hold almost all products with the same bank. Customers holding current accounts with several banks cannot be modelled on a customer basis.

Appendix B
Liquidity Management

B.1 Brownian Transfer Prices for Large and Homogeneous Portfolios

Given (5.11), γ and γ^p simplify to:

$$
\begin{aligned}
\gamma &= \frac{\sigma^A}{\sigma^P + \sigma^M} \\
&= \frac{\sqrt{\sum_{i=1}^d (\sigma^p)^2 + (\sum_{i=1}^d \sigma^m)^2}}{\sqrt{\sum_{i=1}^d (\sigma^p)^2} + \sum_{i=1}^d \sigma^m} \\
&= \frac{\sqrt{d \cdot (\sigma^p)^2 + (d \cdot \sigma^m)^2}}{\sqrt{d \cdot (\sigma^p)^2} + d \cdot \sigma^m} \\
&= \frac{d}{d} \cdot \frac{\sqrt{\frac{(\sigma^p)^2}{\sqrt{d}} + (\sigma^m)^2}}{\frac{\sigma^p}{\sqrt{d}} + \sigma^m} \\
&= \frac{\sqrt{\frac{(\sigma^p)^2}{\sqrt{d}} + (\sigma^m)^2}}{\frac{\sigma^p}{\sqrt{d}} + \sigma^m} \\
\gamma^p &= \frac{\sigma^P}{\sum_{i=1}^d \sigma^p} \\
&= \frac{\sqrt{\sum_{i=1}^d (\sigma^p)^2}}{\sum_{i=1}^d \sigma^p} \\
&= \frac{\sqrt{d} \cdot \sigma^p}{d \cdot \sigma^p} \\
&= \frac{1}{\sqrt{d}}
\end{aligned}
$$

Having a large product spectrum ($d \to \infty$) yields:

$$\lim_{d\to\infty} \gamma = \frac{\sqrt{\frac{(\sigma^p)^2}{\sqrt{d}} + (\sigma^m)^2}}{\frac{\sigma^p}{\sqrt{d}} + \sigma^m}$$

$$= 1$$

$$\lim_{d\to\infty} \gamma^p = \frac{1}{\sqrt{d}}$$

$$= 0$$

Appendix C
Liquidity Optimization

C.1 Optimization in Origination Department

We use the following differentiation rule[1]:

$$\frac{d}{dx}\int_a^x f(t)dt = f(x)$$

and:

$$\frac{d}{dx}\int_a^{g(x)} f(t)dt = f(x)\cdot g'(x) \tag{C.1}$$

Based on this initial relation, we derive two lemmata.

Lemma C.1. *It holds:*

$$\frac{\partial E[\max(x(\alpha)-\beta,0)]}{\partial\alpha} = \frac{\partial x}{\partial\alpha}\cdot P(\beta \le x(\alpha))$$

Derivation of lemma C.1:

[1] See [I.N.Bronstein et al., 2000, p.468].

$$
\begin{aligned}
E[\max(x(\alpha)-\beta,0)] &= \int_0^{x(\alpha)} (x(\alpha)-\beta)f(\beta)d\beta \\
&= x(\alpha)\int_0^{x(\alpha)} f(\beta)d\beta - \int_0^{x(\alpha)} \beta f(\beta)d\beta \\
\frac{\partial E[\max(x(\alpha)-\beta,0)]}{\partial\alpha} &= \frac{\partial\left(x(\alpha)\int_0^{x(\alpha)} f(\beta)d\beta - \int_0^{x(\alpha)}\beta f(\beta)d\beta\right)}{\partial\alpha} \\
&= [1\cdot\frac{\partial x}{\partial\alpha}]\cdot[\int_0^{x(\alpha)} f(\beta)d\beta] \\
&+ [x]\cdot[f(x)\frac{\partial x}{\partial\alpha}] \\
&- x(\alpha)f(x(\alpha))\frac{\partial x}{\partial\alpha} \\
&= \frac{\partial x}{\partial\alpha}\cdot[\int_0^{x(\alpha)} f(\beta)d\beta] \\
&= \frac{\partial x}{\partial\alpha}\cdot P(\beta\le x(\alpha)) \\
\frac{\partial E[\max(x(\alpha)-\beta,0)]}{\partial\alpha} &= \frac{\partial x}{\partial\alpha}\cdot P(\beta\le x(\alpha))
\end{aligned}
$$

Lemma C.2. *It holds:*

$$\frac{\partial E[\max(x(\alpha)-\beta)^2]}{\partial \alpha} = 2 \cdot \frac{\partial x}{\partial \alpha} \cdot (x(\alpha) - E[\beta|\beta \leq x(\alpha)]) \cdot P(\beta \leq x(\alpha)) \tag{C.2}$$

Derivation of lemma (C.2):
Note the following:

$$\begin{aligned} E(\max(x(\alpha)-\beta,0)^2 &= \int_0^{x(\alpha)} (x(\alpha)-\beta)^2 f(\beta)d\beta \\ &= \int_0^{x(\alpha)} (x(\alpha)^2 - 2x(\alpha)\beta + \beta^2) f(\beta)d\beta \\ &= \int_0^{x(\alpha)} (x(\alpha)^2 - 2x(\alpha)\beta + \beta^2) f(\beta)d\beta \\ &= x(\alpha)^2 \int_0^{x(\alpha)} f(\beta)d\beta \\ &\quad - 2x(\alpha) \int_0^{x(\alpha)} \beta f(\beta)d\beta \\ &\quad + \int_0^{x(\alpha)} \beta^2 f(\beta)d\beta \end{aligned} \tag{C.3}$$

The derivation of (C.3) w.r.t. α yields:

$$
\begin{aligned}
\frac{\partial E[TV]}{\partial \alpha} &= [2x(\alpha)\cdot\frac{\partial x}{\partial \alpha}]\cdot[\int_0^{x(\alpha)} f(\beta)d\beta] \\
&+[x(\alpha)^2]\cdot[f(x(\alpha))\frac{\partial x}{\partial \alpha}] \\
&-2([1\cdot\frac{\partial x}{\partial \alpha}]\cdot[\int_0^{x(\alpha)} \beta f(\beta)d\beta]+[x(\alpha)]\cdot[x(\alpha)\cdot f(x(\alpha))\frac{\partial x}{\partial \alpha}]) \\
&+[x(\alpha)^2]\cdot[f(x(\alpha))\frac{\partial x}{\partial \alpha}] \\
&=2x(\alpha)\cdot\frac{\partial x}{\partial \alpha}]\cdot\int_0^{x(\alpha)} f(\beta)d\beta \\
&+2\frac{\partial x}{\partial \alpha}]\cdot([x(\alpha)^2]\cdot f(x(\alpha))-[x(\alpha)^2]\cdot f(x(\alpha))) \\
&-2\frac{\partial x}{\partial \alpha}]\int_0^{x(\alpha)} \beta f(\beta)d\beta \\
&=2\cdot\frac{\partial x}{\partial \alpha}]\cdot[x(\alpha)\cdot\int_0^{x(\alpha)} f(\beta)d\beta-\int_0^{x(\alpha)} \beta f(\beta)d\beta] \\
&=2\cdot\frac{\partial x}{\partial \alpha}]\cdot[x(\alpha)\cdot P(\beta\leq x(\alpha))-E[\beta|\beta\leq x(\alpha)]\cdot P(\beta\leq x(\alpha))] \\
&=2\cdot\frac{\partial x}{\partial \alpha}]\cdot[x(\alpha)-E[\beta|\beta\leq x(\alpha)]]\cdot P(\beta\leq x)
\end{aligned}
$$

C.2 Optimization in Money Market Department

C.2.1 Approximation of Cash Flow SDE by Binomial Cash Flow Model

According to section 6.1 Money Market manages the following cash flow on a daily basis:

$$CF_{t_i}^{MMD} = \underbrace{\mu \cdot \Delta t}_{\substack{\text{Deterministic Cash Flow}\\ \text{Next Quarter}}} + \underbrace{\sigma^A \cdot \Delta W_{t_i}^A}_{\text{Brownian Component}} \tag{C.4}$$

$$CF_0 : \text{ given}$$

The balance (cumulated cash flow) of (C.4) writes as:

$$\begin{aligned} B_0 &= CF_0 \\ B_{t_{k+1}} &= CF_0 + \sum_{i=1}^{k+1} CF_{t_i} \\ &= B_{t_k} + CF_{t_{k+1}} \\ &= B_{t_k} + \mu \cdot \Delta t + \sigma^A \cdot \Delta W_{t_{k+1}}^A \end{aligned} \tag{C.5}$$

(C.5) is normally distributed. We approximate (C.5) with the following binomial model:

$$\begin{aligned} B_0 &= CF_0 \\ B_{t_{k+1}} &= B_{t_k} + CF_{t_{k+1}} \\ &= B_{t_k} + \begin{cases} CF^+, & P(CF_t = CF^+) = p \\ CF^-, & P(CF_t = CF^-) = 1-p \end{cases} \end{aligned} \tag{C.6}$$

We assume that cash flows of different time points are independent.

The resulting binomial tree is displayed in figure C.1. Instead of an infinite number of possible cash flows, only two cash flows are possible: an inflow of CF^+ at probability p and an outflow of CF^- at probability $(1-p)$. The probabilities are constant. The cash flow at t_0 is given.

In the following, we map CF^+ and CF^- to the parameter μ and σ of the original cash flow process (C.4).

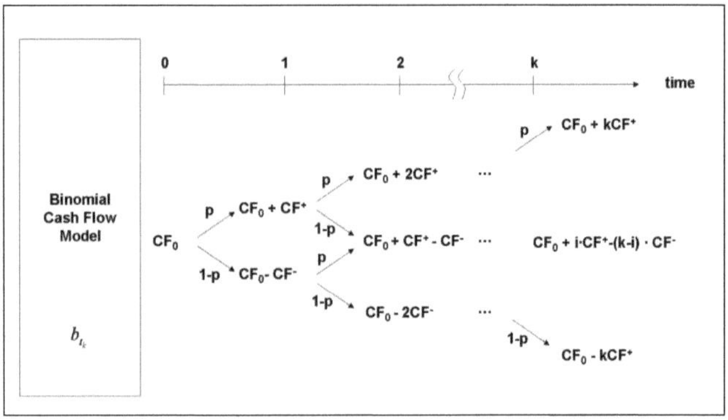

Fig. C.1 Model Dynamic as Binomial Tree

Obviously, a particular realization $b^i_{t_k}$ of (C.6) can be written as:

$$
\begin{aligned}
b_0 &= CF_0 \\
b^i_{t_k} &= CF_0 + i \cdot CF^+ - (k-i) \cdot CF^- \\
&= CF_0 + i \cdot (CF^+ + CF^-) - k \cdot CF^-
\end{aligned}
$$

Being:

i : Number of up-steps

k : Number of time steps

$i \sim Bin(k, p)$

We want to determine CF^+ and CF^- such that the de-leveled binomial approximation $(b^i_{t_k} - CF_0)$ matches expectation and variance of the de-leveled original process (C.5).

$$
\begin{aligned}
E[b_{t_k} - CF_0] &\stackrel{!}{=} E[B_{t_k} - CF_0] = k\mu\Delta t \\
Var[b_{t_k} - CF_0] &\stackrel{!}{=} Var[B_{t_k} - CF_0] = \sigma^2 k\Delta t
\end{aligned}
$$

We have:

$$E[b_{t_k}] = E[i \cdot CF^{+} - (k-i) \cdot CF^{-}]$$
$$= E[i \cdot (CF^{+} + CF^{-}) - k \cdot CF^{-}]$$
$$= (CF^{+} + CF^{-})E[i] - k \cdot CF^{-}$$
$$= (CF^{+} + CF^{-})k \cdot p - k \cdot CF^{-} \stackrel{!}{=} k\mu\Delta t \tag{C.7}$$
$$Var[b_{t_k}] = Var[i \cdot (CF^{+} + CF^{-}) - k \cdot CF^{-}]$$
$$= (CF^{+} + CF^{-})^2 \cdot Var[i]$$
$$= (CF^{+} + CF^{-})^2 \cdot kp(1-p) \stackrel{!}{=} \sigma^2 k \cdot \Delta t \tag{C.8}$$

From (C.7), we get:

$$(CF^{+} + CF^{-})k \cdot p - k \cdot CF^{-} \stackrel{!}{=} k\mu\Delta t$$
$$\Leftrightarrow$$
$$(CF^{+} + CF^{-}) \cdot p - CF^{-} \stackrel{!}{=} \mu\Delta t$$
$$CF^{-} = \frac{p \cdot CF^{+} - \mu\Delta t}{1-p} \tag{C.9}$$

Substituting CF^{-} in (C.8) yields:

$$(CF^{+} \frac{p \cdot CF^{+} - \mu\Delta t}{1-p})^2 \cdot kp(1-p) \stackrel{!}{=} \sigma^2 k \cdot \Delta t$$
$$\Leftrightarrow$$
$$p(1-p)[\frac{CF^{+} - CF^{+}p + CF^{+}p - \mu\Delta t}{1-p}] = \sigma^2 \Delta t$$
$$CF^{+} = \sqrt{\frac{\sigma^2 \Delta t(1-p)}{p}} + \mu\Delta t$$

Setting $p = \frac{1}{2}$, we obtain:[2]

$$CF^{+} = \sigma\sqrt{\Delta t} + \mu\Delta t$$

Using (C.9), CF^{-} writes as:

$$CF^{-} = \frac{p \cdot (\sigma\sqrt{\Delta t} + \mu\Delta t) - \mu\Delta t}{1-p}$$
$$= \sigma\sqrt{\Delta t} - \mu\Delta t$$

[2] The probability is a free parameter. See [Schmidt, 1997].

Finally, we obtain the binomial approximation b_{t_k}:

$$b_0 = CF_0$$

$$b_{t_k} = b_{t_{k-1}} + \begin{cases} CF^+, & P[CF_{t_k} = CF^+] = \frac{1}{2} \\ -CF^-, & P[CF_{t_k} = CF^-] = \frac{1}{2} \end{cases}$$

Being:

$$CF^+ = f(\mu, \sigma) = \sigma\sqrt{\Delta t} + \mu\Delta t$$
$$CF^- = g(\mu, \sigma) = \sigma\sqrt{\Delta t} - \mu\Delta t$$

C.2.2 Determination of Optimality Candidates

Within this section, we verify whether the optimal decisions $d_{12}[i,j]$ are always finite. In particular, we check whether the optimum of unbounded intervals $[-\infty, k]$ or $[l, +\infty]$ is the lower/ higher well-defined interval boundary. We start with node [1,1].

The maximum is determined by following the derivation into the positive direction to the end of the interval.

For the derivation of (6.41) w.r.t. $d_{1,2}[1,1]$ only expressions containing $d_{1,2}[1,1]$ are of interest. Splitting up the value function into $d_{1,2}[1,1]$ expressions and a constant c leads to (C.10).

$$\begin{aligned} f(d_{1,2}[1,1]) = & \\ & p^{CF}(1-p^c)\cdot(\\ & ([CF_0 + CF^+ - d_{02} - d_{12}[1,1]]^+ + 2\cdot[d_{12}[1,1]]^+)r^+ \\ & +([CF_0 + CF^+ - d_{02} - d_{12}[1,1]]^- + 2\cdot[d_{12}[1,1]]^-)r^- \\ & +p^{CF}(1-p^c)\cdot((([CF_0 + CF^+ + CF^+ - d_{12}[1,1]]^+)r^+ \\ & +([CF_0 + CF^+ + CF^+ - d_{12}[1,1]]^-)r^-) \\ & +p^{CF}p^c\cdot((([CF_0 + CF^+ + CF^+ - d_{12}[1,1]]^+)r^+ \\ & +([CF_0 + CF^+ + CF^+ - d_{12}[1,1]]^-)r^{--}) \\ & +(1-p^{CF})(1-p^c)\cdot((([CF_0 + CF^+ - CF^- - d_{12}[1,1]]^+)r^+ \\ & +([CF_0 + CF^+ - CF^- - d_{12}[1,1]]^-)r^-) \\ & +(1-p^{CF})p^c\cdot((([CF_0 + CF^+ - CF^- - d_{12}[1,1]]^+)r^+ \\ & +([CF_0 + CF^+ - CF^- - d_{12}[1,1]]^-)r^{--}) \\ & +c) \end{aligned} \tag{C.10}$$

We observe that $d_{12}[1,1]$ appears in 3 expressions (A,B,C):

$$\begin{aligned}
A :& [CF_0 + CF^+ - d_{02} - d_{12}[1,1]]^{+/-} \\
& \leftrightarrow CF_0 + CF^+ - d_{02} - d_{12}[1,1] \gtrless 0 \\
B :& [d_{12}[1,1]]^{+/-} \\
& \leftrightarrow d_{12}[1,1] \gtrless 0 \\
C :& [CF_0 + CF^+ + CF^+ - d_{12}[1,1]]^{+/-} \\
& \rightarrow CF_0 + CF^+ + CF^+ < d_{12}[1,1] \\
& [CF_0 + CF^+ - CF^- - d_{12}[1,1]]^{+/-} \\
& \rightarrow CF_0 + CF^+ - CF^- > d_{12}[1,1]]
\end{aligned}$$

The expressions can be positive and negative leading to eight possible cases that are displayed as 'case tree' in figure C.2. The structure of figure C.2 can be seen at the left margin in form of blocks. The blocks A-C refer to the expressions A-C. Each expression can be either positive or negative. The blocks A',...,C' refer to their derivations with respect to $d_{12}[1,1]$. The block 'Max' states the condition for a maximum, i.e. $\frac{\partial()}{\partial d_{12}[1,1]} > 0$. If the condition is fulfilled, the optimal $d_{12}[1,1]$ is the highest value of the interval noted 'D'. Otherwise, it is the lowest interval value noted 'd'. For case '1', the optimal value is the maximum value if the crisis probability is lower than $\frac{r^- - r^+}{r^- - r^{--}}$. This can not to be as $r^- - r^{--}$ is negative but probabilities are always positive. Hence, for this case, the maximizing value is the interval minimum. For case '2', we obtain that the objective value is independent on $d_{1,2}[1,1]$ allowing every value within the interval to be optimal.

Figure C.3 charts the case tree from figure C.2, the intervals and optima across $d_{1,2}[1,1]$. The interval boundaries $CF_0 + CF^+ - CF^-$ and $CF_0 + CF^+ + CF^+$ can lay around zero (= block I), can both be negative (= block II) and/ or both be positive (= block III). The situation relative to zero is important as at zero, the weights (= interest rates) in the value function change: positive amounts are invested at r^+, negative amounts are funded at r^- or at r^{--}. The link between figure C.2 and figure C.3 is as follows: the block C of figure C.2 tells us the cases where $d_{1,2}[1,1]$ is beyond $CF_0 + CF^+ + CF^+$. These are cases No 1,5 and 3,7. In figure C.2, 1,5 and 3,7 are in different B-blocks, i.e. $d_{1,2}[1,1]$ is positive for 1,5 and negative for 3,7. Therefore, in figure C.3, 1,5 is in block I ('0' separates $CF_0 + CF^+ + CF^+$ and $CF_0 + CF^+ - CF^-$) and 3,7 in block II (both values are negative). We have chosen the outside intervals that have one unbounded interval limit. Figure C.3 clearly shows that the optimal value lays on the well-defined interval limit but does not go to infinity.

We first discuss block I: for decision values smaller than $CF_0 + CF^+ - CF^-$, the optimal decision is the minimum value, i.e. the interval boundary. For decision values larger than $CF_0 + CF^+ + CF^+$, the optimal decision is the maximum value, i.e. the interval boundary. For the special case that both boundaries are negative (block II)[3], there is the subcase that $d_{12}[1,1]$ is negative. For those cases (cases 3 and 7), the optimal values are the minimum

[3] This might be the case for a small starting balance CF_0 that cannot be overcompensated by cash inflows, e.g. $CF_0 + CF^+ + CF^+ = -20 + 5 + 5 = -10 < 0$.

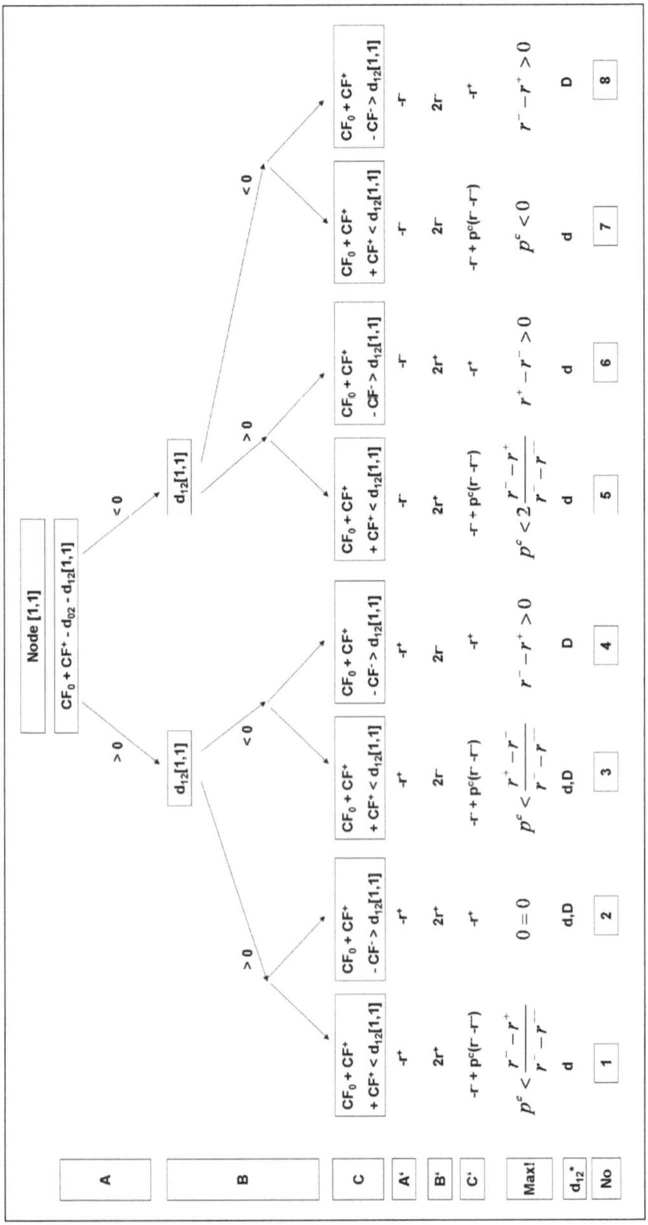

Fig. C.2 Relevant Constellation for Node [1,1]

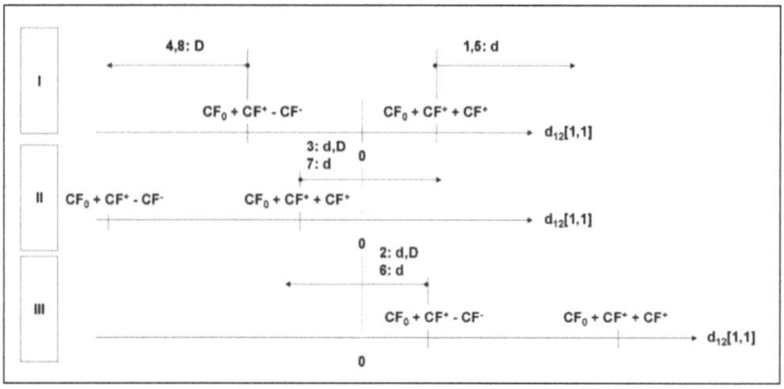

Fig. C.3 Decision Regions and Optima, Node $d_{12}[1,1]$

and maximum value (case 3) or the minimum value (case 7). The maximum value of case 3 is somewhat disturbing, as this seems to lead to an unbounded decision. However, at the critical value 0, case 3 converts to case 1 ($d_{1,2}[1,1]$ becomes positive) and the optimal value for case 1 is a minimum, here 0. Thus, a bounded solution exists also for this setup. An optimal value of zero is plausible as it means that the optimal decision is 'no reserve'. In contrast, by only considering the two positive boundaries we would exclude the possibility of 'no reserve'.

For the setup that both boundaries are positive (Block III), both cases include the minimum value as optimal. However, as cases 4 and 8 (Block I) indicate, at zero the optimality changes and the maximum value (i.e. 0) is optimal.

As unbounded solutions do not exist, candidates for optimal $d_{12}[1,1]$ are the corner values:

$$d^*_{12}[1,1] \in \{CF_0 + CF^+ + CF^+, CF_0 + CF^+ - CF^-, 0\}$$

We verify the boundedness for node $d_{12}[1,2]$ the same way. Node [1,1] and [1,2] only differ in the funding conditions (node [1,1]: normal funding at r^-, node [1,2]: crisis funding at r^{--}). The funding rates in block A' and B' are changed from r^- to r^{--} (see figure C.4). This slightly changes conditions, but only in case 7 it also changes the optimium to the maximum value. However, as argued, the optimium changes at '0' to a minimum (here: zero) which makes the problem bounded again. Hence, we confirm the boundedness of the optimization and $d_{12}[1,2]$ has the same optimal candidates as node [1,1].

The boundedness for nodes [2,1] and [2,2] can be argued the same way: the intervals of [2,i] and [1,i] only differ in their levels, but not their signs:

$$\begin{aligned}
\text{level[1,i]} &: CF_0 + CF^+ + / - CF^{+/-} \\
\text{level[2,i]} &: CF_0 - CF^- + / - CF^{+/-} \\
\text{level[1,i]} &: - \text{level[2,i]} = CF^+ + CF^-
\end{aligned}$$

The level difference only affects the (absolute) location of the intervals, but not the derivatives. As we already checked all possible interval configurations (0 included/ left-/ right-

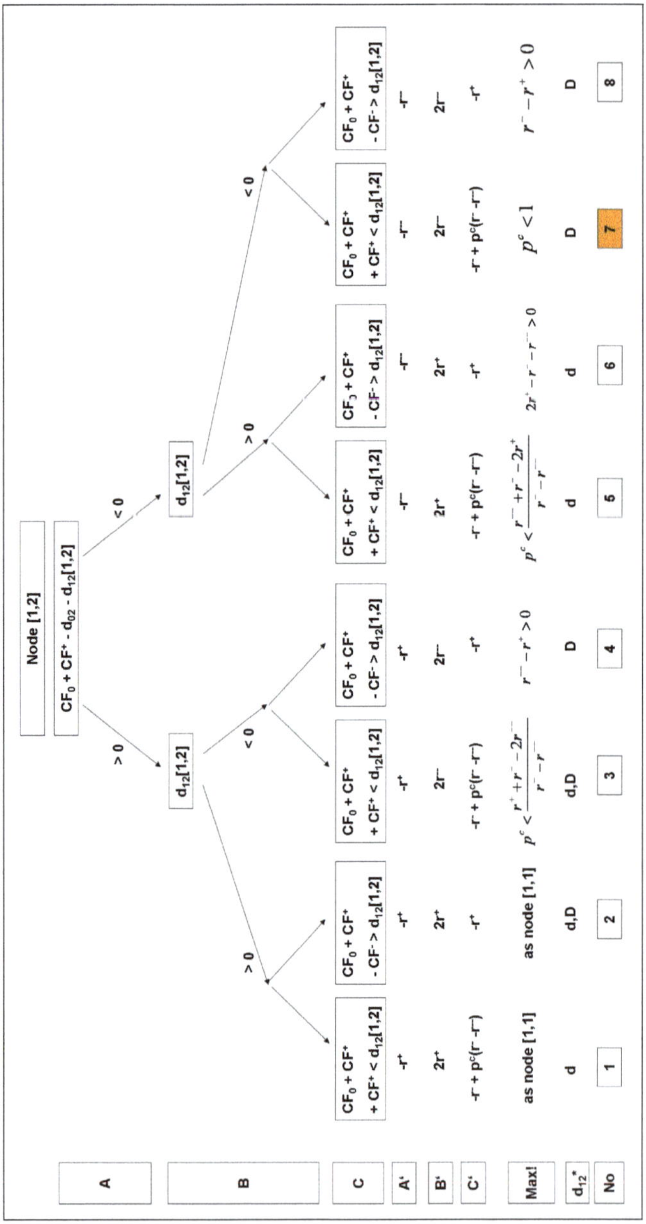

Fig. C.4 Possible Cash Flow Setups

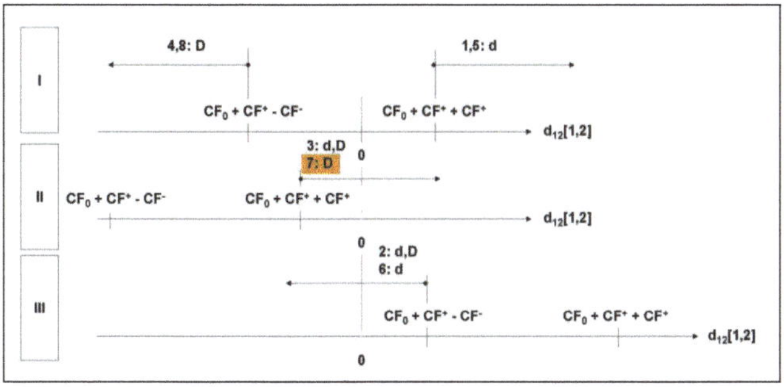

Fig. C.5 Decision Regions and Optima, Node $d_{12}[1,2]$

sided from interval) and the derivatives remain the same, the analysis would lead to the same results but at a modified level: in node [2,i] instead of $CF_0 + CF^+ + CF^+$ as in node [1,i], we have $CF_0 + CF^+ - CF^-$. And instead of $CF_0 + CF^+ - CF^-$ we have $CF_0 - CF^- - CF^-$. Hence, for $d_{12}[2,i]$ we obtain as optimal candidates:

$$d_{12}^*[1,1] \in \{CF_0 - CF^+ + CF^+, CF_0 - CF^+ - CF^-, 0\}$$

Till now we have checked the existence of an optimal strategy for $d_{12}[i,j]$ and determined the candidates. However, we also have to check for the existence of an optimal d_{02}.

C.2.2.1 Candidates for t0

The objective function where all non-d_{02}-elements are summarized in a constant c is given by (C.11).

$$\begin{aligned}
\max_{d_{02}, d_{12}[i,j]} & ([CF_0 - d_{02}]^+ + 2 \cdot [d_{02}]^+) r^+ + ([CF_0 - d_{02}]^- + 2 \cdot [d_{02}]^-) r^- \\
& + p^{CF}(1-p^c) \cdot ((([CF_0 + CF^+ - d_{02} - d_{12}[1,1]]^+) r^+ \\
& + ([CF_0 + CF^+ - d_{02} - d_{12}[1,1]]^-) r^-) \\
& + p^{CF} p^c \cdot ((([CF_0 + CF^+ - d_{02} - d_{12}[1,2]]^+) r^+ \\
& + ([CF_0 + CF^+ - d_{02} - d_{12}[1,2]]^-) r^{--}) \\
& + (1-p^{CF})(1-p^c) \cdot ((([CF_0 - CF^- - d_{02} - d_{12}[2,1]]^+) r^+ \\
& + ([CF_0 - CF^- - d_{02} - d_{12}[2,1]]^-) r^-) \\
& + (1-p^{CF}) p^c \cdot ((([CF_0 - CF^- - d_{02} - d_{12}[2,1]]^+) r^+ \\
& + ([CF_0 - CF^- - d_{02} - d_{12}[2,1]]^-) r^{--}) \\
& + c)
\end{aligned} \tag{C.11}$$

Substituting the $d_{12}[i,j]$-candidates, we obtain:

$$\begin{aligned}
\max_{d_{02},d_{12}[i,j]} & ([CF_0-d_{02}]^{+}+2\cdot[d_{02}]^{+})r^{+}+([CF_0-d_{02}]^{-}+2\cdot[d_{02}]^{-})r^{-} \\
&+(p^{CF}(1-p^{c})\cdot((([CF_0+CF^{+}-d_{02}]^{+})r^{+} \\
&\ +([CF_0+CF^{+}-d_{02}]^{-})r^{-}+s))\cdot 1_{\{d_{12}[1,1]=0\}} \\
&+(p^{CF}(1-p^{c})\cdot((([-CF^{+}-d_{02}]^{+})r^{+} \\
&\ +([-CF^{+}-d_{02}]^{-})r^{-}+s))\cdot 1_{\{d_{12}[1,1]=CF_0+CF^{+}+CF^{+}\}} \\
&+(p^{CF}(1-p^{c})\cdot((([CF^{-}-d_{02}]^{+})r^{+} \\
&\ +([CF^{-}-d_{02}]^{-})r^{-}+s))\cdot 1_{\{d_{12}[1,1]=CF_0+CF^{+}-CF^{-}\}} \\
&+(p^{CF}p^{c}\cdot((([CF_0+CF^{+}-d_{02}]^{+})r^{+} \\
&\ +([CF_0+CF^{+}-d_{02}]^{-})r^{--}+s))\cdot 1_{\{d_{12}[1,2]=0\}} \\
&+(p^{CF}p^{c}\cdot((([-CF^{+}-d_{02}]^{+})r^{+} \\
&\ +([-CF^{+}-d_{02}]^{-})r^{--}+s))\cdot 1_{\{d_{12}[1,2]=CF_0+CF^{+}+CF^{+}\}} \\
&+(p^{CF}p^{c}\cdot((([CF^{-}-d_{02}]^{+})r^{+} \\
&\ +([CF^{-}-d_{02}]^{-})r^{--}+s))\cdot 1_{\{d_{12}[1,2]=CF_0+CF^{+}-CF^{-}\}} \\
&+((1-p^{CF})(1-p^{c})\cdot((([CF_0-CF^{-}-d_{02}]^{+})r^{+} \\
&\ +([CF_0-CF^{-}-d_{02}]^{-})r^{-}+s))\cdot 1_{\{d_{12}[2,1]=0\}} \\
&+((1-p^{CF})(1-p^{c})\cdot((([-CF^{+}-d_{02}]^{+})r^{+} \\
&\ +([-CF^{+}-d_{02}]^{-})r^{-}+s))\cdot 1_{\{d_{12}[2,1]=CF_0-CF^{+}+CF^{+}\}} \\
&+((1-p^{CF})(1-p^{c})\cdot((([CF^{-}-d_{02}]^{+})r^{+} \\
&\ +([CF^{-}-d_{02}]^{-})r^{-}+s))\cdot 1_{\{d_{12}[2,1]=CF_0-CF^{-}-CF^{-}\}} \\
&+((1-p^{CF})p^{c}\cdot((([CF_0-CF^{-}-d_{02}]^{+})r^{+} \\
&\ +([CF_0-CF^{-}-d_{02}]^{-})r^{--}+s))\cdot 1_{\{d_{12}[2,2]=0\}} \\
&+((1-p^{CF})p^{c}\cdot((([-CF^{+}-d_{02}]^{+})r^{+} \\
&\ +([-CF^{+}-d_{02}]^{-})r^{--}+s))\cdot 1_{\{d_{12}[2,2]=CF_0-CF^{+}+CF^{+}\}} \\
&+((1-p^{CF})p^{c}\cdot((([CF^{-}-d_{02}]^{+})r^{+} \\
&\ +([CF^{-}-d_{02}]^{-})r^{--}+s))\cdot 1_{\{d_{12}[2,2]=CF_0-CF^{-}-CF^{-}\}}
\end{aligned} \tag{C.12}$$

As before, we want to check whether the optimal value of one-sided unlimited intervals $(d_{02} \in (\Xi, +\infty)$ is the well-defined boundary.

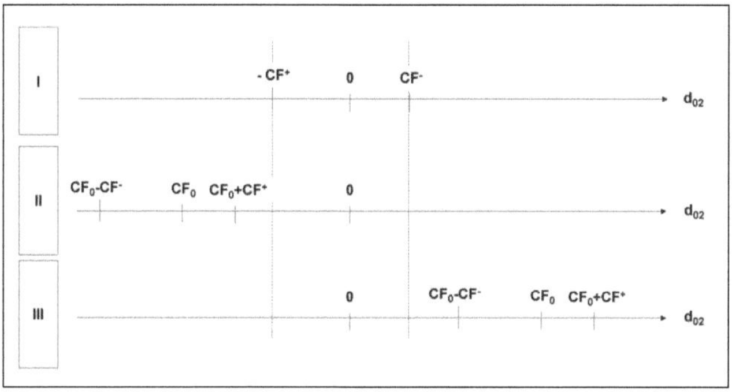

Fig. C.6 Candidates for Unlimited Intervals of d_{02}

Based on (C.12), we obtain the following interval boundaries:

$$
\begin{aligned}
[CF_0 - d_{02}]^{+/-} &: d_{02} \gtrless CF_0 \\
[d_{02}]^{+/-} &: d_{02} \gtrless 0 \\
[CF_0 + CF^+ - d_{02}]^{+/-} &: d_{02} > CF_0 + CF^+ \\
[-CF^+ - d_{02}]^{+/-} &: d_{02} < -CF^+ < 0 \\
[CF_0 - CF^- - d_{02}]^{+/-} &: d_{02} < CF_0 - CF^- \\
[CF^- - d_{02}]^{+/-} &: d_{02} > CF^- > 0
\end{aligned}
$$

In order to determine the unlimited intervals, figure C.6 visualizes the previous interval boundaries. As CF^- and CF^+ are assumed to be positive[4], CF^- is a candidate for the interval $[\Xi, \infty]$ and $-CF^+$ a candidate for the interval $[-\infty, \xi]$ (see block I in figure C.6. It is obvious that zero can not be the interval boundary of an unlimited interval. It is always within the $[-CF^+, CF^-]$-interval. Therefore, we do not have to explicitly test for $d_{02} \gtrless 0$. Just like the interval $[-CF^+, CF^-]$ is situated around zero, we have a similar interval situated around CF_0: $[CF_0 - CF^-, CF_0 + CF^+]$. Depending on the situation of CF_0, its lower bound $CF_0 - CF^-$ is a candidate for the lower unbounded interval (see block II) whereas its upper bound $CF_0 + CF^+$ is a candidate for the upper unbounded interval (see block III).

[4] CF^- is an outflow, because it is always used with a negative sign.

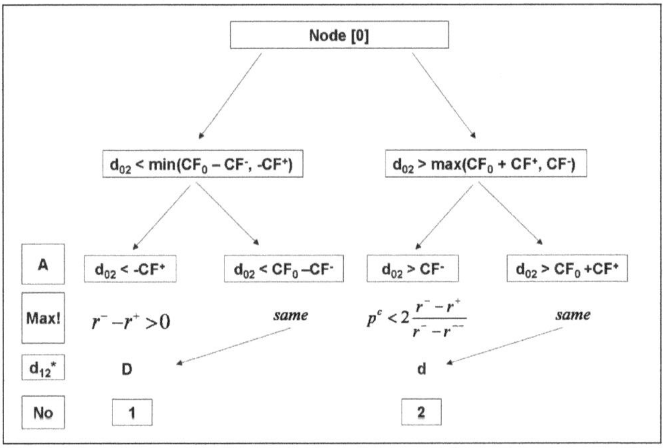

Fig. C.7 Case Tree for Unlimited Intervals of d_{02}

We conclude that we have to check the derivations for $max(CF_0 + CF^+, \ CF^-) < d_{02}$ and $d_{02} < min(-CF^+, CF_0 - CF^-)$. The resulting case tree summarizes figure C.7. It turns out that for the two possible ∞-intervals, the crisis probability has to be negative to have an infinity optimal d_{02}-value. Therefore, for all eligible crisis probabilities, the optimal value is the minimum in that interval, i.e. $d^*_{02} = CF^-$ or $d^*_{02} = CF_0 + CF^+$, respectively. For the −∞-intervals, the maximum condition is always fulfilled. We can state that the optimal value is the maximum (interval boundary) $d^*_{02} = -CF^+$ or $d^*_{02} = CF_0 - CF^-$, respectively.

References

[PLC, 2007] (2007). *Public Limited Company Law*. Version: 6.9.1965. dtv, Munich.

[Acharya and Pedersen, 2005] Acharya, V. V. and Pedersen, L. H. (2005). Asset pricing with liquidity risk. *Journal of Financial Economics*, 77 (2):375–410.

[Akmann et al., 2005] Akmann, M., Beck, A., Herrmann, R., and Stückler, R. (2005). Die Liquiditätsrisisken dürfen nicht vernachlässigt werden. *Betriebswirtschaftliche Blätter*, 10:556–559.

[Amihud et al., 2005] Amihud, Y., Mendelson, H., and Pedersen, H. (2005). Liquidity and asset prices. *Foundations and Trends in Finance*, 1:269–364.

[Baetge et al., 2004] Baetge, J., Kirsch, H.-J., and Thiele, S. (2004). *Bilanzanalyse*. IDW, 2nd edition.

[Baker et al., 2003] Baker, M., Greenwood, R., and Wurgler, J. (2003). The maturity of debt issues and predictable variation in bond returns. *Journal of Financial Economics*, 70(2):261–291.

[Bank for International Settlement, 2006] Bank for International Settlement (2006). Annual Report 2006. Download: http://www.bis.org/publ/annualreport.htm, Time Stamp: 16.04.2007.

[Bartetzky, 2008] Bartetzky, P. (2008). Liquiditätsmanagement - status quo. In Bartetzky, P., Gruber, W., and Wehn, C. S., editors, *Handbuch Liquiditätsrisiko*, pages 1–27. Schäfer-Poeschel Verlag, Stuttgart,.

[Bartetzky et al., 2008] Bartetzky, P., Gruber, W., and Wehn, C. S. (2008). *Handbuch Liquiditätsrisiko*. Schäffer-Poeschel Verlag, Stuttgart.

[Basel Committee on Banking Supervision, 2006] Basel Committee on Banking Supervision (2006). International convergence of capital measurement and capital standards.

[Basel Committee on Banking Supervision, 2008] Basel Committee on Banking Supervision (2008). Liquidity risk: Management and supervisory challenges.

[BCBS, 2008] BCBS (2008). Principles for Sound Liquidity Risk Management and Supervision (Draft for Consultation). Basel Committee on Banking Supervision.

[Bedendo et al., 2004] Bedendo, M., Cathcart, L., and El-Jahel, L. (2004). The shape of the term structure of credit spreads: An empirical investigation. Discussion Paper, Tanaka Business School (Imperial College).

[Biais et al., 2005] Biais, B., Glosten, L., and Spatt, L. (2005). Market microstructure: A survey of microfoundations, empirical results, and policy implications. *Journal of Financial Markets*, 8:217–264.

[Brealey and Myers, 2000] Brealey, R. A. and Myers, S. C. (2000). *Principles of Corporate Finance*. Irwin McGraw-Hill, Singapore, 6th edition.

[Brealey and Myers, 2003] Brealey, R. A. and Myers, S. C. (2003). *Principles of Corporate Finance*. Irwin McGraw-Hill, Singapore, 7th edition.

[British Bankers' Association, 2006] British Bankers' Association (2006). Credit derivatives report 2006.

[Brunner, 1996] Brunner, A. (1996). *Messkonzepte zur Liquidität auf Wertpapiermärkten*, volume 13 of *Beiträge zur Theorie der Finanzmärkte*. Frankfurt am Main.

[Brunnermeier, 2008] Brunnermeier, M. K. (2008). Deciphering the 2007-08 Liquidity and Credit Crunch. *Journal of Economic Perspectives (forthcoming)*.

[Brunnermeier and Pedersen,] Brunnermeier, M. K. and Pedersen, L. H. forthcoming, Market Liquidity and Funding Liquidity. *Review of Financial Studies*.

[Bundesanstalt für Finanzdienstleistungsaufsicht, 2005] Bundesanstalt für Finanzdienstleistungsaufsicht (2005). Mindestanforderungen an das Risikomanagement (MaRisk). Rundschreiben 18/2005 (20.12.2005).

[Bundesanstalt für Finanzdienstleistungsaufsicht, 2006a] Bundesanstalt für Finanzdienstleistungsaufsicht (2006a). Die Verordnung über die angemessene Eigenmittelausstattung von Instituten, Institutsgruppen und Finanzholding-Gruppen (Solvabilitätsverordnung - SolvV). Bundesgesetzblatt (Jahrgang 2006 Teil I Nr. 61, S. 2926 ff.), Effective by: 1. Januar 2007.

[Bundesanstalt für Finanzdienstleistungsaufsicht, 2006b] Bundesanstalt für Finanzdienstleistungsaufsicht (2006b). Die Verordnung über die Liquidität der Institute (Liquditätsverordnung - LiqV). Bundesgesetzblatt (Jahrgang 2006 Teil I Nr. 61, S. 3117 ff.), Effective by: January 1, 2007.

[Buraschi and Menini, 2002] Buraschi, A. and Menini, D. (2002). Liquidity risk and specialness. *Journal of Financial Economics*, 64:243–284.

[Büttler, 1999] Büttler, H.-J. (1999). The optimal capital structure of a liquidity-insuring bank. *Econometrics Journal*, 2(2):268–292.

[CEBS, 2007] CEBS (2007). First part of CEBS's technical advice to the european commission on liquidity risk management. Technical report, Committee of European Banking Supervisors.

[CEBS, 2008] CEBS (2008). Second part of CEBS's technical advice to the european commission on liquidity risk management. Technical report, Committee of European Banking Supervisors.

[Centre for the Study of Financial Innovation, 2008] Centre for the Study of Financial Innovation (2008). Banking banana skins.

[Chiu and Xu, 2004] Chiu, K.-C. and Xu, L. (2004). NFA for factor number determination in APT. *International Journal of Theoretical and Applied Finance*, 7(3):253–267.

[Choudhry, 2006] Choudhry, M. (2006). *The Credit Default Swap Basis*. Bloomberg Press, New York.

[Choudhry, 2007] Choudhry, M. (2007). *Bank Asset and Liability Management*. John Wiley & Sons (Asia) Pte Ltd, New York.

[Chowdhry and Nanda, 1998] Chowdhry, B. and Nanda, V. (1998). Leverage and market stability: The role of margin rules and price limits. *Journal of Business*, 71 (2):179–210.

[Commerzbank AG, 2008] Commerzbank AG (2008). Annual report 2007.

[Committee on the Global Financial System, 2008] Committee on the Global Financial System (2008). Ratings in structured finance: what went wrong and what can be done to address shortcomings? Working Paper No 32.

[Cont and Tankov, 2004] Cont, R. and Tankov, P. (2004). *Financial Modelling with Jump Processes*. Chapman & Hall, London.

[Cornuejols and Tütüncü, 2007] Cornuejols, G. and Tütüncü, R. (2007). *Optimization Methods in Finance*. Cambridge University Press, Cambridge.

[Crouhy et al., 2008] Crouhy, M., Jarrow, R. A., and Turnbull, S. M. (2008). The subprime credit crisis of 2007. *The Journal of Derivatives*, Fall:81–110.

[Dempster and Ireland, 1988] Dempster, M. and Ireland, A. (1988). A financial expert decision support system. *Nato Asi Series*, pages 415–440.

[Deutsche Bank Group, 2007] Deutsche Bank Group (2007). Annual report 2007.

[Deutsche Bundesbank, 2007] Deutsche Bundesbank (2007). Geschäftsbericht 2006.

[Diamond, 1991] Diamond, D. (1991). Debt maturity structure and liquidity risk. *Quarterly Journal of Economics*, 106:709–738.

[Doms et al., 2007] Doms, M., Furlong, F., and Krainer, J. (2007). House prices and subprime mortgage delinquencies. *FRBSF - Economic Letter*, 14:1–4.

[Economist, 2007] Economist, T. (2007). Sold down the river rhine. *The Economist*, Aug 9th 2007.

[E.Orgler, 1969] E.Orgler, Y. (1969). An unequal-period model for cash management decisions. *Management Science*, 16:B77–B92.

[European Central Bank, 2002] European Central Bank (2002). Developments in bank's liquidity profile and management.

[European Central Bank, 2006] European Central Bank (2006). The implementation of monetary policy in the euro area.

[European Central Bank, 2007] European Central Bank (2007). Monthly bulletin september.

[Faulkender, 2005] Faulkender, M. (2005). Hedging or Market Timing? Selecting the Interest Rate Exposure of Corporate Debt. *Journal of Finance*, 60(2):931–962.

[Ferstl and Weissensteiner, 2008] Ferstl, R. and Weissensteiner, A. (2008). Cash Management Using Multi-Stage Stochastic Programming. *SSRN eLibrary*.

[Fiedler, 2000] Fiedler, R. E. (2000). Liquidity risk. In Lore, M. and Borodovsky, L., editors, *The professional's handbook of financial risk management*, pages 441–472. Butterworth-Heinemann, Oxford.

[Fiedler, 2007] Fiedler, R. E. (2007). A concept for cash flow and funding liquidity risk. In Matz, L. and Neu, P., editors, *Liquidity Risk Measurement and Management*, pages 173–203. John Wiley & Sons (Asia) Pte Ltd., Singapore.

[Financial Stability Directorate, 2008] Financial Stability Directorate (2008). Liquidity in a time of financial turbulences. *Financial Stability Review*.

[Fitch, 2007] Fitch (2007). Short-term ratings criteria for corporate finance. p. 15: Liquidity Questions for Banks.

[Flannery, 1986] Flannery, M. J. (1986). Asymmetric information and risky debt maturity choice. *Journal of Finance*, 41:19–37.

[Frank De Jong and Joost Driessen, 2005] Frank De Jong and Joost Driessen (2005). Liquidity Risk Premia in Corporate Bond Markets. Downloadable from: http://w4.stern.nyu.edu/salomon/docs/Credit2006/SSRN-id686681.pdf.

[Freidank, 2008] Freidank, C.-C. (2008). *Kostenrechnung*. Oldenbourg, Munich, 8th edition.

[FTD, 2008b] FTD (10.10.2008b). Schwere Krise am Geldmarkt hält an. *Financial Times Deutschland*, page 22.

[FTD, 2008a] FTD (13.03.2008a). Banken buhlen um EZB-Geld. *Financial Times Deutschland*, page 21.

[FTD, 2008c] FTD (25.9.2008c). SMS stürzen Bank ins Chaos. *Financial Times Deutschland*, page 1.

[German Bankruptcy Code, 1995] German Bankruptcy Code (1995). German Bankruptcy Code. Bundesgesetzblatt (Jahrgang 1994 Teil I, S. 2866 ff.), Effective by: 1. Januar 1995.

[Gibson and Mougeot, 2004] Gibson, R. and Mougeot, N. (2004). The pricing of systematic liquidity risk: Empirical evidence from the us stock market. *Journal of Banking and Finance*, 28:157–178.

[Glosten and Milgrom, 1985] Glosten, L. and Milgrom, P. (1985). Bid, ask and transaction prices in a specialist market with heterogeneously informed traders. *Journal of Financial Economics*, 14 (1):71–100.

[Graham and Harvey, 2001] Graham, J. R. and Harvey, C. R. (2001). The theory and practice of corporate finance: evidence from the field. *Journal of Financial Economics*, 60:187–243.

[Grossman and Miller, 1988] Grossman, S. J. and Miller, M. H. (1988). Liquidity and market structure. *Journal of Finance*, 43 (3):617–633.

[Hartmann-Wendels et al., 2007] Hartmann-Wendels, T., Pfingsten, A., and Weber, M. (2007). *Bankbetriebslehre*. Springer, Heidelberg, 4th edition.

[Heffernan, 1996] Heffernan, S. (1996). *Modern Banking in Theory and Practice*. John Wiley & Sons, New York.

[Hoitsch and Lingnau, 2007] Hoitsch, H.-J. and Lingnau, V. (2007). *Kosten- und Erlösrechnung*. Springer.

[Holtemöller, 2008] Holtemöller, O. (2008). *Geldtheorie und Geldpolitik*. Mohr Siebeck.

[Horváth, 1996] Horváth, P. (1996). *Controlling*. Franz Vahlen, Munich, 6th edition.

[IIF, 2007] IIF (2007). Principles of liquidity risk management.

[IKB, 2008] IKB (2008). Restated annual report 2006/07.

[I.N.Bronstein et al., 2000] I.N.Bronstein, K.A.Semendjajew, G.Musiol, and H.Mühlig (2000). *Taschenbuch der Mathematik*. Harri Deutsch, 5 edition. HB.

[Issing, 2001] Issing, O. (2001). *Einführung in die Geldtheorie*. Vahlen, Munich.

[Jórasz, 2003] Jórasz, W. (2003). *Kosten- und Leistungsrechnung*. Schäffer-Poeschel, Stuttgart, 3rd edition.

[Jun and Jen, 2003] Jun, A. and Jen, F. (2003). Trade-off model of debt maturity structure. *Review of Quantitative Finance and Accounting*, 20:5–34.

[Kale and Noe, 1990] Kale, J. and Noe, T. (1990). Risky debt maturity choice in a sequential game equilibrium. *Journal of Financial Research*, 13(2):155–166.

[Keynes, 1936] Keynes, J. M. (1936). *Allgemeine Theorie der Beschäftigung, des Zinses und des Geldes*. Duncker & Humblot, Berlin, 10th edition.

[Koch and MacDonald, 2000] Koch, T. W. and MacDonald, S. S. (2000). *Bank Management*. Dryden, Fort Worth.

[Körnert, 1998] Körnert, J. (1998). *Dominoeffekte im Bankensystem - Theorien und Evidenz*. Berlin-Verl. Spitz, Berlin.

[Krishnan et al., 2006] Krishnan, C., Ritchken, P., and Thomson, J. (2006). On credit-spread slopes and predicting bank risk. *Journal of Money, Credit, and Banking*, 38(6):1545–1574.

[Krumnow et al., 2002] Krumnow, J., Gramlich, L., Lange, T. A., and Dewner, T. M. (2002). *Gabler Bank Lexikon*. Gabler, Wiesbaden, 13th edition.

[Küting and Weber, 2001] Küting, K. and Weber, C.-P. (2001). *Die Bilanzanalyse*. Schäffer-Poeschel, Stuttgart, 6th edition.

[Leistenschneider, 2008] Leistenschneider, A. (2008). Methoden zur Ermittlung von Transferpreisen für Liquiditätsrisiken. In Peter Bartetzky, Walter Gruber, C. W., editor, *Handbuch Liquidität*, pages 171–192. Schäffer-Poeschel, Stuttgart.

[Longstaff et al., 2005] Longstaff, F. A., Mithal, S., and Neis, E. (2005). Corporate yield spreads: Default risk or liquidity? New evidence from the credit default swap market. *Journal of Finance*, 60 (5):2213–2253.

[Mankiw, 2001] Mankiw, N. G. (2001). *Grundzüge der Volkwirtschaftslehre*. Schäffer-Poeschel, Stuttgart.

[Marohn, 1998] Marohn, C. (1998). *Stochastische mehrstufige lineare Programmierung im Asset- & Liability Management*. Haupt, Bern.

[Martin et al., 2006] Martin, M. R. W., Reitz, S., and Wehn, C. S. (2006). *Kreditderivate und Kreditrisikomodelle : eine mathematische Einführung*. Vieweg, Wiesbaden.

[Matz and Neu, 2007] Matz, L. and Neu, P. (2007). *Liquidity Risk Measurement and Management*. John Wiley & Sons (Asia), Singapore.

[McNeil et al., 2005] McNeil, A. J., Frey, R., and Embrechts, P. (2005). *Quantitative Risk Management*. Princeton University Press, Princeton.

[Mönch, 2005] Mönch, B. (2005). *Strategic Trading in Illiquid Markets*. Springer, Heidelberg.

[Myers, 1977] Myers, S. C. (1977). Determinants of corporate borrowing. *Journal of Financial Economics*, 5(2):147–175.

[Neu, 2007] Neu, P. (2007). Liquidity risk measurement. In Matz, L. and Neu, P., editors, *Liquidity Risk Measurement and Management*, pages 15–36. John Wiley & Sons (Asia) Pte Ltd., Singapore.

[Neu et al., 2007] Neu, P., Leistenschneider, A., Wondrak, B., and Knippschild, M. (2007). Market Developments in Banks' Funding Markets. In Matz, L. and Neu, P., editors, *Liquidity Risk Measurement and Management*, pages 146–169. John Wiley & Sons (Asia), Singapore.

[Northern Rock plc, 2007] Northern Rock plc (2007). Annual Report and Accounts 2007.

[Novosyolov and Satchkov, 2008] Novosyolov, A. and Satchkov, D. (2008). Global term structure modelling using principal component analysis. *Journal of Asset Management*, 9(1):49.

[Pástor and Stambaugh, 2003] Pástor, L. and Stambaugh, R. F. (2003). Liquidity risk and expected stock returns. *Journal of Political Economy*, 111:642–685.

[Persaud, 2003] Persaud, A. D. (2003). Liquidity black holes. In Persaud, A. D., editor, *Liquidity Black Holes*, pages 85–104. Risk Books, London.

[Pohl and Zaby, 2008] Pohl, M. and Zaby, S. (2008). Das bankbetriebliche Reputationsrisikomanagement und dessen Umsetzung. *WWZ-Forschungsbericht, University of Basle*, 01.

[Preat and Herzberg, 2008] Preat, P. and Herzberg, V. (2008). Market liquidity and banking liquidity: linkages, vulnerabilities and the role of disclosure. *Financial Stability Review*, pages 95–109.

[Reichardt, 2006] Reichardt, R. (2006). Kapitalmarktorientierte Risikosteuerung in Banken: Marktwertsteuerung statt Marktzinsmethode. *Kredit und Kapital*, 39(2):233–280.

[Reimund, 2003] Reimund, C. (2003). *Liquiditätshaltung und Unternehmenswert*. Handelshochschule Leipzig, Leipzig.

[RISK, 2005] RISK (2005). The challenge of CDO squared. *RISK Magazine*, 18(3):12.

[Robichek et al., 1965] Robichek, A., Teichrow, D., and Jones, J. (1965). Optimal short-term financing decision. *Management Science*, 12:1–36.

[Saunders and Hugh, 2001] Saunders, A. and Hugh, T. (2001). *Financial Institutions Management*. McGraw-Hill, Ryerson, London.

[Schierenbeck, 2003a] Schierenbeck, H. (2003a). *Ertragsorientiertes Bankmanagement*, volume 2. GablerWiesbaden, 8 edition.

[Schierenbeck, 2003b] Schierenbeck, H. (2003b). *Ertragsorientiertes Bankmanagement*, volume 1. GablerWiesbaden, 8 edition.

[Schmalenbach, 1908] Schmalenbach, E. (1908). Über Verrechnungspreise. *Zeitschrift für handelswissenschaftliche Forschung*, 3(9):165–185.

[Schmid, 2000] Schmid, O. (2000). *Management der Unternehmensliquidität*. Paul Haupt, Stuttgart.

[Schmidt, 1997] Schmidt, W. M. (1997). On a general class of one-factor models for the term structure of interest rates. *Finance & Stochastics*, 1:3–24.

[Shanken, 1992] Shanken, J. (1992). The current state of the arbitrage pricing theory. *The Journal of Finance*, 47(4):1569–1574.

[Shiryaev, 1996] Shiryaev, A. N. (1996). *Probability*. Springer, 2 edition.

[Shreve, 2004] Shreve, S. E. (2004). *Stochastic Calculus for Finance II - Continuous-Time Models*. Springer, New York.

[SIFMA, 2008] SIFMA (2008). Securitization report 2008/ q2.

[Stoll, 1978] Stoll, H. R. (1978). The supply of dealer services in security markets. *Journal of Finance*, 33 (4):1133–1151.

[Süchtig and Paul, 1998] Süchtig, J. and Paul, S. (1998). *Bankmanagement*. Schäffer-Poeschel, Stuttgart, 4th edition.

[Timothy W. Koch, 2000] Timothy W. Koch, S. S. M. (2000). *Bank Management, Dryden, Fort Worth.* Dryden, Fort Worth.

[Wagner, 2007] Wagner, W. (2007). The liquidity of bank assets and banking stability. *Journal of Banking & Finance*, 31(1):121–139.

[Weber and Norden, 2006] Weber, M. and Norden, L. (2006). Funding modes of german banks: structural changes and their implications. DGF-Conference, October 2006, European Business School.

[Wetmore, 2004] Wetmore, J. L. (2004). Panel data, liquidity risk and increasing loans-to-core deposit ratio of large commercial bank holding companies (1992-2000). *American Business Review*, 06/2004:99–107.

[Witt, 1994] Witt, M. (1994). *Der Eigenhandel von Universalbanken*. Deutscher Universittsverlag.

[Zeranski, 2005] Zeranski, S. (2005). *Liquidity at Risk zur Steuerung des liquiditätsmässig-finanziellen Bereichs von Kreditinstituten*. Verlag der Gesellschaft für Unternehmensrechnung und Controlling, Chemnitz.

MIX
Papier aus verantwortungsvollen Quellen
Paper from responsible sources
FSC® C105338

If you have any concerns about our products,
you can contact us on
ProductSafety@springernature.com

In case Publisher is established outside the EU,
the EU authorized representative is:
Springer Nature Customer Service Center GmbH
Europaplatz 3, 69115 Heidelberg, Germany

Printed by Libri Plureos GmbH
in Hamburg, Germany